AN UNEXPECTED WILDERNESS

AN UNEXPECTED WILDERNESS

Christianity and the Natural World

Colleen Mary Carpenter
Editor

**THE ANNUAL PUBLICATION
OF THE COLLEGE THEOLOGY SOCIETY
2015
VOLUME 61**

ORBIS BOOKS
Maryknoll, New York 10545

ORBIS BOOKS
Maryknoll, New York 10545

Fathers and Brothers
MARYKNOLL™

Founded in 1970, Orbis Books endeavors to publish works that enlighten the mind, nourish the spirit, and challenge the conscience. The publishing arm of the Maryknoll Fathers and Brothers, Orbis seeks to explore the global dimensions of the Christian faith and mission, to invite dialogue with diverse cultures and religious traditions, and to serve the cause of reconciliation and peace. The books published reflect the views of their authors and do not represent the official position of the Maryknoll Society. To learn more about Maryknoll and Orbis Books, please visit our website at www.maryknollsociety.org.

Library of Congress Cataloging-in-Publication Data

Names: Carpenter, Colleen Mary, editor.
Title: An Unexpected wilderness : Christianity and the natural world / Colleen Mary Carpenter, Editor.
Description: Maryknoll : Orbis Books, 2016 | Series: College Theology Society annual ; 2015, VOLUME 61 | Includes bibliographical references.
Identifiers: LCCN 2015045632 (print) | LCCN 2015048976 (ebook) | ISBN 9781626981652 (pbk.) | ISBN 9781608336326 (ebook)
Subjects: LCSH: Nature—Religious aspects—Christianity. | Wilderness (Theology)
Classification: LCC BR115.N3 U54 2016 (print) | LCC BR115.N3 (ebooks) | DDC 261.8/8—dc23
LC record availabl at http://lccn.loc.gov/2015045632

With gratitude and love,
this volume is dedicated to
Sisters Kay and Annette Fernholz, SSND,
whose work in ecotheology and ecospirituality
has so deeply blessed the world.
You welcomed me to Earthrise Farm
and taught me about stardust and storytelling;
your wisdom, kindness, and love are always with me.

Contents

Part III
Spiritual Practices for a Changing Earth

Part IV
The Human Person in the Community of Creation

Part V
Exploring a Particular Wilderness

Introduction

At Home in the Wilderness

Colleen Mary Carpenter

> *God is not to be fenced in, under human control, like*
> *some domestic creature; He is the wildest being in ex-*
> *istence. The presence of His spirit in us is our wildness,*
> *our oneness with the wilderness of Creation.*
> —Wendell Berry[1]

In his explorations of the words *wild* and *wilderness*, poet and environmental activist Gary Snyder points out that *wild* is primarily defined in terms of what it is not—not tame, not cultivated, not inhabited, not civilized, not restrained—and *wilderness*, too, has a plethora of negative meanings: a wasteland, a place of danger or difficulty, a place untamed by human habitation and cultivation.[2] Yet for all this, the wild and the wilderness also hold a compelling attraction for human beings: the wilderness is a place of beauty as well as danger, of freedom as well as chaos, of abundance as well as emptiness. We define wilderness in opposition to civilization, and our attraction to wilderness, then, waxes and wanes as we reject or embrace the civilization around us. In early colonial America, with European settlers precariously making their way in a new land, wilderness was seen as "'gloomy,' 'dreary,' and 'unhallowed,'"[3] not to mention "a dark and dismal place where all manner of wild beasts dash about uncooked";[4] but by the early twentieth century, with the frontier long since closed, wilderness was seen instead as "a spiritual necessity, an antidote to the high pressure of modern life, a means of regaining serenity and equilibrium."[5]

In John Muir's famous words, "Thousands of tired, nerve-shaken, over-civilized people are beginning to find out that going to the mountains is going home; that wildness is a necessity; and that mountain parks and reservations are useful not only as fountains of timber and irrigating rivers, but as fountains of life."[6]

Wilderness as an idea also has deep biblical resonance, calling to mind the forty years the Israelites spent wandering in the wilderness after leaving Egypt, the temptations of Jesus in the wilderness after his baptism, and Jesus' frequent retreats from active ministry to spend time praying "in a deserted place" (Luke 4:42). Wilderness is thus the desolate place through which we must pass in order to reach the Promised Land; the place where we are tested; and it can also be the place where we meet God.

Whether dismal or delightful, wilderness has always been clearly separated from civilization: it is a place apart. Yet today that bright line defining the wilderness as something distinctly "other" seems to be fading. As the planet changes around us—due to our own actions, yet not easily traceable to any one person's decisions or acts—the world we thought we knew is becoming unfamiliar, even dangerous. Insects that were once regularly killed by the cold of winter are surviving the now-warmer winters, and vast stretches of forest in the mountain west have been devastated as a result.[7] Hurricanes are larger; droughts are more frequent; storms more unpredictable and more destructive. The wilderness we have created is not the saving wilderness imagined by Muir and others, nor is it necessarily the quiet place to which we can retreat to seek God.

It is also important to note that as the planet changes, places that once were thought of as reliably "conquered" by human beings are being reclaimed by the wild, and also that we have made the deliberate choice to degrade and destroy places inhabited by people who are not valued by those in power. Thus wilderness and civilization are tangling together in ways that make it difficult to sort out which is which. Inhabited islands are slowly returning to the sea; garbage pits and toxic waste dumps are both wild and urban; cities and even entire countries become newly wild and hostile to human life under the onslaught of hurricanes, typhoons, and earthquakes. Moreover, these post-storm/post-disaster "wildernesses" disproportionately affect the poor: Pope Francis points this out in his 2015 encyclical *Laudato Si'*, insisting that the cry of the poor is deeply connected to the cry of the Earth.[8] Later in this volume, Agnes Brazal offers the reader an intimate vision of this broad truth, interviewing survivors of Typhoon Haiyan, which devastated the Philippines in 2013.

How, then, are we to understand wilderness today? The desolate waste "out there" is no longer distant, separate, and avoidable; instead, the terrifying chaos is just outside the front door—or perhaps it has even swept the house off its foundations. Similarly, the sublime spiritual haven to which we long to escape is polluted or melting or overrun with ATVs; nowhere on Earth can any longer be described as wilderness, if by that we mean a place "untrammeled by man . . . retaining its primeval character and influence," as the 1964 Wilderness Act defined the term.[9] In our zeal to conquer the wilderness, to tame it, and even to save it, we have forever altered it. Perhaps, then, it is time to remember, with Wendell Berry, that wildness and wilderness are not "out there" at all, but are instead connected to us, and deeply connected to the spirit of God. "The presence of His spirit in us is our . . . oneness with the wilderness of Creation," Berry argues. If all of creation is indeed a wilderness, and we are one with that wilderness in and through the Holy Spirit, then perhaps we need to find a way to understand wilderness neither as threatening nor as paradise, but simply as *home*. It is, after all, the place where we live, and move, and have our being—in God, yes, and also in God's good creation.

Coming to see the wilderness neither as a threatening nor enticing Other but simply as our home: this seems contradictory, but it is not. Rather, it is a recognition of the dazzling, startling, wild creativity of our God, and the dazzling, startling, wild Creation in which we live. The Earth is wild, and we not only live on Earth but are part of it: we exist in the wilderness of Creation and it is right to call this wilderness, this wild and strange and wonderful gift of God, our home. *Laudato Si'*, whose title in English is *On Care for Our Common Home*, takes for granted that when we speak of the Earth as a whole we are speaking of the home God has given to all people (and indeed, all creatures). Quoting St. Francis, the pope reminds us that "our Sister, Mother Earth . . . sustains and governs us," and he then goes on to remind us that "We have forgotten that we ourselves are dust of the earth (cf. Gn 2:7); our very bodies are made up of her elements, we breathe her air and we receive life and refreshment from her waters."[10]

This world is our home; this good and wild creation is our home.

Yet it is also true that our home is in trouble; it has been "gravely damaged by our irresponsible behavior."[11] A long yet disturbingly incomplete list of the problems we face today includes pollution, overfishing, deforestation, loss of topsoil, ocean acidification, loss of biodiversity, a growing scarcity of fresh, clean drinking water, and of course, climate change, which is already causing more extreme weather events, including more powerful hurricanes, increased frequency and intensity of droughts and wildfires, and the melting of glaciers around the world. In *Laudato Si'*, Pope Francis describes the state of our world—the condition of our home—and calls on all the people of the world to "come together to take charge of this home which has been entrusted to us."[12] We have much work to do to repair the damage we have done to our home; we also have much work to do in learning how to care for it properly and how to live in it respectfully, generously, and peacefully.

There are countless ways in which we are called to take charge of our home, and Pope Francis discusses many of them in *Laudato Si'*.[13] However, in order to illustrate how we might begin to engage the world both as wilderness and as home, I would like to focus on just one: access to clean water. Water is necessary for life—and we are faced today with the knowledge that not only is access to water difficult for far too many people, it is also likely to become more difficult for more and more people as the effects of climate change intensify in coming years. Access to fresh, clean water is one of the most significant environmental problems Francis addresses in the opening chapter of *Laudato Si'*; he points out that water poverty is a matter not only of lack of water (drought, desertification), but also of problems with water quality (unsafe, chemically-poisoned or disease-carrying water).[14] Currently, the World Health Organization estimates that three-quarters of a billion people lack access to clean water; globally, one-third of all schools lack access to safe water and adequate sanitation; and in low- and middle-income countries, one-third of all hospitals lack a safe water source.[15] In this context, I would like to talk about a group of women who are deliberately and purposefully changing their relationship with water, women who live in places where water has become hard to get and even harder to trust (because the deadliest pollution is not always visible). These women are working together to transform their water, their communities, and themselves—they are working to make the wilderness their home.

In developing countries, women are usually the ones tasked with collecting clean water—or any water at all—for their families. "The United Nations Development Fund for Women estimates that 'women and children in Africa alone spend approximately forty billion hours every year fetching and carrying water.' "[16] Some women (and girls, often of school age; many cannot attend school because of their water-gathering responsibilities) spend up to eight hours every day collecting water.[17] Despite the fact that it is women who are responsible for collecting water, "they are often left out of development schemes and policies" meant to address water supply issues.[18] Planning is done by experts, usually experts from halfway around the world; the thought of consulting local women—uneducated, poor women—simply never occurs to many planners and agencies. As a result, technologies are introduced that do not meet local needs: wells are placed where women cannot go, or pump handles are located too high off the ground.[19] The United Nations Food and Agriculture Organization has finally recognized that this refusal to consult with and work with women has been disastrous: the "exclusion of women from the planning of water supply and sanitation schemes is a major cause of their high rate of failure."[20]

For water supply and sanitation problems to be adequately addressed, then, women must be involved from the beginning. One organization that has recognized this and that has built its programs around and for women is the Global Women's Water Initiative, an organization whose goal is to educate local women to be able to plan and implement water projects in their own communities. Building on the work of several founding partner organizations, the Global Women's Water Initiative held its first training for African women in 2008. Their "Grassroots Women and Water Training" project is a year-long training program that introduces WASH (water, sanitation, and hygiene) strategies and technologies, as well as ongoing leadership development, to select pairs of women who have already proven themselves as community organizers and project managers. The first training project brought together thirty women from eight African nations; the women learned about rainwater harvesting, biosand filters, portable microbiology lab water testing, solar cooking, microlending and microbusiness, applying for grants, and how to advocate for women's participation in local water policy and decision making.[21] More training sessions for new groups of women have followed every year: the women who have been through the training have returned to their communities to educate their neighbors and build WASH technologies offering clean water and improved sanitation to thousands of people. A partner organization, the Katosi Women's Development Trust, won the 2012 World Water Forum grand prize for their work in addressing water issues in Uganda. The Katosi Women's Development Trust not only trains women in WASH strategies and technologies, but also offers masonry training for building "tanks, filters, hand-washing stations, dishwashers, and toilets."[22]

Here it should be noted that in *Laudato Si'*, Pope Francis warns that "the dominant technocratic paradigm" through which most of us understand the world today lies at the root of much of the ecological damage we have inflicted on the planet.[23] He argues that technology should in many ways be celebrated, but that "reality, goodness and truth" do not in fact "automatically flow from technological and economic power as such."[24] Instead, technology needs to be limited and directed; it needs to serve "another type of progress, one which is healthier, more human, more social, more integral."[25] And this is exactly the kind of technology being used by the Global Women's Water Initiative. This is technology that does not replace human work but instead—as in Francis's vision for truly fulfilling human work—is "the setting for . . . rich personal growth, where many aspects of life enter into play: creativity, planning for the future, developing our talents, living out our values, relating to others, giving glory to God."[26] This can be seen in the stories of what women have achieved through the Katosi Women's Development Trust and the Global Women's Water Initiative. Their websites host a blog that chronicles the triumphs of specific women in specific communities: for example, Angella and Martha in Uganda raised $1,500 to purchase a brick-making machine, and their first project was a rainwater harvesting tank for a local school. Catherine Wanjohi was hired to install biosand filters at a women's prison in Kenya. Rachel and Grace in Tanzania learned how to build a rainwater catchment system, worked with their neighbors to build one—and also learned how to apply for grants to raise the money to build more. They now have three in their local community, and have been teaching women in neighboring villages how to do the same work. Anna Anatoli not only trains the other women in her community to use the various WASH technologies, but also is the Regional Secretary of the Girl Guides in Tanzania and has brought Girl Guides to Global Women's Water Initiative trainings, so that young girls are growing up knowing how to do the things that their mothers are just now learning about.[27] In Ghana, Victoria Norgbey and Benedicta Datsomor learned how to build composting toilets, and then trained fifty schoolchildren to do so as well. They hope that the young people will lead the way in both using and demanding Ecosan toilets in their region—a region in which 90 percent of homes have no toilet, and the busy public market has only one.[28]

These are small victories—fifty schoolchildren building toilets in a world where three-quarters of a billion people lack access to clean water and sanitation might seem nearly pointless—but what is happening is incredibly powerful. Local women are not only learning how to solve the problems particular to their own home and community, they are also learning how to train others to do the same. Change, hope, and empowerment are being built along with the filters, water tanks, and toilets; the women are making positive changes in themselves and in their relationship to both creation and society. They are creating a home—a safe, nurturing, truly human place; the difficult, hostile wilderness in which water was scarce and change seemed impossible turned out to be exactly the place where they could engage in creative, positive work. They found ways to be at home in the wilderness.

Mapping the Volume

In planning this volume, I had assumed that it would have three sections, with the essays in each section connected to one of the three plenary addresses. As it turned out, the theme of wilderness led the members of the Society in so many fascinating directions that containing their creativity in just three categories was impossible. Several papers addressed the "big-picture" issue of how to understand and name what is happening to the Earth right now; others focused tightly on one particular area of wilderness; and some used wilderness as one category among others in examining the broader relationship between human beings and creation.

Other essays, addressing how we might respond to the dramatic changes we are seeing in our world, fell into two groups: those that described a particular virtue that could aid us in dealing with those changes, and those that described not an overarching virtue but concrete practices that could do the same.

Two of the three plenary addresses appear in the volume: I will say more about each of those below. First, however, I would like to reflect on the address that is not here, the one given by Brent Olson. Titled "Fireflies, Wood Ticks, and Gloria the Two-Legged Cat: Wonders in the Wilderness," Olson's address was not a typical theological lecture—and that, of course, was the point. My own journey to theological reflection on the state of the Earth today began in the farm country of western Minnesota, and I remain convinced that doing ecotheology solely from the perspectives of the city, the suburbs, and the academy leaves an enormous gap in our understanding of the human relationship to creation. Farming is central to the human relationship to the Earth, in part because we all eat, but also because so many people are farmers. This was once true around the world, even though it is no longer true in the developed world—in the United States, for example, only 2 percent of the population farms[29]—but 70 percent of the world's poor live in rural areas, and agriculture is their main source of income and employment.[30] Thus one of the plenary addresses was given by a farmer: his perspective on the conference theme grew out of experiences and daily realities that few theologians ever encounter. He asked, however, that his address not be included in the volume, which—while it makes sense in terms of the volume's theological and scholarly aims—was still a real loss. In order to remedy that, at least partially, I offer here a brief introduction to Olson, and a few glimpses of the things he spoke about at the conference.

Brent Olson is a nationally syndicated, award-winning columnist, and has published four books of essays: *Letters from a Peasant; The Lay of the Land; Still Whistling;* and *Papa.*[31] He lives in Big Stone County, Minnesota, which is about two hundred miles west of Minneapolis, right next door to South Dakota. He farmed there for thirty years before turning to writing full-time. His c.v. says that he can castrate thirty-pound pigs by himself, at a rate of thirty seconds per pig. One might think that castrating farm animals is not particularly theologically relevant, but as

Frederick L. Kirschenmann argues in "Theological Reflections while Castrating Calves," the work of understanding the incarnation, and living our lives in response to that astonishing reality, comes in part through cultivating an "awareness that *all* of the members of the biotic community of which we are a part are our 'neighbors' " and that we "encounter the divine in the flesh-and-blood experiences of daily life on a farm, including the simple act of castrating calves."[32]

In 2012, Olson became a Bush Foundation Fellow, receiving a $75,000 grant to reopen the town café in Clinton, MN.[33] He is now the owner, manager, executive chef, head waiter and fry cook at the Inadvertent Café. The idea behind the café is two fold: first, it fills a need for breakfast; and second, for the rest of the day, its licensed commercial kitchen is available to community members who are interested in producing value-added food to sell commercially. For those of us who are neither farmers nor residents of small rural communities, this might seem a bit curious, but in fact both the restaurant and the kitchen meet profound needs. Perhaps surprisingly, it is often difficult to get good and interesting local food in many small towns; it's also very difficult to survive today as a small farmer, or to run a locally-owned grocery store in a rural community. The café's kitchen is an experiment in trying to change all of that. Having the kitchen available to budding entrepreneurs means that local farmers find a cooking customer; the local grocery store gets innovative products; people get good local food; and community members can develop new businesses.

The Inadvertent Café is not of course Olson's first foray into making his community a stronger place, more livable, more inviting. He served as a county commissioner for ten years, and is the chair of the Pioneerland Library System Board, which serves nine counties in western Minnesota. He's active in the Methodist Church, and says that he "takes that whole John Wesley thing really seriously": *Do all the good you can, by all the means you can, in all the ways you can, in all the places you can, at all the times you can, to all the people you can, as long as ever you can.* Grounded in the Methodist tradition, then, Olson's perspective as a farmer, social justice activist, and community leader shaped his reflections on the conference themes of wilderness and the search for God on a changing planet. Those reflections were not presented in the form of a familiar, academic, theological argument but instead as a personal narrative, one constructed as a series of interlocking, overlapping stories that slowly built into a very particular vision of what this world is, what it means, and how we as human creatures fit into it.

Contemplating "the stunning variety of wonders in the wilderness" provided the structure of Olson's address, and the first wonder he presented to us was rather startling: the wood tick. "Wood ticks are disease-ridden, disgusting vermin that make life a torment for all sorts of creatures . . . [but] I fully expected to find some nifty ecological niche to justify their existence on this earth, which would help illustrate a stunning metaphor about the least among us." Unfortunately, as it turns out, wood ticks are not a particularly essential form of life on earth. "Oh sure, they're a food source for some critters, but not in any sort of critical way. They do spread diseases, but mostly to moose and nowhere in the weight class of the Black Death or avian flu. So what purpose do they serve? None. At least none that we can tell. And that's what is so cool."[34] Yes, *cool*—our ignorance here, about such an odd and seemingly insignificant thing, fascinates Olson.

And it should fascinate us as well, for despite our intelligence and vast scientific knowledge, human beings do not in fact know what purpose wood ticks serve, nor even if they serve a purpose at all. And this reminds us that, despite our theological claims about the significance and uniqueness of humanity, we are not in the end masters of this world, nor are we its center. In their sheer mystery, wood ticks remind us that:

> It's not about us. That's hard for many folks to hear. This is a glorious, magnificent, puzzling, dangerous world and we're not a particularly important part of it. Despite the claims, humanity is in no danger of destroying the world. We have it within our grasp to kill ourselves off and most other living creatures but the world will be just fine . . . no matter what we do, in a few million years there will be a whole new thriving ecosystem.[35]

Olson also spoke about fireflies, and the risks inherent in "projecting our own illusions and feelings on . . . a meadow full of fireflies on a June evening,"[36] and eventually came to the story of Gloria, the two-legged cat:

In the midst of a brutally cold January my son-in-law came across a cat literally frozen to the ground at the end of our driveway. . . . Gloria's story could be a Disney movie, if Disney movies were made by Tim Burton. She's missing her ears, one leg to the hock and has another one that ends at the ankle. Her tail is two inches long with a scratchy stump at the tip. She is a gruesome-looking individual, always anxious to sit on your lap and cuddle, purring and rubbing her ear holes against you.[37]

Despite her injuries and distressing appearance, Gloria is a perfectly happy cat. More than that, even: she "is the very personification of joie de vivre," of the kind of joy in living that teaches us that there is a difference, and an enormous one, between being alive and living. Yet Gloria is also, for Olson, a lesson in wilderness. "What happened to her was not an act of malevolence; there was no evil intent. There was simply someone's lost cat and a hard January cold. Nature is neither kind nor cruel; wilderness holds no special benefit or vice. It simply is."[38]

The stories we tell about wilderness, Olson insists, tend to ignore the reality of Nature—and this is dangerous. It is dangerous because it means we misunderstand the world around us, which can have serious, even fatal, consequences, and not just during January in western Minnesota. More important, it is dangerous because when we are focused on the frightening or compelling or beautiful or overwhelming wilderness "out there," we find it all too easy to ignore the wilderness that is part of our own being:

Most of the true wilderness left in the world isn't out there; it's in here. Our hearts are the only place where there are no rules, where chaos exists, and danger is everywhere. It's a place where we need to walk carefully, tend our garden with care and keep the wolves at bay. We're all a little broken, a little scarred, and that isn't our weakness; that is our strength and our beauty and if we are going to save the wilderness, and the garden, and seek God along the way, that is where the work begins.[39]

The more traditionally theological work of the conference, too, focused on what it might mean to save the wilderness, and to understand it properly, and how the human quest for God engages that project in our particular circumstances. Part I, "Naming Our New Era," comprises three essays that each wrestle with the question of how to understand the world in which we now live. The Earth is not the same as it once was: the human impact on our planet has fundamentally changed it. Journalist and climate activist Bill McKibben once suggested that we stop calling it Earth and identify it instead as "Eaarth," thus indicating that the planet that most of us knew as children is essentially lost to us.[40] In the opening essay of the volume, Catherine Keller takes up this challenge of climate change as an all too practical issue—and argues that it is also more than that, as climate change is inevitably "entangled in questions of God, of creation and apocalypse, of beginnings and catastrophes." Her lyrical consideration of the wild Spirit of God, *creatio ex nihilo*, and the possibility of understanding creation "tehomophilically" leads her to argue that there is still reason for hope, even as we face the growing possibility of ecological catastrophe. Next, Elizabeth Groppe explores the new designation for the geologic age in which we live: the Anthropocene. Its name points to what once was an unimaginable reality: human activity is now the determinative factor in the geological "state of the world." Groppe's essay asks how we as Christians might tell the story of the Anthropocene: "How will we speak of God, Christ, creation, grace, sin, humanity, and eschatology in this context? How will we express this theological narrative in poetry, literature, song, and art?" She examines the art of Samuel Bak as one possible answer to these questions. J. Leavitt Pearl, too, is interested in what story we are telling about our time and our planet. He argues that the popular, romantic model of ecological thinking epitomized by David Abram cannot in fact do the work it is attempting, and suggests that an apocalyptic model would in fact better describe where we are and how to understand our current plight.

In the next section, "Virtues for the Wilderness," Agnes Brazal starts from a consideration of Super-typhoon Haiyan as an example of unexpected wilderness. Haiyan, which struck the Philippines in November 2013, killed over six thousand people and displaced more than four million. In interviews with survivors, Brazal explores their responses to the devastating storm and constructs an understanding of their resilience that enables her to propose that resilience is indeed a virtue that is particularly needed in today's changing world. Bridget O'Brien turns to the biblical story of Hagar as interpreted by Delores Williams in order to explore the risks of ecological despair—and the power of the virtue of hope. Looking not at a single virtue but at the connections between the virtues, Nancy Rourke examines the intersection of wilderness and integrity, arguing that chaos is and should be part of our understanding of moral character.

Part III, "Spiritual Practices for a Changing Earth," introduces three different approaches to the spiritual activities we might undertake in confronting the problems of the Earth today. Julia Brumbaugh speaks movingly of grief; Katherine Greiner advocates cultivating a sense of rootedness and belonging. Greiner's essay provides a counterpoint to J. Leavitt Pearl's: how, in the end, should we understand the human yearning to root oneself, to dwell in a particular place to the point where we identify as part of it? The final essay in this section, Regina Boisclair's, turns to practices of biblical interpretation and proclamation. She explains and advocates a change in the Sunday lectionary that would aid the Church in fostering a greater sense of ecological responsibility.

Next, in Part IV, three essays address "The Human Person in the Community of Creation." David Gentry-Akin offers an account of the life and work of Thomas Berry, whose ecological writings are central to a substantial body of Catholic thinking today on the relationship between humanity and creation. Berry's critique of our long-standing anthropocentrism, and his insistence that the universe is "not a collection of objects but a communion of subjects" opened the door to conversations that profoundly challenged ideas we had too long taken for granted. John Thiede, too, addresses the problem of anthropocentrism as he describes Leonardo Boff's revisioning of the human relationship to the world, and links that vision to a renewed understanding of martyrdom today. Mary Doak and Thomas Hughson offer us a dialogic essay exploring a specific instance of the human relationship to the world: the American relationship to wilderness. By examining the idea of wilderness in American cultural history and in American political ideals, Doak and Hughson demonstrate that engaging wilderness is necessary to any US public theology today.

Finally, in Part V, "Exploring a Particular Wilderness," we have the opportunity to move from consideration of the planet as a whole to a more intimate consideration of particular places. Jessica Wrobleski takes us on a journey to Appalachia, where the beauty and wildness of the mountains is and long has been under assault by those who profit by stripping the land of its rich resources. Christine Fletcher takes us to a Benedictine monastery outside of Chicago, and describes contemporary challenges to the Benedictine commitment to living on the border between wilderness and garden. Finally, Jessica Coblentz offers us a vision not of a place on the Earth but a place within the human mind. Her essay considers the imagery of "melancholic landscapes" used by those struggling through the wilderness of depression, and turns to Delores Williams's understanding of wilderness and of suffering to construct a theology of depression.

Acknowledgments

Both the conference and this volume were the work of many hands, and I am profoundly grateful to all the people who contributed so generously to this project. I remain utterly amazed at all of David Gentry-Akin's work as the Executive Director of National Conventions for the College Theology Society; coordinating all of the practical aspects of the conference program and venue is an enormous and difficult task. The smooth operation of the annual convention does not call attention to itself, which makes it all the more necessary to thank Dave for all the behind-the-scenes work that makes that smooth operation possible. Carol Dempsey served as Local Coordinator for the convention, welcoming the Society once again to the University of Portland, where we enjoyed rich hospitality through her work and the work of many others at the university. The section leaders are the heart of the conference and have my gratitude for their hard work over the many months preceding our time together in Portland: they wrote the calls for papers, evaluated proposals, put together and moderated fascinating sessions, and encouraged their presenters to submit their papers to the volume. Dozens of members of the Society gave of their time in order to serve as reviewers for this volume, and I am grateful to all of them for their expertise and thoughtful responses to the papers. Dana Dillon, the Executive Coordinator of Digital Media, designed a wonderful system for people to volunteer to be reviewers; it was amazing to open a Google Docs spreadsheet and have at my fingertips a long list of reviewers, including their specializations and email addresses. The days of yellow legal pads covered in semilegible script seem to have come to a blessed end.

I am deeply grateful to the three plenary speakers, Agnes Brazal, Brent Olson, and Catherine Keller, who agreed to accompany us through our meditations on wilderness and on the state of the Earth today. Their provocative, insightful presentations anchored the conference; their voices and their wisdom started lively conversations and charted new paths forward in both theological and practical ways. I am also grateful to the thirteen other contributors to the volume, each of whom approached the theme in thoughtful and rich ways and worked quickly to prepare their manuscripts under the tight time constraints required by the publication schedule. I owe further gratitude to the many other members of CTS who submitted their work for consideration for the volume; there were far too many excellent papers to choose from, and I regret that there was not room enough for all of them. Many thanks, too, go to William Collinge, Chairperson and Editor of Research and Publications for the CTS, whose keen eye and careful editing were invaluable, and to Jim Keane of Orbis Books, especially for his patience and his creativity in finding ways to make the deadlines meet me when it looked like I was not going to meet them. Finally, I would like to thank my own institution, St. Catherine University, for giving me the time to work on this volume through the support of the Sister Mona Riley Endowed Chair in the Humanities.

Notes

[1] Wendell Berry, "Christianity and the Survival of Creation," in Norman Wirzba, ed., *The Art of the Commonplace: The Agrarian Essays of Wendell Berry*, ed. Norman Wirzba (Washington, D.C.: Counterpoint Press, 2002), 310.

[2] Gary Snyder, *The Practice of the Wild* (Berkeley, CA: Counterpoint Press, 1990), 9-12.

[3] Roderick Nash, *Wilderness and the American Mind* (New Haven: Yale UP, 1967), 24.

[4] "What Is Wilderness?" in The Wilderness Institute at the University of Montana, wilderness.net.

[5] Sigurd F. Olson, "We Need Wilderness," in *The Meaning of Wilderness: Essential Articles and Speeches*, ed. David Backes (Minneapolis: University of Minnesota Press, 2001), 61. Originally published in *National Parks Magazine* 84 (1946).

[6] John Muir, *Our National Parks* (Boston: Houghton Mifflin, 1901), 1.

[7] "Forest Health: Mountain Pine Beetle," Rocky Mountain National Park Colorado, National Park Service, nps.gov.

[8] *Laudato Si'*, 48–52. Pope Francis is of course not the first to make this connection. For two other examples, see Leonardo Boff, *Cry of the Earth, Cry of the Poor* (Maryknoll, NY: Orbis Books, 1997), especially chapter 5, "Liberation Theology and Ecology: Rivals or Partners?" 104–14, and James H. Cone, "Whose Earth Is It Anyway?" *Cross Currents* 50, no.1–2 (Spring/Summer 2000): 36–46, Crosscurrents.org.

[9] The full definition of wilderness in the 1964 Wilderness Act is as follows: "A wilderness, in contrast with those areas where man and his works dominate the landscape, is hereby recognized as an area where the earth and its community of life are untrammeled by man, where man himself is a visitor who does not remain. An area of wilderness is further defined to mean in this Act an area of undeveloped Federal land retaining its primeval character and influence, without permanent improvements or human habitation, which is protected and managed so as to preserve its natural conditions and which (1) generally appears to have been affected primarily by the forces of nature, with the imprint of man's work substantially unnoticeable; (2) has outstanding opportunities for solitude or a primitive and unconfined type of recreation; (3) has at least five thousand acres of land or is of sufficient size as to make practicable its preservation and use in an unimpaired condition; and (4) may also contain ecological, geological, or other features of scientific, educational, scenic, or historical value." The Wilderness Act, Public Law 88-577 (16 U.S.C. 1131-1136), section 2(c).

[10] *Laudato Si'*, 1, 2.

[11] Ibid., 6.

[12] Ibid., 244.

[13] The problems facing the world are outlined in chapter 1, "What Is Happening to Our Common Home," and Pope Francis's suggestions for how we might begin to respond can be found in chapters 5 and 6, "Lines of Approach and Action," and "Ecological Education and Spirituality."

[14] *Laudato Si'*, 28.

[15] "Drinking-water," Fact sheet 391, June 2015. World Health Organization, www.who.int.

[16] "Watering the Grassroots: Training African Women to Solve Water Problems," *World Rivers Review*, 26, no.1 (March 2011): 4.

[17] www.globalwomenswater.org.

[18] "Watering the Grassroots," 4.

[19] www.globalwomenswater.org.

[20] "Watering the Grassroots," 4.

[21] www.globalwomenswater.org.

[22] "GWWI Women and Water on Wednesdays: Katosi Women's Development Trust Wins 3rd Kyoto World Water Grand Prize!" Women's Earth Alliance blog, March 21, 2012, www.womensearthalliance.blogspot.com.

[23] *Laudato Si'*, 101.

[24] Ibid., 105.

[25]Ibid., 112.

[26]Ibid., 127.

[27]www.womensearthalliance.blogspot.com.

[28]www.womensearthalliance.org.

[29]"Fast Facts about Agriculture," *The Voice of Agriculture*, American Farm Bureau Federation. www.fb.org.

[30]"Agriculture and Rural Development," World Bank. www.data.worldbank.org.

[31]*The Lay of the Land: A View from the Prairie* (Lincoln, NE: J & L Lee, 1998); *Letters from a Peasant: The Wit and Wisdom of a Prairie Farmer* (Edina, MN: Kirk House, 2001); *Still Whistling: The Only Sane Response to a Complicated World* (Edina, MN: Kirk House, 2004); *Papa: Figuring Out What Matters* (Edina, MN: Kirk House, 2009).

[32]Frederick L. Kirschenmann, "Theological Reflections while Castrating Calves," *Cultivating an Ecological Conscience: Essays from a Farmer Philosopher* (Lexington: University Press of Kentucky, 2010), 20.

[33]Bob Collins, "You Should Meet: Brent Olson," Minnesota Public Radio News (April 2, 2013). www.blogs.mprnews.org.

[34]Brent Olson, "Wood Ticks, Fireflies, and Gloria the Two-Legged Cat: Wonders in the Wilderness," unpublished speaking text, 6.

[35]Olson, 7.

[36]Ibid., 9.

[37]Ibid., 10.

[38]Ibid., 11.

[39]Ibid., 15.

[40]Bill McKibben, *Eaarth: Making a Life on a Tough New Planet* (New York: Henry Holt, 2010), 2.

PART I

NAMING OUR NEW ERA

Spirit Wilds

Climate and Theology

Catherine Keller

It is a pleasure to join the unexpected and refreshing wildness of this conversation among theologians. But theology can feel wild in a less inviting sense these days. Theology itself feels like an endangered species within the changing, poorly protected wilderness park of higher education—whether in church-related liberal arts colleges or in theological schools. The ecologies of uncertainty we address in this conference are not those of an academic discipline, however, even one so vulnerable as theology.

The uncertainty as to the human future that climate change signifies comes fraught with theological meanings. It bears opposite senses of "wild": our planetary ecology is being made turbulent and dangerous through the economic-political secularizations of a theology of human dominion; and the earth remains wild in an opposite sense, the sense of the spirit of the wilderness—the Holy Spirit. Let me cite a great Catholic authority: "for all this, nature is never spent; There lives the dearest freshness deep down things." Ah, bright wings. Ah, winged Hopkins. Ah, bright Jesuits. If we are in this event seeking God—the deep down of things—on a changing planet, we have come already entangled in questions of God, of creation and apocalypse, of beginnings and catastrophes.

Where to start seeking with you now? There have been so many honorable starts, indeed a proliferation of ecotheological starts, all tinged with the wildness of the prophets, for nearly half a century. Well, we do not start from nothing. Indeed, the whole notion of starting from nothing—of *creatio ex nihilo*—can be read as one long campaign against the wilderness. I'll get to that. How do you start talk about climate change with your students? Scare them with well-aimed facts and postapocalyptic imaginaries? Reassure them with action-galvanizing hope? I worry I may be just swinging between privileged Pollyanna and climate killjoy. How do we catalyze change in the face of catastrophe—that is, when honest hope must face the wilderness to come, not that of a restored balance between human culture and nonhuman nature but of a disastrous imbalance already to an unknown degree locked into the human future? If the best we can now expect to achieve through an unbelievably difficult and unlikely historical shift is partial mitigation and painful adaptation—how shall we generate enough hope to break through the layered logics of denial and the daily comforts of distraction?

In what follows I hope to reflect with you a bit further on the idea of wilderness as it pertains to the climate, theologically speaking, and specifically to the beginnings and endings that theology encodes; and then to think about the kind of knowledge that is at stake in the wildness of the climate, in the discussion of climate change in general. It is a kind of wildness of our knowing, an intensified uncertainty, that responds to the indeterminacy of our world. And theologically that uncertainty goes deep, deep down things, to the apophatic unknowing—which is where I get even closer to Catholicism. Named or unnamed, the divine is a deep wellspring of action that we as theologians must help our collectives, religious and secular, to tap. Not just to face the unpredictabilities of life but to subvert the causes of climate catastrophe. But finally I will also suggest a couple of strategically concrete reasons for, yes, hope.

Serendipitously the lyrical book of Robert Macfarlane, *The Wild Places,* landed in my hands just as I was considering this lecture. Asking whether there are any genuinely wild places left in his homeland, he narrates a series of journeys through the archipelago of the United Kingdom. On Ynys Enlli, Island of the Currents, around which "several fierce tide races meet," he contemplates the particular erratic wave formations, menacing to mariners.[1] Later he likens ideas to waves:

> They arrive with us having travelled vast distances, and their pasts are often invisible, or barely imaginable. "Wildness" is

such an idea: it has moved immensely through time. And in that time, two great and conflicting stories have been told about it. According to the first of these, wildness is a quality to be vanquished; according to the second, it is a quality to be cherished.[2]

On this island, "its beauty and its riotous fecundity,"[3] he finds himself tracking the monks who found their way there already in the sixth century. They called themselves *peregrini*, and left traces of their wonder: one wrote of "the wind's voice against a branchy wood on a day of grey cloud."[4]

"The etymology of the word 'wild' is vexed and subtle," Macfarlane writes, "but the most persuasive past proposed for it involves the Old High German *wildi*, and the Old Norse *villr.*" If these words signify disorder and irregularity, they also carry from "the English root-word 'will' 'a descriptive meaning of . . . wilful or uncontrollable.' " Thus independence from human management, or wild land, can be said to be "*self-willed* land."[5] So on the one hand, he continues, "wildness has been perceived as a dangerous force that confounds the order-bringing pursuits of human culture and agriculture. Wildness . . . is cognate with wastefulness. Wild places resist conversion to human use, and they must be destroyed or overcome. . . . 'Except for the true civilization builders,' hallelujahed the popular preacher and writer James Stalker in 1881, 'the very land in which we live would still be an undiscovered wilderness. These men see teeming cities, and thriving factories upon the desert, where others see only sagebrush and alkali plains. . . . These men have tunnelled our mountains, have spanned our great rivers, and opened our mines of wealth!' "[6]

Mines of wealth indeed. The ecotheologian Michael Northcott, also of the UK, describes how definitive were those mines for modernity, for the structuring of Western civilization in terms of an economy of extraction. Coal mining in fact "set the pattern for the new form of wage labour which grew outside of the moral constraints of guild or manor after the failure of the English revolution and the restoration of the monarchy. Hence coal not only made industrial civilisation materially possible. It also shaped the relations of production that predominate in both capitalist and communist forms of mercantilism until the present."[7] Indeed the material culture enabled by coal, in which "the earth is dominated and reengineered from its depths to its outer atmospheric limits, also sustains the cultural objects and values that until today make it difficult for industrial societies to respond to or to resolve the ecological and climate crisis." At the heart of this lack of response is manifest a "new attitude to human making as a form of conscious rational dominion over a material earth that is empty of moral or spiritual significance apart from humanity's rational reordering."[8]

In other words, dominion is exercised at once in knowledge and in power—over all that is otherwise wild, waste, disorderly, even revolting, except as extrinsically ordered by the man—the white man—made in the image of divine dominance. Bacon's "knowledge as power" then energized what he called "The Masculine Birth of Time,"[9] the modern form of dominion. It focused a whole paradigm of penetrating and pumping, based on his own metaphors of the Christian practice of drilling into the bodies of women with the torture instruments of interrogation, as willful women—in early modernity—were for their wild natures routinely suspected of witchcraft. (Catholics and Protestants were equal opportunity witch hammerers, though as Weber nailed it, we Protestants early outdid you Catholics in terms of drilling the earth. Anyway, you see how feminist theology, led by that stubbornly R.C. Rosemary Ruether, so soon became ecofeminism.)

The extraction of fossil fuels is inextricable then from the rising middle class, and from the development of a democracy now increasingly turning into corporatocracy. In the interest of not wasting, it lays waste the creaturely context of life, human and nonhuman. The CO_2 released as a result of all the drilling from still-proliferating coal-fired energy plants, along with the oil and gas emissions, is producing the vast wastelands of earth and water and air that characterize the culture of extractivism.

Yet coal in the ground is "stored sunlight . . . the effect of the activities of millions of plants and other creatures which in the Carboniferous geological era gradually sank into the earth's crust. . . . They locked down sufficient quantities of CO_2 to change the balance of carbon and oxygen in the atmosphere, thus creating the climatic conditions which enabled the evolutionary rise of mammals."[10] In other words, coal is a wild thing, benign on its own. It becomes another kind of wild when exploited.

Of course this modern attitude to making, with its fundamental sense of taking or taming the wild things, the wilderness, is not at its root secularist. It is powered by its secularization of the theology of dominion over an earth that is—in its initial condition—construed as empty of intrinsic value or spiritual meaning. In other words: waste and void. Oops, isn't that what the Bible says the earth is? Literally, in the American Standard version of Genesis.

Actually no, the Hebrew says *tohu va bohu . . . tohu* means without form, uninhabitable, wild; and *bohu* was added just as a poetic intensifier, a rhyme wedged right into that second verse for beauty. In France, *tohubohu* is in dictionaries, and a German student of mine said her mother used to scold her for making a *tohuvabohu* of her room. When in the beginning Elohim was creating it all, the earth was already there in this unformed condition, this potentiality, as darkness was upon the face of the *tehom*. The deep. And the *ruach*, no tame bird this, vibrating like a gull upon the waters. A scene of oceanic wilderness, this, pulsing with theopoetic possibility, a chaos not of disorder but of vibratory intensity and of uncertain outcomes, its virtual earth a dark precursor of the later habitable materiality called forth in such congenial co-creativity.

Ok, but isn't that all nothing? Nada. *Nihil.* So the orthodoxy of *creatio ex nihilo* teaches. For after all, there had always been those two possibilities for reading the wildness of creation itself, weren't there—as a disorder to be vanquished, its sea monsters destroyed; or as the chaotic virtuality to be cherished, the very deep of the freshness deep down things, the womb of every beginning? These alternate readings begin biblically—the first, in which the Lord smites the Leviathan, I nicknamed *tehomophobia*; the other, in which YHWH as in Job and Ps 104 adores the sea monsters, *tehomophilia*. (Potentials for a queer reading noted.) In our civilization, the heroic tehomophobia triumphed, as *Face of the Deep*[11] tells it leviathanically. But the mythic battle with chaos, while opposing order to disorder antagonistically, does not yet simply repress and deny the primal chaos. *Creatio ex nihilo*, however, offers an image of serene omnipotence with no troublingly original wilderness to conquer in the first place, a metaphysical upgrade of control to the absolute: in other words, the wilderness gets vanquished after the fact and a priori by theology. The creation from mere nothingness vanquishes the wilderness of creation so totally that Christians never need to face their own fear of that deep down of things. Will climate change change that too?

Indeed, how you teach your students to interpret the *imago dei* and its dominion in verses 26–29 will depend on how you read verse 2. For if you go the route of the conquest of the chaos and more, of its precreation reduction to *nihil*, then you may comfortably read the dominion as mirroring the image of the sovereign deity—in His [*sic*] infinite dominance. So then man (oh, and woman) is made in His Image to fill the earth and subdue it: the one commandment, as John Cobb quips, that our species has consistently obeyed. But even theologians who insist upon a strong image of divine rule may worry about the *Wirkungsgeschichte* of this text. They can see that the political theology of the West shares responsibility for the limitless extractivism and unfettered capitalism that fuel climate change. They may, Barth style, pit the sovereign God against the idols of human sovereignty. And surely any responsible reading will read the *imago dei* in the context of all those "God saw that it was good!" exclamations, which is to say dominion can only mean responsibility; even if we fancy ourselves the culmination of the creative process, does that that give us license to exploit and extinguish all the good that leads up to us?

But if you read tehomophilically, you find in the wilds of the universe evidence of an originative wilderness, mysterious and fecund, something like the quantum void that is no nothing at all but that, as Karen Barad explicates it, comes queerly replete with electrons touching each other infinitely.[12] If you can translate the Holy Spirit as the wild spirit of verse 2, you bring your cherishing of wilderness right to the *imago dei*: we are created in the image of a creator in order to be—creative, in a creativity that is from the start a collaboration. Elohim calls and creatures respond by *becoming*, each time fresh and somehow surprising to the creator. Not only humans co-create: the earth itself is called to bring forth, as are the waters, and the delegation intensifies the feedback loops of evolutionary interactivity that do yield us, here, naming it all, even now.

If you are reading tehomophilically, cherishing wildness, you are no doubt already some sort of ecotheologian. You might wish those verses of dominion would just disappear, along with the great *kabash* of the earth. (Yes, I kid you not, *kabash* is the Hebrew for 'subdue.') I cannot disagree with Lynn White Jr.'s classic argument that the standard rendition of dominion lies at the root of the problem. But with a theological public, I find it more effectual to reinterpret the dominion than to denounce it. I

can share with enlightened ex-nihilists the sense that this dominion can only mean responsibility. But one must historicize that
dominion: in its context it is an exilic work of resistance to the
Babylonian empire and Marduk their warrior god, who kabashes
Tiamat—the etymological sister of Tehom. He pierces her through
and creates—or shall we say extracts—from her body the world
he will dominate. Humans were meant to be slaves to the gods;
other creatures are hardly mentioned. So instead, in Genesis, all
humans are created to be god-like, all royal, not meant to be slaves.
The *imago dei* expresses a companionate creativity of God, men,
women, and nonhumans. Then look at the text itself: make your
more fundamentalist students get really literal: like, *read* the verses
immediately following the dominion:

> God said, "See, I have given you every plant yielding seed
> that is upon the face of all the earth, and every tree with seed
> in its fruit; you shall have them for food. And to every beast
> of the earth, and to every bird of the air, and to everything
> that creeps on the earth, everything that has the breath of
> life, I have given every green plant for food." And it was so.
> God saw everything that he had made, and indeed, it was
> very good.[13]

What the biblical God literally deems really good, then, is our
responsible inhabitation of a planet in which we are vegans. Like
the other breathers. That's dominion for you!

If you want to be literal.

Of course, the context is that of a mainly wild planet, with
minimal cultivated land—in that original sense, with nutrients
botanically free to pluck. Indeed, it suggests precisely the garden of
Eden. Which not accidentally the editors set as the next chapter. But
then it would be the garden as wilderness. But isn't a garden what
we mean by cultivation, and so the very opposite of a wild place?
Language gets ambiguous. The Edenic story of sin and expulsion
transitions the humans into the familiar punitively heavy labor of
reproduction and cultivation. This wilderness being plowed loses
the sense of refreshment that is remembered as Edenic.

But Eden would in the future take on the meaning of the
original wilderness as restorative. The place to which, like the
old monks, the *peregrini*, whose traces Macfarlane tracks in the

lingering wild spaces, one seeks to return. We cannot return to the ambiguously gardened Eden, but it somehow promises to return to us—as the hoped-for future, the new heaven and earth. But differently. It is called also the New Jerusalem. And then, in The Book of Revelation, it is nothing if not an immense urban park. By Stephen Moore's exegesis, it has a couple of trees, and resembles a "continent-sized shopping mall."[14] *Oy vey.* Is that the best we can hope for, at the end of the age? The New Jerusalem with its absolute artifice cultivated for the small number of the elect—what, the 1%?

I wrote an end-of-the-millennium book about apocalypse, proposing a counterapocalypse: deconstructing absolute ending as I would later do with absolute beginning.[15] Even though my feminist mistrust of this text persists, I imagine returning to the scene of John's apocalypse, ruminating on its eerie prophecy of floods and forest fires and the desertification of the land and of the seas, the violence and hunger and wild devastation that our species brings upon itself and all the rest—in other words, its anticipation of what we so calmly call climate change. . . . Its mythic vision of the lascivious imperial greed, including its merchant navy and its trade in luxury products, that triggers doom, is precise. In the vision, the wildness is all about destruction, doom, the punishing effects of our systemic sinful power; and so redemption means—no more wilderness: literally "no more sea." And then the geometric garden-city. In the text—literally—there is not, nonetheless, "the end of the world." It is a barely imaginable new beginning after great catastrophe. It is fundamentalism, not biblical eschatology, that offers the end of the world.

As I find no escape from these codes of beginning and ending and beginning again, their garden patches uncultivated or over-cultivated, I might write a little book called *Apocalypse After All?* The question mark would not mark a rhetorical question, but a real uncertainty. An uncertainty as to whether we are caught up in a self-fulfilling prophecy of doom: its glyphs of dominion pressed into the reign of the market, guided by the invisible hand through the myth of the sovereignty of the individual consumer, which conceals the sovereignty of the corporate elite. The wild elements of earth and water and atmosphere are either expropriated—vanquished and enslaved—as market commodities or else are considered waste and void, so-called externalities irrelevant to the calculus of growth. And so indeed endless waste and wasteland are produced, not as a void, not as *nihil*, but as a new and spreading uninhabitability, an earth being artificially rendered *tohuvabohu* in the name of the conquest of that very chaos.

The great uncertainty of the Anthropocene is whether the determinisms of the mechanisms of deregulation and extraction will play themselves out. What seems clear is that all we have to do in order to make the ancient prophecies of doom come true is to do nothing. To let the determinisms of capital and its fossil fuel emissions take their course. Will we let these deterministic outcomes play out the certainty represented by 97% of all climate scientists? Perhaps. Or not.

I consider this uncertainty dire and deep—and weirdly hopeful. It does not answer to the deterministic logic of modernity or to the random gambles of high stakes capitalism. It does not justify either nihilistic despair or ex nihilist triumph. It answers instead to the spirit of a universe in which every determinate process enfolds microcosmic indeterminacies from the bottom up, and every complex system unfolds, as Prigogine put it, at the edge of chaos.[16] It makes of the creation one great ecology of uncertainty—a Joycean chaosmos, not mere chaos, not mere cosmos.[17]

In other words, there is a wild space of thought that we need now—a transdisciplinary thinking that embraces an uncertainty at the edge of any trusty knowledge: for it is a thinking of the entanglements of vast diversity, a thinking across unexpected wildernesses dire.

Differently, the monocropping rationality of late capitalism operates with an economics that with its quantitative models, as Cobb demonstrated already in *For the Common Good*,[18] remains the most resistant discipline of all to interdisciplinarity and so to interlinkages of the economy with every other dimension of our *oikos*, our dwelling. Yet theology is transdisciplinary to the core, constructed of biblical stories and Greek philosophy put into practice in every register of life, art, and liturgy. Your thinking is crucial now—not because theology can trump the certitudes of late capitalism with a greater certainty. Faith may be assurance, it may be trustworthy, but it is not certainty. No, it offers a deeper unknowing: that of creativity from the deep itself. From life's wild places, where there may be great suffering, vulnerability and loss, where wilderness may quickly turn inhospitable. And yet these

are places of intense affect, places that can open into alternative
wisdoms, publics, ritual communities, social movements. But these
wild places do not open as mere knowledge but as what the old
fifteenth-century Nicholas of Cusa—yes, the cardinal—called the
"knowing ignorance."

And it originates in biblical interpretation. Indeed, it lets us
return to an ancient wilderness, indeed to the wilderness of the
Exodus. Full of daunting dangers, certainly no garden—it was the
only way to liberation. Moses is invited to meet God in a dark
cloud. And from this image would be born in another millennium
the whole tradition of apophatic theology: with Gregory of Nyssa
discerning in that peak experience the brilliant darkness: God
as a nonknowable infinity contemplated in the dark cloud. This
mystical thread extrudes itself through Dionysius and Eckhart,
unsaying every claim about God—father, light, person—as any
entity that we could name and know. Yet this does not create a
distant transcendence but energizes a mystical ubiquity, a mysterious intimacy of the infinite.

And there old Cusa captures me in his rendition of the dark
cloud in the wild: in what he called "the cloud of the impossible."[19]
But what does this have to do with climate change and the all
too literal, material wildernesses at stake? This much, *in nuce*:
his apophatic method led him to rethink the universe as radically
interconnected: "all in all and each in each"; and only *so* is God
in all and all in God. It is a mystical panentheism for an ecology
of uncertainty: for the noncertitude, the unknowability, of what
we name as God lends itself to the universe, in which we do not
know anything with simple certainty. With Cusa, we conjecture
perspectivally. And contradictions throw us into the cloud, in pain
. . . to struggle with impossibility. It opens into a paradise in the
cloud, an Eden concealed by the wall of our binary constructions,
and so into a God who is *posse ipsum*, possibility itself. But we
creatures do the actualizing.

In process theology, the dependence of God on the creature to
materialize the possible becomes fully explicit. And the wildness of
the ultimate creativity becomes cosmology in Whitehead's 1920s
reception of quantum uncertainty. We are called to responsibility
not just for our bit of the creation, but for our self-creation—as
selves boundlessly entangled with our creaturely neighbors—"we
find ourselves in a . . . democracy of fellow creatures."[20]

Is it possible that the contemplative hospitality of the cloud, as *docta ignorantia*, can shed its dark luminosity on the specific uncertainty that plagues climate science itself? For what the deniers use is *uncertainty—doubt* about the facts. Oreskes' and Conway's *Merchants of Doubt* exposed the ancestry of the denial of climate science in the earlier denial of the effects of tobacco smoke. The merchandising of doubt has been able to work so well "because we have an erroneous view of science. We think that science provides certainty, so if we lack certainty, we think the science must be faulty or incomplete."[21] Contra positivist science, we know of no more complex system than that of the earth, so of course there are layers of uncertainty. Climate science can predict the general patterns of Arctic ice melt, methane release, Gulf Stream shifts, sea risings, and droughts. But it cannot tell us how long the California drought will last. Or which part of Oregon's fabulous forests will go up in flames or down to insects this summer.

We can draw upon the depths of our contemplative tradition of knowing ignorance—humble rigorous attention to the limits of our knowledge—both to support good science and to minister to fear in the face of uncertainties. Learning to live with the wildernesses of human making, urban and rural wastelands that will be populated with hungry and frantic crowds, may require a spiritually charged, contemplative and activist, cloud-practice. It may inspire new gardens in the wilderness, like collective gardens in churchyards and on city roofs, and with these, modes of collaboration and locality that may build up the publics with which to confront the causes of the planetary crisis.[22]

Still, an ecology of uncertainty does not by itself generate hope—but it makes hope possible. It does not of itself activate a multitude that hope can provoke. Hope as a virtue springs not eternal but from the Mosaic liberation tradition. Ignorance as a virtue has a Socratic heritage, and mixes in the cloud of the impossible with the prophetic heritage of hope. Hope for a new heaven and earth, or for what we may translate as a renewed atmosphere and earth, will not then signify hope for a *nova creatio ex nihilo* but for a *nova creatio ex profundis*. And I want that hope to display a bit of its concrete edge. So let me end with two great current sources of strategic hope.

The first is Naomi Klein's important book, *This Changes Everything: Capitalism vs. the Climate*. She conveys the need to shift deep civilizational habits pretty much within a generation. She recognizes that:

> the kind of counter-power that has a chance of changing society on anything close to the scale required is still missing. It is a painful irony that while the right is forever casting climate change as a left-wing plot, most leftists and liberals are still averting their eyes, having yet to grasp that climate science has handed them the most powerful argument against unfettered capitalism since William Blake's "dark Satanic Mills" blackened England's skies (which, incidentally, was the beginning of climate change).[23]

It seems word is getting out that the same neoliberal free trade capitalism that demands the sacrifice of most of the world's poor is also thereby trading the wilderness that sustains life for the new anthropogenic wilderness.

So might we be outgrowing the old alienation between white hiker environmentalism (preoccupied with the uninhabited paradise-wilderness) and social justice movements (preoccupied with the overinhabited urban wildernesses)? Could we—starting with the left—cease to be divided against ourselves? As Klein puts it: "The environmental crisis—if conceived sufficiently broadly—neither trumps nor distracts from our pressing political and economic causes: it supercharges each one of them with existential urgency."[24] For instance, she writes carefully about the colonial synergy of extractivism and racism, providing peoples and cultures as "sacrifice zones." The theological ethicist Cynthia Moe-Lobeda writes similarly of "the race debt of climate change."[25] The point is that this double jeopardy of social injustice and global warming need not discourage us. Climate change, with its rising flood waters, "could become a galvanizing force for humanity, leaving us all not just safer from extreme weather, but with societies that are safer and fairer in all kinds of other ways as well." It is a matter of collectively using "the crisis to leap somewhere that seems, frankly, better than where we are right now."[26] To take on "the corporate forces arrayed against science-based emission reduction will require the broadest possible spectrum of allies." And if we "seize the climate moment," this might be possible.[27] Turn catastrophe into catalyst?

Klein recognizes that "the climate movement has yet to find its full moral voice on the world stage, but it is most certainly clearing its throat—beginning to put the very real thefts and torments that ineluctably flow from the decision to mock international climate commitments alongside history's most damned crimes."[28] She finds her major hope in the arising of "blockadia"—a coalescence of multiple coalitions no longer waiting for governments to act or markets to find green solutions, but willing to put their collective bodies in the way of extractivist progress. Klein stresses the new moral force of the emergent coalitions between first peoples, indigenous groups, with environmentalists and farmers and students around the world. Check out the statement of gratitude up now on 350.org, sent to the Shell No! activists of the Pacific Northwest by the Pacific Climate Warriors, who in traditional hand-carved canoes paddled into the port of Newcastle in Australia to blockade one of the largest coal-shipping terminals in the world. They were met by thousands of people on land. Blockadia is an emergent phenomenon, bubbling up from below around the planet.

Klein considers the despondent question, "How can you persuade the human race to put the future ahead of the present?" And she answers: "You don't. You point out . . . that for a great many people, climate action is their best hope for a better present, and a future far more exciting than anything else currently on offer."[29] A wild hope? And so all the more energizing?

As to new moral forces, one voice is trumpeting down from the most hierarchical old above. And it is insisting that we treat climate change and poverty as joint global emergencies. The head of the Yale Forum for Religion and Ecology, allied with the forestry school, emailed me in the summer of 2014 already that her new motto is "hope with the pope." Pope Francis's encyclical *Laudato Si'* (still several weeks away from publication at the time of this conference) does not merely address climate change and humanity's obligation of planetary stewardship. Francis addresses those issues within the context of what he calls an "integral ecology" that encompasses concerns of economic justice, true human development, and global solidarity. I suspect I do not have to fill this audience in on his definition of ecologically irresponsible lifestyles as sin.

Naturally the right rose immediately to the occasion: Before the encyclical was even published, the conservative journal *First*

Things wrote that "Francis sullies his office by using demagogic formulations to bully the populace into reflexive climate action with no more substantive guide than theologized propaganda."[30] At the same time, Timothy Wirth, vice chair of the UN Foundation, said: "We've never seen a pope do anything like this. No single individual has as much global sway as he does. What he is doing will resonate in the government of any country that has a leading Catholic constituency."[31]

The pope is not the messiah. But the resonance of his impact with movements on the ground—and in the waters—reinforces Klein's conclusion: we have "just enough time for impossible."[32] Not that an integral ecology displaces the ecology of uncertainty. Hope, far from an eschatological guarantee, bears instead the fragile promise that catastrophe itself can—might—catalyze the needed change. Etymologically kata-strophe means *turning down*. Maybe it can turn us back down to earth. Deep down things. Such a hope arises—*creatio ex profundis*—out of profound loss and deepening uncertainty. In the old and new wildernesses of our entangled differences, we may find the wild spirit of God blowing through unpredictable assemblages.

The feedback loop between papacy and blockadia may be just one more windy start. But it is my guess that something has shifted, that we have the wild chance we need. And we grasp that chance not only by stopping everything and becoming climate activists. We need to use our gifts wisely: the contemplative and the active paths need each other more than ever. The impossible breaks into the possible as we prepare our students for adventures in communal activism and teaching, for cherishing the chaos of the transition and the precious forms of life, new and ancient, that can live into the wilds of a changing planet. Macfarlane imagines at the end of his book the wind moving through all the places he has explored, places that were "separated from one another by roads and housing, fences and shopping-centers, street lights and cities, but that were joined across space at that time by their wildness in the wind. We are fallen in mostly broken pieces, but the wild can still return us to ourselves."[33] The return is not to the same old selves, in their same old separative normalcies; but there is return nonetheless. The new creation of our planet is the new creation of ourselves: and the new creation comes not ex nihilo but *nova creatio ex profundis*: out of the oldest and newest wildness of Spirit.

Notes

[1]Robert Macfarlane, *The Wild Places* (New York: Penguin, 2007), 23.
[2]Ibid., 29-30.
[3]Ibid., 31.
[4]Ibid., 29.
[5]Ibid., 30.
[6]Ibid., 30-31.
[7]Michael S. Northcott, *A Political Theology of Climate Change* (Grand Rapids, MI: William B. Eerdmans, 2013), 56.
[8]Ibid., 63.
[9]Francis Bacon, "The Masculine Birth of Time," *The Philosophy of Francis Bacon: An Essay on its Development from 1603 to 1609,* ed. and trans. Benjamin Farrington (Liverpool: Liverpool University Press, 1964).
[10]Northcott, *Political Theology,* 50.
[11]Catherine Keller, *Face of the Deep: A Theology of Becoming* (New York: Routledge, 2003).
[12]See Karen Barad, "On Touching—The Inhuman that Therefore I Am," *differences* 23, no. 3 (2012): 206–23.
[13]Gn 1: 29–31.
[14]Stephen D. Moore, *Untold Tales from the Book of Revelation: Sex and Gender, Empire and Ecology* (Resources for Biblical Study 79; Atlanta: SBL Press, 2014), 227.
[15]Catherine Keller, *Apocalypse Now and Then: a Feminist Guide to the End of the World* (Boston: Beacon, 1996).
[16]See Ilya Prigogine and Isabelle Stengers, *Order Out of Chaos: Man's New Dialogue with Nature* (New York: Bantam, 1984).
[17]See Keller, *Face of the Deep,* 12–14.
[18]Herman E. Daly and John B. Cobb, Jr., *For the Common Good: Redirecting the Economy toward Community, the Environment, and a Sustainable Future,* 2nd edition (Boston: Beacon Press, 1994).
[19]See "On the Vision of God" *Nicholas of Cusa: Selected Spiritual Writings,* trans. H. Lawrence Bond, Classics of Western Spirituality (New York: Paulist, 2005), 43–55. See my interpretation of this tradition vis-à-vis constructive theological concerns, *Cloud of the Impossible: Negative Theology and Planetary Entanglement* (New York: Columbia University Press), 2015.
[20]Alfred N. Whitehead, *Process and Reality: An Essay in Cosmology,* ed. David R. Griffin and Donald W. Sherburne (New York: Free Press, 1978), 50.
[21]Naomi Oreskes and Erik M. Conway, *Merchants of Doubt: How a Handful of Scientists Obscured the Truth on Issues from Tobacco Smoke to Global Warming* (New York: Bloomsbury, 2011), 267. I strongly recommend the recent documentary film version.
[22]For a contemporary take on knowing ignorance and its relationship to wildernesses and gardens of human making, see Wes Jackson and Bill Vitek, eds., *The Virtues of Ignorance: Complexity, Sustainability, and the Limits of*

Knowledge, Culture of the Land (Lexington: University Press of Kentucky, 2008), esp. their introduction, "Taking Ignorance Seriously" (1–17). They don't mention the *docta ignorantia.* But this eco-ignorantia is the very opposite of the willful ignorance of climate denial.

[23]Naomi Klein, *This Changes Everything: Capitalism vs. the Climate* (New York: Simon and Schuster, 2014), 156–57.

[24]Ibid., 153.

[25]Cynthia Moe-Lobeda, *Resisting Structural Evil: Love as Ecological-Economic Vocation* (Minneapolis: Fortress Press, 2013), 36ff.

[26]Klein, *This Changes Everything,* 7.

[27]Ibid.,157, 153.

[28]Ibid., 464.

[29]Ibid., 156.

[30]Maureen Mullarkey, "Francis and Political Illusion," *First Things,* January 15, 2015, firstthings.com

[31]Coral Davenport and Laurie Goodstein, "Pope Francis Steps Up Campaign on Climate Change, to Conservatives' Alarm," *New York Times,* April 27, 2015, nytimes.com.

[32]Klein, *This Changes Everything,* 449.

[33]Macfarlane, *Wild Places,* 320.

A Broken Paradise

The Art of Samuel Bak and Spirituality in the Anthropocene

Elizabeth Groppe

"In the day that the Lord God made the earth and the heavens
. . . no plant of the field was yet in the earth" (Gn 2:4). Without
benefit of knowledge of paleontology, the ancient Israelites told a
story of creation in which the earth is transformed from a dry and
barren state into a moist and fertile garden, from which Adam and
Eve are banished after transgressing divinely established limits. The
dramatic Genesis narrative that has shaped the imaginations of
both Christians and Jews is given a visual reinterpretation in the
work of Samuel Bak, a Jewish artist and survivor of the Shoah. In
this essay, I will introduce Bak and then discuss the "Anthropocene," a term that scientists have coined to designate a new period
of geologic time distinguishable by the determinative influence of
one species, our own. I conclude with brief comments on several
of Bak's paintings from his *Bereyshiss* (Genesis) series, which are
suggestive of ways we might give visual expression to some of
the theological dimensions of our existence in our unexpected
wilderness.

The Life and Work of Samuel Bak

As an adult, Samuel Bak travels the world, at home both "everywhere and nowhere,"[1] but, as a child, his life was tethered very
closely to one place: Vilna. This Eastern European city known as
the "Jerusalem of Lithuania" was home to many generations of

learned rabbis and host to numerous Jewish theological centers and yeshivas. In the nineteenth century, Vilna also raised up secular Jewish Zionist and socialist leaders. At the time of Bak's birth in 1933, Jews constituted one-third of a population of 500,000 people. Vilna was, Bak reminisced, "a magical place."[2]

An only child, Samuel was the center of the lives of Jonah Bak and Mizia Yochel. The family dwelt in an apartment at 10 Wilsenska Street, five flights up from the office where Jonah made dental prostheses. Jonah often joked and laughed with his son, and he loved to play games. Elegant and athletic, he set the standard for masculine attire when he and Mizia attended evening social events. Mizia, who worked as an accountant in her mother's successful grocery business, adored Yiddish poetry and was a superb storyteller. Seated with Samuel at their round dining room table below a silken lampshade, she told him stories from *Bereyshiss* as she coaxed him to taste unwanted vegetables or eat sticky porridge on a silver spoon. "Eat, my child, eat. . . .Take a bite from this pear and you shall again hear the story of Paradise, and if you promise to finish all your lentil soup, I'll tell you about Jacob's stew."[3] You must build "good reserves," she insisted, "for bad times."[4]

The Bak family flat was walking distance from the homes of Samuel's paternal and maternal grandparents. One day a week, he walked past cinema posters and through door frames ornamented with carved angels to enter Grandmother Rachel's domain. The living room sofa routinely became a boat, the brass draping rod a mast for its sail, and the kitchen broom an oar. A gramophone's turntable became a merry-go-round for porcelain figurines—a boy and a dog, a ballerina, two elderly gentlemen—pieced back together with a father's dental skills when centripetal force sent the figurines flying across the room. A weekly activity that continued even after the gramophone was locked with a key was the lengthening of young Samuel's pants. Grandmother Rachel heartily disapproved of Mizia's practice of clothing her grandson in pants cut one finger below the crotch, and each week she extended Samuel's pants to a length just above the knee with a swatch of fabric that his mother would deftly remove on his return home. Looking back on his childhood, Bak describes Rachel and Chayim's home as a "beloved world" and "lost Paradise."[5]

Equally beloved was the home of his maternal grandparents, Shifra and Khone. His grandmother Shifra was the only religiously observant Jew in Samuel's extended family, and she never failed to return from work on Friday evening in time to bless the *Shabbat* candles at the dinner table, to which she regularly welcomed beggars encountered in the synagogue courtyard. On her Saturday outings with Samuel, the pair listened to live music at Café Sztral or enjoyed a Yiddish film at the cinema. Dismissive of a pediatrician's counsel that her grandson was to eat ice cream only in a warm liquefied state due to his chronic bronchitis, she led him on feet swollen in high heels to a kiosk called the "Little Paradise" in the municipal gardens, where they sampled every flavor of frozen cream, bound by the solemn oath that Samuel was to keep this "very naughty and unforgivable behavior" a secret from the entire family.[6]

It was through parents and grandparents, Bak reflects, that he came to know the reality of unconditional love.[7] For years, the adults sheltered Samuel from the anxieties occasioned by the political tug-of-war that pulled Vilna between Poland, Lithuania, and the Soviet Union. But there was no way to hide the waves of people fleeing Poland after the 1939 Nazi occupation, some of whom sought the services of Samuel's father, who constructed false teeth with cavities to hide precious stones that could be essential barter for refugees as they tried to make their way to Japan, Palestine, or the United States. The migrations stopped abruptly on June 24, 1941, when Vilna itself came under Nazi occupation, and the dental lab stood idle when Jonah was conscripted to cut turf in a labor camp outside the city.

In early September 1941, Lithuanian police banged their guns and clubs on the door of the Baks' flat so hard that they shook the lintels. Mizia and Samuel were ordered to take whatever they could carry and descend quickly to the courtyard, where they sloshed in the rain through the gutters in the streets, forced by the local enforcers of Nazi decrees into a Jewish ghetto. Thus began a three-year odyssey that would take mother and son in and out of a Vilna ghetto, into hiding in a Benedictine convent, back into the Vilna ghetto, into labor camps just outside Vilna, and then back into hiding.

Of all the memories of these years, one that most haunts Bak is the Nazi *Aktion* that took place in the Herren Kommando Platz labor camp on March 27, 1943. "All the children out into the courtyard! Vaccinations!" the Gestapo cried in shrill voices under a leaden sky. "Get out! Quickly you *schweine*!" Mizia knew that the Gestapo were not piling children into the back of a truck to take them for vaccinations. Expressionless, she took Samuel's hand. "I am staying with you," she declared.[8] She moved slowly toward the door leading out onto a square courtyard thronging with soldiers, women, and children. There were, Samuel recalls, "terrifying, piercing screams."[9] Suddenly a woman who was a friend of Mizia grabbed her arm and pulled her back into the corridor. The two mothers pushed Samuel under a bed in a bunk room where three other children were hiding, and Jonah began scheming a way to get Mizia and Samuel out of the camp.

At least ten miracles, Bak reflects, were necessary to spare any Jew who survived the Nazi era. When the Red Army liberated Vilna on July 13, 1944, after a battle that took 8,000 lives, only 200 members of Vilna's Jewish community were still alive. Samuel and his mother stumbled across the corpses of soldiers in the streets where the smells of human bodies mingled with the acrid scent of smoke. Bak would later learn that his father was shot just days before the liberation outside Vilna at Ponar. This mass grave had previously received the murdered bodies of his grandfathers Chayim and Khone, who were arrested while standing together in a bread line, and the bodies of his grandmothers Rachel and Shifra, shot on Yom Kippur in 1941.

From 1944 to 1948, Mizia and Samuel navigated the chaos and dangers of post-Nazi Europe and the Soviet system in a harrowing journey that eventually would take them at Mizia's insistence to Israel. In a camp in Bavaria for Displaced Persons where they spent more than two years awaiting passage, Mizia married Nathan Markovsky, a survivor of Dachau bereaved of his wife and two daughters. Once in Israel, this brilliant chess player and mathematician found employment with a bank. "He was," Bak remembers, "sensitive, tender and intelligent, but in him there was something that had broken beyond repair. There was hardly a night when he did not jump up from his nightmares and awaken us with his screams."[10] For many years the Shoah was not openly discussed in Israel, and those who passed through its horrors, Bak writes, lived silently with the guilt of surviving.

The artistic gifts of Samuel Bak were evident from a very young age. The first exhibition of his work took place in the Vilna ghetto under Nazi occupation in 1942 when he was only nine years old.

His mother nurtured his artistic talent and sought instruction for him even in dire circumstances. Once settled in Israel, he began formal study at Bezalel Art School in Jerusalem, and from 1956 to 1959 he continued study at the Ecole des Beaux-Arts in Paris. In 1959, he moved to Rome, where his first exhibition of the abstract painting that was the art world's norm was highly acclaimed. Then, between 1963 and 1964, he began to break the rules of the guild. "Storytelling," he recounts, "was anathema to what art was allowed to be," but Bak had a story to tell.[11] With oil paints and canvas, he began to transfer raw experience into metaphor, giving expression to a complex narrative that cannot be captured on a single canvas—or even in the output of an entire lifetime.[12] His paintings, in his own words, are "metaphorical visions of a terrain transformed by the Shoah."[13] Among these is a series of works named *Pardes*, the Hebrew word for "orchard" and a cognate to the English "Paradise."

Samuel Bak, *Pardes III*, 1994. Courtesy Pucker Gallery, Boston.

The stone structure in *Pardes III*, painted in 1994,[14] has the shape of the tablets of the law—or, could they be tombstones?

Four doors invite entry, and above each of the four portals are the Hebrew letters: פ (P), ר (R), ד (D), ס (S) which are to be read from right to left. In Rabbinic Judaism, the Torah is the way back to paradise, and the four doors signify the four dimensions of biblical interpretation: Peshat (the literal sense), Remez (the allegorical sense), Derash (the legal and theological sense), and Sed (the mystical). The first door, Peshat, is open and leads to a tree of life—but there is smoke wafting across its upper branches. Through the second door marked with the letter ר (R) we glimpse other portals that may or may not provide passage to the tablets of the law, which provides the moral and spiritual scaffold of Jewish life. The door of Derash is closed and blocked, but from our privileged bird's-eye view, we can see that passage would lead us only into mazes with no clear exit. The fourth door, Sed, the portal to the mystical way that the Rabbis considered Scripture's most important sense, is entirely boarded up. From our privileged view, however, we see a rickety Jacob's ladder with missing steps rising out of a crematorium. "My childhood paradise," writes Bak in his memoir, "was not simply lost, as any Eden must be, but rather destroyed by eager human cruelty and meditated violence, and my art is centered on the memory and meaning of that destruction." [15]

The Anthropocene

Bak's art can help those of us who are not Jewish to empathize with the Jewish experience. Moreover, the catastrophe of the Shoah poses to all of us fundamental questions about the character of human existence. It also calls Christians to a historical examination of corporate conscience about the anti-Jewish theologies and practices that contributed to the development of a European culture in which the ghettoization and genocide of six million people was possible.[16] Bak paints, however, not only out of his experience as a Jew, but also out of his concern for the future of the entire human family. "I feel the necessity," he writes, "to remember and to take it upon myself to bear witness to the things that happened in those times, so that human beings today and those of tomorrow—if only it were possible—are spared a similar destiny on earth."[17]

Today, the context in which we gather to ask fundamental human questions is one that has been unofficially named the "Anthropocene." The Geological Time Scale established by the International Commission on Stratigraphy divides Earth's 4.5-billion-year history into ages nested within epochs, periods, eras, and eons. Within the Cenozoic era in which we live, the last epoch on the charts that paper the walls of many geology and biology classrooms is the Holocene, which began approximately 12,000 years ago, at the end of the last Ice Age. The Holocene is notable for its stable and temperate climate that has been so hospitable to the development of human civilization. Atmospheric chemist and Nobel laureate Paul Crutzen coined the term "Anthropocene" to name a new Cenozoic epoch. "I was at a conference," he explained, "where someone said something about the Holocene. I suddenly thought this was wrong. The world has changed too much. So I said: 'No, we are in the Anthropocene.' I just made up the word on the spur of the moment. Everyone was shocked. But it seems to have stuck."[18] In the 1980s, independently of Crutzen, biologist Eugene F. Stoermer at the University of Michigan began using the same term to convey that we live in a new period of geologic time in which human activity has a determinative influence on the geology, chemistry, biology, and climate of the entire planet. Crutzen dates the beginning of the Anthropocene to the Industrial Revolution in the eighteenth century, whereas others believe the Anthropocene begins with the human transition from hunting and gathering to the agricultural production of food. The International Commission on Stratigraphy's Anthropocene Working Group is expected to issue a formal decision about the addition of the Anthropocene epoch to the Geological Time Scale in 2016 or 2017.[19]

Meanwhile, the thesis that we now dwell in the Anthropocene has already generated intense discussion in scientific disciplines and portends paradigm changes in the humanities and social sciences. It challenges assumptions that have shaped the humanistic disciplines in modernity, such as the presumption of the externality of a law-governed realm of Nature to a human society that acts in free self-determination, and the way in which we have conceptualized the distinction of nature and culture and the relationship of subject and object.[20] Awareness of the Anthropocene also requires us to face the reality that the one epoch of geologic time that may bear the name of our species will be shaped by more erratic and extreme weather, changes in the hydrologic cycles of the planet that will precipitate floods and droughts, higher average global temperatures, inexorably rising sea levels, the acidification of the oceans, soil erosion, deforestation, the dispersal throughout the biosphere of synthetic chemicals and radioactive particles, and the sixth mass extinction of species in the biotic history of the planet. All of this poses important theological questions. How, for example, will we tell the story of humanity's relation to God in our new context? The way that we narrate the Anthropocene, Christophe Bonneuil emphasizes, will shape our understanding of our context, our psyches, and our actions. As a historian, Bonneuil highlights four emerging narratives of this epoch—a tale of scientific shepherds and green geotechnologies, a postnature narrative, a story of dystopian collapse, and an eco-Marxist account.[21] What, we must consider, is a Christian narrative of the Anthropocene? How will we speak of God, Christ, creation, grace, sin, humanity, and eschatology in this context? How will we express this theological narrative in poetry, literature, song, and art?

Narrative Art in the Anthropocene

"I have made paintings," Bak reflects, "that evoke the concerns of our time and invite observers to invest them with their own reflections."[22] Moving back and forth between literature on the Anthropocene and contemplation of paintings from Bak's *Bereyshiss* series, a number of his works strike me as suggestive of some of the dimensions of our context. There are fundamental differences between Bak's Shoah experience and the challenges facing humanity in the Anthropocene, and these two contexts must not be equated. The destruction of the European Jewish community was an intentional act of genocide, whereas the advent of the Anthropocene is the consequence of both human ignorance and willfulness; creativity and the limitations of human inventiveness; greed and excess and the good desire to develop economies that would alleviate suffering and support human flourishing. We will face, nonetheless, some realities that are similar to those that Bak experienced, including the displacement of peoples, the exacerbation or instigation of violent conflict or even genocide,[23] the fracturing of things that on this side of the eschaton cannot be put back together, and the agony of parents who find themselves in a situation in which they cannot protect their children from harm. Below, I share and comment briefly on some of the paintings in the *Bereyshiss* series named for the book of the Bible that was the source of the stories Mizia recounted to young Samuel as she lovingly coaxed him to eat sticky porridge from a spoon.

Michelangelo, *The Creation of Adam*, c.1511. Available at www.CanStockPhoto.com.

Samuel Bak, *Adam with His Own Image*, 2000. Courtesy Pucker Gallery, Boston.

The first image, a pencil and oil on paper, is one in a series of works that recasts Michaelangelo's dramatic creation scene on the ceiling of the Sistine Chapel (above). There, God the Father, surrounded by angels, extends his powerful forefinger to touch the finger of a reclining Adam, bringing the first human being to life. In Bak's rendition, a lifeless Adam clad in human garments extends a stone hand waiting for a vivifying touch. In place of Michaelangelo's God, however, there is only the stone Adam's inverted reflection, with foot nailed to a wooden stud exposed in a broken brick wall. Behind the wall are two smokestacks, signs of the use of industrial power to build factories of death. Contemplating this image in awareness of the Anthropocene, the painting heightens my consciousness of the reality that there is no longer any place on Earth untouched by human influence. In Scripture, the wilderness (*midbar*) is a place of purgation and purification where we seek God at a distance from the dynamics of human societies imbued with the consequences of the sin (e.g., Ex 3:1, 3:18, 4:27, 5:1, 5:3; Nm 1:1a). Today, however, even on a remote mountaintop we will find signs of anthropogenic ecological degradation, whether this be in the form of melting glacial ice or conifers that are dying en masse because the winter season has not been sufficiently cold to reduce the population of bark beetles. Wherever we look, we see reflections of ourselves.

Samuel Bak, *Banishment*, 1999. Courtesy Pucker Gallery, Boston.

In the Genesis narrative, God compassionately clothes Adam and Eve with garments of skin to cover them in their state of lost innocence (Gn 3:20). In Bak's painting, in contrast, the bodies of Adam and Eve familiar to us from Michaelangelo's banishment scene are fractured into pieces, and a weapon of industrial warfare is bound to a fragment of Adam's leg. "We are dealing here," writes Lawrence Langer in a commentary on Bak's work, "with a different kind of expulsion . . . a violence that violates the physical integrity of the human couple. . . . If punishment for sin has culminated in mass murder, then something has clearly gone awry."[24] Contemplating this image in our context of potentially catastrophic anthropogenic climate change, I think of Francis Bacon, who believed modern man [*sic*] would use science and technology to create a new Eden that would free us from the misery that followed the biblical Fall.[25] Something, however, has gone terribly awry.

Samuel Bak, *Reflecting*, 1999. Courtesy Pucker Gallery, Boston.

In this painting, despondent angels sit below a broken rainbow that has been clumsily cobbled back together, its pieces mismatched. In the background is a pale ark still as stone with tall smokestack masts. "I am establishing my covenant with you and your descendants after you," God said to Noah, "and with every living creature that is with you, the birds, the domestic animals, and every animal of the earth with you, as many as came out of the ark . . . never again shall there be a flood to destroy the earth" (Gn 9:9–11). Beholding the angel who sits on a coffin-shaped seat that is already partially covered with water, I think of the people of the Carteret Atoll, displaced by rising sea level from the South Pacific islands where they have lived for nearly three thousand years. "The sea," said clan chief Bernard Tunim, who is a Roman Catholic, "is destroying our island paradise." He does not fault the sea itself, nor God, but the failure of those of us in industrialized countries to respond appropriately to the climate emergency.[26]

Samuel Bak, *Adam and Eve and the Ongoing Repair*. 2009. Courtesy Pucker Gallery, Boston.

In covenant relationship with God, the Jewish people have committed themselves to *tikkun 'olam*, the repair of the brokenness of the world. "The premise behind *tikkun*," Langer explains, "is that a successful repair can restore some of the equilibrium lost when a particular disruption of the human community temporarily violates the order implicit in creation." Bak's art, however, illustrates the limitations of this principle. "As survivors of the Holocaust slowly pieced together a Jewish world from its European remnants, it became clear to unsentimental observers that the resulting society could never equal its former state. An irreplaceable cultural void lay at its very heart."[27] In *Adam and Eve and the Ongoing Repair*, Adam tries to cobble together a rainbow, but the pieces don't match, and one of the planks bears the blue and white stripes of a labor camp uniform. As I behold in this scene the attempt to brace back together large trees that have been slashed into sections, I think of a woods restoration project in which I have been involved. A multiyear community effort to remove invasive species that are choking out native wildflowers, shrubs, and saplings from three acres of woodland has thus far cleared only a small patch of ground. The honeysuckle and ivy that have become invasive were introduced into our region for landscaping purposes and are now wreaking havoc on native ecosystems. This is small local example of a much greater global reality. We have a moral and spiritual responsibility to ameliorate the ecological harm that we have caused, but we cannot reconstitute the climatic patterns or full biological integrity of the Holocene.

Contemplation and Action

As I contemplate Bak's paintings, I lament the catastrophic destruction of the European Jewish community. In like vein, beholding fractured Genesis scenes as metaphors of ecological degradation in the Anthropocene may invite the "gift of tears" that Douglas E. Christie considers essential to a Christian spirituality in our time.[28] Perhaps Bak's Genesis art could inspire Catholic artists to consider how they might portray the full drama of creation and redemption in our context. Such art would invite both contemplation and action. As Michael Fishbane has observed, Bak's work poses insistent questions and asks us to make a choice. "Conjured by the colors we are entranced. But a decision awaits us."[29]

Notes

[1]Samuel Bak, *Painted in Words* (Bloomington: Indiana University Press, 2001), 66.

[2]Ibid., 91.

[3]Samuel Bak, "My Mother's *Bereyshiss*," in *In a Different Light: The Book of Genesis in the Art of Samuel Bak,* by Lawrence L. Langer (Boston: Pucker Gallery, 2001), 83.

[4]Samuel Bak, "My Adams and Eves," in *Adam and Eve in the Art of Samuel Bak,* by Lawrence L. Langer (Boston: Pucker Gallery, 2012), 121.

[5]Bak, *Painted in Words,* 167.

[6]Ibid., 254.

[7]Ibid., 282.

[8]Ibid., 74.

[9]Samuel Bak, *The Past Continues* (Boston: Pucker Gallery, 1988), 70.

[10]Ibid., 68.

[11]Ibid.

[12]Bak, *Painted in Words,* 4–6.

[13]Ibid., 95.

[14]For commentary, see Lawrence L. Langer, *Landscapes of Jewish Experience* (Boston: Pucker Gallery, 1997), 100–105; Michael Fishbane, "Visions: The Paintings of Samuel Bak," in *Bak: Myth, Midrash and Mysticism: Paintings 1973–1994* (Boston: Pucker Gallery, 1995), 8–10.

[15]Bak, *Painted in Words,* 297.

[16]See, for example, Secretariat for Ecumenical and Interreligious Affairs, *Catholic Teaching on the Shoah* (Washington, DC: United States Catholic Conference, 2001), 8–11.

[17]Bak, *Past Continues,* 70.

[18]Fred Pearce, *With Speed and Violence: Why Scientists Fear Tipping Points in Climate Change* (Boston: Beacon, 2007), 21.

[19]For a survey of various ways of defining and validating this term, see Clive Hamilton, Christophe Bonneuil, and François Gemenne, "Thinking the Anthropocene," in their volume *The Anthropocene and the Global Environmental Crisis: Rethinking Modernity in a New Epoch* (New York: Routledge, 2015), 1–3.

[20]Ibid., 3–9.

[21]Christophe Bonneuil, "The Geological Turn: Narratives of the Anthropocene," in *The Anthropocene and the Global Environmental Crisis,* 17–31.

[22]Bak, *Painted in Words,* 91.

[23]On the relationship of climate change to genocide, see Alex Alvarez, *Genocidal Crimes* (New York: Routledge, 2010), 127–34.

[24]Langer, *Adam and Eve,* 18.

[25]Francis Bacon, *New Atlantis* (Oxford: Clarendon, 1915).

[26]"Bernard Tunim, Clan Chief," *Telegraph,* December 7, 2009, http://www.telegraph.co.uk.

[27]Bak, *Painted in Words,* 60–61.

[28]Douglas E. Christie, *The Blue Sapphire of the Mind: Notes for a Contemplative Ecology* (New York: Oxford, 2013), 70–101.

[29]Fishbane, "Visions," 10.

From the Autochthonous to the Apocalyptic

Toward a Radical Ecotheology

J. Leavitt Pearl

And when he had opened the seventh seal, there was silence in heaven about the space of half an hour. And I saw the seven angels which stood before God; and to them were given seven trumpets. . . . And the seven angels which had the seven trumpets prepared themselves to sound. The first angel sounded, and there followed hail and fire mingled with blood, and they were cast upon the earth: and the third part of trees was burnt up, and all green grass was burnt up. And the second angel sounded, and as it were a great mountain burning with fire was cast into the sea: and the third part of the sea became blood; And the third part of the creatures which were in the sea, and had life, died; and the third part of the ships were destroyed. And the third angel sounded, and there fell a great star from heaven, burning as it were a lamp, and it fell upon the third part of the rivers, and upon the fountains of waters. (Rv 8:1–2, 6–10, KJV)

If ever there were a discourse ill-suited for the present ecological crisis, it appears that it would be the apocalyptic. "The third part of trees was burnt up, and all green grass was burnt up" is hardly a text that one would find as a bumper sticker on a Prius or as a slogan printed on the next Sierra Club brochure. Nonetheless, I would like to suggest that the specific apocalyptic discourse of radical theology constitutes a fruitful alternative to the romantic idealism of "nature" and autochthonous dwelling that one finds throughout much environmental thought.

In particular, I would here like to break an unstated rule of theological thinking and invoke the so-called "third rail" of academic theology, Thomas J. J. Altizer. [1] While ecology was certainly far from the mind of Altizer's "Christian atheism" when it was first proclaimed in the 1960s, it will here be shown that the apocalyptic logic of Christian atheism—particularly as manifest in Altizer's theological successor, Slavoj Žižek—may provide a language uniquely suited to the present ecological crisis. When the status quo has so wholly failed to protect the interests of humans or our environmental compatriots, then the prophetic declaration of the "absolutely new" may provide the ideological and rhetorical tools necessary to think an authentic alternative.

In order to frame a radical theological response to traditional ecological models, Altizer's and Žižek's specific brand of apocalyptic radical theology will be contrasted with David Abram's *Spell of the Sensuous* (1996) and its recourse to Heideggerian themes. This text is paradigmatic of the romantic, autochthonous model of ecological thinking dominant in much of the present ecological discourse, though one might just as well substitute any number of theological ecologies instead. Following an analysis and critique of Abram's model, the particular strength of an apocalyptic model will be presented as a viable alternative.

On Autochthony

Although David Abram's own disposition is largely anti-Christian, it is nonetheless the case that Abram's work presents a distinctly theological view of the world: he postulates an Edenic paradise (the world prior to the alienation of conceptual language), a fall (the invention of abstract language, particularly writing), and a means toward salvation (a return to "nature"). Nonetheless, while such a view is theological, it is certainly not Christian.[2] Rather, for Abram, the very fall of humankind into a destructive alienation from nature emerges from a distinctly Western theological paradigm, with its emphasis on transcendence.[3]

This concern for Western alienation leads Abram to draw generously from phenomenological sources. As Abram rightly notes, the status of the world cannot be disentangled from the perspective that one takes upon it and the language that one uses to speak about it; as Heidegger famously suggested, "language is the house of Being."[4] Thus, for Abram, a proper account of our current alienation from nature requires a phenomenological analysis of the very "how" (Husserl: *Wie*) of our perception.[5] Abram must undertake a phenomenalization of the mode of phenomenality endemic to modern humanity. It is for this reason that Abram's largely poetic account of nature opens with a discussion and explication of Husserl and Merleau-Ponty's phenomenological projects and methods. In his own words, "It is natural that we turn to the tradition of phenomenology in order to understand the strange difference between the experienced world, or worlds, of indigenous, vernacular cultures and the world of modern European and North American civilization."[6]

Although it is certainly the case that Husserl and Merleau-Ponty play a central methodological role in Abram's project, it is nevertheless surprising that Heidegger is left out of this initial discussion.[7] Indeed, this late introduction of Heidegger *masks* a deep indebtedness to the Heideggerian project. Whereas Merleau-Ponty provides Abram with a method, *Heidegger provides an ideology*.

This indebtedness may best be explicated with a turn to a Heideggerian term, absent from Abram's text, but indicative of his central motivation: *autochthonous*. Derived from the Greek ("oneself") and chthon ("earth"), autochthonous refers to a rootedness in the earth, an indigenous character. It is an authentic dwelling in the land, a dwelling in a *place* that is more than a mere space. Marking this distinction, Abram suggests "space, for the oral culture, is directly experienced as place, or as places—as a differentiated realm containing diverse sites, each of which has its own power, its own way of organizing our senses and influencing our awareness."[8] For Abram, it is the Western world's inability to experience the speaking-sensuous world that has broken its capacity to dwell autochthonously. A nearly identical fear can be found in Martin Heidegger's *Discourse on Thinking*, where he writes, "The rootedness, the autochthony, of man [*sic*] is threatened today at its core! . . . The loss of autochthony springs from the spirit of the age into which all of us are born."[9] For Abram as much as Heidegger, this loss of autochthony is a symptom of human civilization's, or at least Western civilization's, failure to find its proper place in its environing world. It is a symptom whose disease can only be overcome by the recovery of a proper thinking of Being (Heidegger), or a new perception (Abram).

In Abram, this call to an authochthonous dwelling manifests as a romantic idealization of indigenous cultures,[10] a rejection of technology that often approaches the Luddite,[11] and a romanticization of nature. Against this modern technological world, Abram argues for "a new way of speaking, one that enacts our interbeing with the earth rather than binding us to it. A language that stirs a new humility in relation to other earthborn beings . . . a style of speech that opens our senses to the sensuous in all its multiform strangeness."[12] In this way, the three central themes of Abram's project come into relation: Abram wants to develop a new mode of speaking (poetic, natural), in order that we might perceive or "sense" differently, in order that we might once again properly dwell within the earth.

The Danger of the Autochthonous; or, Why You Should Never Listen to Heidegger

Heidegger offers a considerably *more nuanced* account of autochthonous dwelling than Abram. Unlike his predecessor, he resists a total Luddism, acknowledging, for example, that dwelling itself presupposes "building," a *techne*.[13] He also recognizes that one does not merely dwell in the earth, but also lives in the world, the two manifesting in a dialectical relation of dwelling and alienation; "world and earth," he notes, "are never separated."[14] Nonetheless, despite this nuance, the reactionary, even dangerous character of this turn to the autochthonous remains here even more apparent.

This danger, as one might expect, manifests in Heidegger politically as a turn to the regressive ideologies of National Socialism and its anti-Semitism. Certainly, more than enough ink has been spilled on the question of Heidegger's Nazism,[15] but with the recent publication of the *Black Notebooks*, the question has again resurfaced. The advantage of this most recent text is not that it reveals an anti-Semitism in Heidegger's life; such an anti-Semitism is hardly in dispute. Rather, it reveals the specific way in which this anti-Semitism does not spring from merely nonphilosophical, what Heidegger might call "ontic," concerns. Rather, to strike at Heidegger's anti-Semitism is to strike at a central notion of his corpus.

The "Jewish problem," for Heidegger, emerges from the "root-lessness" of the Jews,[16] that is to say, directly from his conception of autochthonous dwelling. As he writes, "The question of the role of world Jewry is not a racial question, but the metaphysical question about the kind of humanity that, without any restraints, can take over the uprooting of all beings from being as its world-historical 'task.' "[17] The reliance on a notion of a pre-alienated nature within which each one finds its proper "place," cannot abide a "rootless" people, any more than a modern-technological society. The immigrant, the stranger, the nomad, the nonnative, and the Jew, all become figures to be feared, because they are figures without a land or a proper place; they are figures that cannot properly dwell.

Certainly, Abram does not share Heidegger's anti-Semitism. Nonetheless, it is certainly worth questioning whether the turn to the autochthonous—which emerges in Abram's thought under the titles of the "indigenous" or the "aboriginal"—can escape a necessary provincialism. When nature is understood as that toward which we must "return," as a harmonious reality in which everything and *everyone* has a place (not merely a space), then it becomes increasingly unclear what is to be done with those who lack a place in this specific sense: the immigrant, the traveler, the stranger, the nomad, the Jew.

The provincialism of this autochthonous dwelling may be understood, in radical theology's terminology as a return to the "pagan cosmos." In Žižek's words:

> The pagan Cosmos [represents] the Divine hierarchical order of cosmic Principles, which, applied to society, produces the image of a congruent edifice in which each member has its own place. Here the supreme Good is the global balance of Principles, while evil stands for their derailment or derangement, for the excessive assertion of one Principle to the detriment of others.[18] [Here Žižek has in mind, particularly, the Christian emphasis on love or charity.]

It is perhaps not surprising then, that Heidegger and Abram's autochthonous philosophies find significant recourse to the language and figures of paganism: Heidegger, turning to Germanic paganism and the myth of a Greek-German inheritance,[19] and Abram turning to various indigenous animisms.[20] Yet this explicit turn to the pagan cosmos is not necessary to understand the striated and parochial character of Abram's thought. Rather, such a view is already perfectly clear in Abram's romantic notion of "nature."

There Was Never Nature

The philosopher and ecocritic Timothy Morton highlights the problematic character of this nature romanticism in his *Ecology without Nature*; suggesting, paradoxically: "The idea of nature is getting in the way of properly ecological forms of culture, philosophy, politics, and art."[21] Perhaps, Morton suggests, there simply never was a nature. His study targets a number of proponents of what he calls a "romanticism" of nature, including Abram. For Morton, the ultimate failure of Abram's autochthonous project is that it ultimately produces exactly that which it ostensibly condemns: alienation and separation. He writes:

> Romantic experiments had already surpassed the conundrum of how embedding yourself in reality can also produce the opposite, a sublime aesthetic distancing. This is the problem that haunts David Abram's utopian prose. The self-defeating routine of puncturing the aesthetic veil, only to have it grow back even stronger.[22]

Rather than opening a juncture to an authentic participation within the environing world, the romanticization and idealization of a prehuman earth forecloses any possible constructive interaction. Rather than operating within a truly univocal field wherein the human is embedded within nature, Abram is operating a zero-sum game: the more the human "is," the less nature "is." Thus, as soon as one turns one's gaze, consciousness, or understanding toward nature, nature is either corrupted or retreats.[23]

This failure may also be expressed in a different language, that of the "Anthropocene." Coined by Eugene F. Stoermer and popularized by Paul Crutzen, the Anthropocene is understood to be the most recent geological era, an era in which human industrialization has resulted in a catastrophically changing environment, changing so rapidly as to constitute an epochal geological shift. Yet as the critical theorist Claire Colebrook has recently suggested, "We have always been post-Anthropocene."[24] For Colebrook, the problem with the hypothesis of the Anthropocene is not—as the so-called "climate deniers" would have it—that nature is not changing or that humans are not affecting nature. Rather, the problem is what the hypothesis presupposes, namely, that there was a period of relative stability, a period without corruption. To again use the language of radical theology: *this view presupposes a primordial harmonious cosmos.*

What Colebrook suggests, to the contrary, is that the world is always already changed and changing. "It is not that humans have destroyed this stable nature," she argues:

> We should reverse that and see that stabilized nature is a product of industrialized technology, and that a desire for a stable or unchanging climate—that you could eat broccoli all year-round, if you like—is what got us into this mess. What I am arguing is that there is no such thing as natural stability, in fact it is the notion of "nature"—this stable, timeless renewing whole—that is a product of industrialized technology.[25]

The source of the present crisis, in Colebrook's eyes, is not that we have taken a stable, harmonious cosmos and "broken" it; there is, for Colebrook, no fall. Rather, it is modern humanity's attempt to restrain the change and evolution of nature, to freeze nature, that has led to our present crisis. Like Nietzsche, who condemns Western thought, arguing that "when these honorable idolators of concepts worship something, they kill it and stuff it; they threaten the life of everything they worship,"[26] Colebrook's analysis shows the romantic ideal of nature to be nothing more than an embalmed idol. In her words, "There never was nature: this untransformed, prehuman presence."[27]

Žižek will similarly center his critique of modern ecological movement on this romanticized state of nature: "Like the anthropomorphic universe magically designed for man's comfort," he writes, "the so-called balance of nature, which humankind brutally destroys with its hubris, is a myth."[28] Such a reification, he will suggest, instead of challenging the industrialized society that stands at the foundation of the present crisis, rather reinforces its very logic: the logic of stasis and hierarchy.[29] Once one affirms a hierarchical nature, a hierarchical social order is not far behind. As Žižek writes:

> With regard to the social body, an individual is "good" when he acts in accordance with his special place in the social edifice (when he respects Nature, which provides food and shelter; when he shows respect for his superiors, who take care of him in a fatherly way); and Evil occurs when some particular strata or individuals are no longer satisfied with this place.[30]

Yet if one abandons the notion of an uninterrupted nature as the proper route out of the present crisis, then it becomes considerably less clear what ideological tool permits an escape from a quietistic resignation to ecological and human violence. The tool that permits such an escape, I would like to here suggest, is precisely the interruption of nature; it is the Žižekian "evil" of not knowing one's place; it is an apocalypse.

Breaking the Seventh Seal;
or, Why We Must Have an Apocalyptic Ecotheology

There is great disorder under Heaven,
the situation is excellent.[31]

In the language of radical theology, and particularly that of Thomas Altizer, Abram stands as a paradigmatic example of a philosophy of the "primordial" or "eternal return." This logic of the eternal return, Altizer argues, "is not only a cyclical return," as in, for example, stoicism, "but is an ultimately backward moving return to a primordial totality, and here the only possible ultimate movement is one of *return*."[32] That is to say, the logic of the primordial return, the logic of the harmonious circular totality, births a reactionary logic, a backward-facing nostalgic conservatism. This nostalgia is evidenced by Heidegger's turn to the pre-Socratics or Abram's condemnation of alphabetic language.

The danger of the ideology of the eternal return is precisely its recourse to harmonious stability. Not only is such a recourse factually untenable, as Colebrook seeks to illustrate, but it is also politically impotent. The eternal return is a philosophy of the same, built on a fear of change and difference, and epitomized by the face of modern ecological thought: "conservation." In a lecture dedicated to Morton's *Ecology without Nature*, Žižek highlights this relation, suggesting that "the underlying message of this predominant ecological ideology is a deeply conservative one: any change can only be a change for the worse."[33] Such an approach cannot help but foster a political and social quietism. Certainly clear culprits of ecological distress can be identified and targeted—hubris, modern technology, writing, the Cartesian subject; everyone has his or her own culprit in the "Fall," but within an ideology that fears change, any notion of forward radical social change becomes nearly impossible. Rather, the only answer, as Altizer suggests, is a logic of return. The primitivist anarchists, then—with their call to an end of all modern technology and a "return to the wild"—stand as paradigmatic of this approach, and equally paradigmatic of its violence. Who survives the catastrophic and sudden abandonment of modern technology? Certainly not the sick, the weak, those with disabilities. In the primitivist logic, those who stand at the bottom of the present social hierarchy, remain trapped there indefinitely. This ideology manifests clearly in the Western imaginary of the pseudo-apocalypse.

A famous quote—attributed to both Fredric Jameson and Slavoj Žižek—states that, for the modern mind, "it is easier to imagine the end of the world than the end of capitalism."[34] The 2009 disaster film *2012*, for example, perfectly models this reactionary character. Here the world is devastated by the eruption of the Yellowstone caldera, countless seismic events, and flooding on a biblical scale. Yet the meager few who survive are, for the most part, precisely the richest and most influential members of the current economic system—those who could afford to purchase a ticket aboard one of the so-called "arks." The world ends, but capitalism survives, more hierarchical than ever.

This view ostensibly affirms the apocalyptic tenor of radical theology and its chief proponents, but an such appearance is misleading. Rather, even the outwardly apocalyptic has been absorbed into the logic of the primordial return. Here the primordial forces of nature swallow up vast swaths of the earth, returning it, as the end of the film shows, to its pristine, "natural" state. Yet even such a cataclysmic event fails to challenge the underlying sociopolitical and economic structures of human society; the principal hierarchies survive. Rather, what this film illustrates is an affinity between the ideology of a harmonious "nature" and the hierarchical structure of the modern, industrialized economic world. *2012* illustrates the apocalypse-without-apocalypse, the faux-apocalypse.

I here draw on *2012* in order to mark a distinction between authentic and inauthentic apocalypse, and to highlight that what is being called for here is not simply arbitrary destruction. What the present ecological crisis demands is not merely the faux-apocalypse of fire and brimstone, tornado and flood, one that may permit—if not actively reinforce—present social hierarchies. On the contrary, it is precisely hierarchical social orders that radical theology's apocalypticism marks as contingent. Such an apocalypse, Altizer writes, "brings an end to all imaginative and mythical orders and structures of the cosmos, and does so by realizing all such order and structure as a paradise lost."[35] If the present crisis demands an absolute turning of social, political, and economic reality, then the possibility of such a turning may find a unique manifestation in the Christian imaginary. As Altizer argues:

> Christianity can know itself as being truly and even absolutely unique, as first proclaimed by Paul . . . [by] its ultimate challenge to the world itself, which was inevitably a challenge to the Roman Empire. . . . Christ is the lord of the new creation or the new aeon, an absolutely new world that has now dawned, a dawning that soon will bring an end to the old aeon or the old creation. . . . Its goal is an absolutely new omega rather than an absolutely primordial past.[36]

The hierarchical logic that dominates the present world must be challenged at a fundamental, ideological level. As Žižek suggests, "Instead of looking to science to stop our world from ending, we need to look at ourselves and learn to imagine and create a new world."[37] For such a change at the level of the communal imaginary to provide a route out of the present crisis, it cannot merely adjust the gears of the present economic and political machinery.

Change must be significant, revolutionary, or to speak theologically, apocalyptic.

It is this uniquely apocalyptic vocabulary that Christianity offers to the present ecological crisis. Yet it is precisely this vocabulary that has been abandoned by Christian ecotheologians. Rather, to offer just a few examples, Michael Northcott's *The Environment and Christian Ethics* argues that the present crisis emerges from the "demise of . . . moral purposiveness in the *global order*" and that the solution is a return to "the Hebrew vision of *created order*."[38] Similarly, Jame Schaefer's *Theological Foundations for Environmental Ethics* draws on the language of "creation" and "cooperative interdependence" to posit a primordial "orderly composition of the world."[39] While both works are commendable, I would here like to provisionally suggest that this notion of an orderly cosmos is profoundly limited—aesthetically, rhetorically, and politically. The scope and depth of the present crisis requires immediate, substantial, and decisive action, an immediate reorientation of society. It is not sufficient to look backwards at agrarian or rural societies in order to develop a response. Against Abram's call for a return to indigenous autochthonous dwelling, radical theological thought suggests precisely the opposite. As Žižek notes, "What this means is that new forms of global cooperation, which do not depend on the market or on diplomatic negotiations, *must be invented*."[40]

It is this capacity to envision or invent a new world, at the apocalyptic heart of Christianity, that has grasped the minds of recent *political* thinkers, Christian and not (e.g., Alain Badiou). If our present crisis demands a new world—a new way of ordering our society, our relation to our environment, and our economic life—than perhaps the apocalyptic tenor of a radical Christianity might also find a new life in the realm of environmental ethics.

> I mean, brothers and sisters, the appointed time has grown short; from now on, let even those who have wives be as though they had none, and those who mourn as though they were not mourning, and those who rejoice as though they were not rejoicing, and those who buy as though they had no possessions, and those who deal with the world as though they had no dealings with it. For the present form of this world is passing away. (1 Cor 7:29–31, NRSV)

Notes

[1]See Adam Kotsko, "Altizer as the Third Rail of Academic Theology," https://itself.wordpress.com.

[2]Abram praises "some historians and philosophers [who] have concluded that the Jewish and Christian traditions, with their otherworldly God, are primarily responsible for civilization's negligent attitude toward the environing earth," a possible reference to the work of Lynn White Jr., particularly "The Historical Roots of Our Ecologic Crisis" (David Abram, *The Spell of the Sensuous* [New York: Pantheon, 1996], 94).

[3]I will "have no such ready recourse to an immaterial realm outside of earthly nature" (Abram, *Spell of the Sensuous*, 15).

[4]Martin Heidegger, "Letter on Humanism," trans. Frank A. Capuzzi and J. Glenn Gray, in *Basic Writings*, ed. David Farrell Krell (New York: Harper Collins, 1977), 217.

[5]"Thus in every noema there lies as point of unification a pure objective something such as the above, and we see at the same time how in respect of the noema two generically different concepts of object are to be distinguished: this pure point of unification, this noematic 'object simpliciter,' and the 'object as modally determined' [*Gegenstand im Wie seiner Bestimmtheiten*]." Although a helpful translation for extracting the technical character intended by Husserl, *Wie* ("modally") may also be simply translated as the "how." Thus Husserl's distinction here is essentially between what appears in a phenomenon and the way in which it appears. It is the latter that will particularly interest Abram, since he is not interested in altering "what" is seen, but rather the way in which we see it. (Edmund Husserl, *Ideas: General Introduction to Pure Phenomenology*, trans. W. T. Boyce Gibson [New York: Routledge, 2002], 274).

[6]Abram, *Spell of the Sensuous*, 31.

[7]Only to return later in the analyses of temporality, where Abram will note, for example, "If we have taken a kind of method from Merleau-Ponty, it is to Martin Heidegger that we should turn for a careful structural description of 'the past' and 'the future' " (ibid., 208).

[8]Ibid., 190.

[9]Martin Heidegger, *Discourse on Thinking* (New York: Harper and Row, 1966), 48–49.

[10]Abram will, for example, draw from his diverse experiences with Nepalese and Balinese shamanism, the Amahuaca Indians of Peru, the Kuyukon of Alaska, the Apache of Arizona, and the Aborigines of Australia. But the generalizations derived from these diverse cultures have led many critics to accuse Abram of both romanticizing and blurring the distinctions between these radically unique peoples. As Anne Zavalkoff writes, "[The] arguments [of *The Spell of the Sensuous*] may be fairly criticized for mythologizing and universalizing the experiences of many diverse oral cultures" (Anne Zavalkoff, "Dis/Located in Nature? A Feminist Critique of David Abram," *Ethics and the Environment* 9, no. 1 [Spring 2004]: 121–39).

[11]Including a rejection of "that strange and potent technology" (Abram,

Spell of the Sensuous, 263): the written alphabet. Space does not permit a turn in this direction here, but it is worth noting the deconstruction of this problematic critique of writing that Jacques Derrida popularized in numerous publications, notably *Of Grammatology*. Certainly, the Derridean argument is not beyond dispute, but it is noteworthy that Abram advances his thesis without an attempted refutation of, or reference to, Derrida.

[12]David Abram, *Becoming Animal: An Earthly Cosmology* (New York: Pantheon Books, 2010), 3.

[13]Albeit a *techne* of a distinctly different character than modern architectural engineering (Martin Heidegger, "Building, Dwelling, Thinking," trans. Albert Hofstadter, in Heidegger, *Basic Writings*, 361).

[14]Full quote: "World and earth are essentially different from one another and yet are never separated. The world grounds itself on the earth, and earth juts through world. Yet the relation between world and earth does not wither away into the empty unity of opposites unconcerned with one another. The world, in resting upon the earth, strives to surmount it. As self-opening it cannot endure anything closed. The earth, however, as sheltering and concealing, tends always to draw the world into itself and keep it there" (Martin Heidegger, "The Origin of the Work of Art," trans. Albert Hofstadter, in Heidegger, *Basic Writings*, 174).

[15]Noteworthy, in this regard, is Dominic Janicaud's *The Shadow of That Thought: Heidegger and the Question of Politics*, trans. Michael Gendre (Evanston, IL: Northwestern University Press, 1996).

[16]It is worth noting that Heidegger also here criticizes the "worldlessness" of the Jews. That is to say, for him, they fail to participate properly in either of the sides of the world/earth dialectic. As he will write, the character of the modern world "is the tenacious skillfulness in calculating, hustling, and intermingling through which the worldlessness of Jewry is grounded" (*Gesamtausgabe* [*GA*] 95: 97 [Überlegungen VIII, 5]; unpublished translation by Richard Polt, http://www.critical-theory.com). To be worldless, for Heidegger, is to be nothing more than an object or an animal. As he remarks in "On the Origin of the Work of Art," "a stone is worldless. Plant and animal likewise have no world" (Heidegger, "On the Origin of the Work of Art," 170).

[17]*GA* 96: 243 (Überlegungen XIV).

[18]Slavoj Žižek, *The Fragile Absolute; or, Why Is the Christian Legacy Worth Fighting For?* (New York: Verso, 2000), 119.

[19]The "late" Heidegger, has consistent recourse to the language of, for example, the "gods." See, e.g., Heidegger, "Building, Dwelling, Thinking"; Heidegger, "Letter on Humanism"; and Martin Heidegger, *Hölderlin's Hymn "The Ister,"* trans. William McNeill and Julia Davis (Bloomington: Indiana University Press, 1996).

[20]See Abram, *Spell of the Sensuous*, 93–135.

[21]Timothy Morton, *Ecology without Nature: Rethinking Environmental Ethics* (Cambridge, MA: Harvard University Press, 2007), 1.

[22]Ibid., 142.

[23]"Abram," Morton suggests, for example, "has tried to link environmental poetics to an attunement to the animal aspects of human being. [But] there is a

zero-sum game going on here. . . . Either one is more conscious and less attuned to the world, or more sensitive to the world and less conscious" (ibid., 58).

[24]Claire Colebrook, "We Have Always Been Post-Anthropocene" (presented at the conference Approaching the Liminal: Pushing the Boundaries of Continental Philosophy, Pittsburgh, PA, September 27, 2014), https://www.youtube.com.

[25]Ibid.

[26]Friedrich Nietzsche, "Twilight of the Idols," in *The Portable Nietzsche*, trans. Walter Kaufmann (New York: Penguin Books, 1984), 479.

[27]Colebrook, "We Have Always Been Post-Anthropocene."

[28]Slavoj Žižek, "The End of Nature," *New York Times*, December 2, 2010.

[29]"It is . . . all too easy to attribute our disbelief in the catastrophe to the impregnation of our minds by scientific ideology. [The] standard thesis of the predominant ecology . . . says something like this: 'The ultimate cause of our ecological problems is modern technology, Cartesian subjectivity, within which we are abstract beings somehow outside nature, who can manipulate nature, dominate nature. . . . What we should rediscover is that nature is not out there, an object of our manipulation. Nature is our very background, we are wired to nature, embedded in nature. You should go out, feel, breathe nature. You should accept that your abstract scientific reification . . . is just an alienating effect of being embedded in the life world.' I think that far from offering a solution, this kind of reference to our immediate living experience is the cause of the problem" (Slavoj Žižek, "Nature Doesn't Exist," Presentation, Panteion University, Athens, Greece, October 3, 2007).

[30]Žižek, *Fragile Absolute*, 119.

[31]Chairman Mao, qtd. in Slavoj Žižek, *Less Than Nothing: Hegel and the Shadow of Dialectical Materialism* (London: Verso, 2012), 233.

[32]Thomas J. J. Altizer, *The New Gospel of Christian Atheism* (Aurora, CO: Davies Group, 2002), 10.

[33]Žižek, "Nature Doesn't Exist."

[34]See Fredric Jameson, "Future City," *New Left Review* 21 (May–June 2003). See Žižek in a number of locations and iterations, including as "the paradox is, that it's much easier to imagine the end of all life on earth than a much more modest radical change in capitalism" (Slavoj Žižek, *Žižek!*, documentary, dir. Astra Taylor [New York: Zeitgeist Films, 2005]).

[35]Thomas J. J. Altizer, *History as Apocalypse* (Albany: State University of New York Press, 1985), 171.

[36]Altizer, *New Gospel of Christian Atheism*, 9–11.

[37]Žižek, "End of Nature."

[38]Michael Northcott, *The Environment and Christian Ethics* (Cambridge: Cambridge University Press, 1996), xiii (emphasis added).

[39]Jame Schaefer, *Theological Foundations for Environmental Ethics: Reconstructing Patristic and Medieval Concepts* (Washington, DC: Georgetown University Press, 2009), 121.

[40]Žižek, "End of Nature" (emphasis added).

PART II

VIRTUES FOR THE WILDERNESS

Resilience

Virtue in the Unexpected Wilderness

Agnes M. Brazal

Wilderness is commonly understood as referring to areas significantly untouched by human modifications, even if indigenous peoples may have lived in these areas.[1] In economically developed countries, wilderness also refers to "land where development is prohibited by law,"[2] for a variety of reasons—aesthetic, biological, recreational, cultural, and scientific. The US Wilderness Act of 1964 further qualifies that humans could have been in these places but only as transient visitors.[3] In the twenty-first century, a shift in wilderness theory occurred with the realization that wilderness cannot be defined by physical boundaries, since all landscapes are connected: climate change, for example, affects the national parks and other "protected" wilderness areas. Furthermore, wilderness ecosystems, like all ecosystems, are no longer thought to be static or stable, but instead are dynamic and in constant flux: thus we need to reevaluate what wilderness preservation means.

The context of this essay, however, is another type of "unexpected wilderness." From an anthropocentric perspective, it is the wilderness that suddenly encroaches upon our existence; or from an ecocentric standpoint, it could be described as nature taking back its own (e.g., nature taking over coasts that should have been populated with mangroves and not peoples, or floodplains that should not have been made the site of subdivisions). This is the return of wilderness due to nature-related disasters—and these disasters are bound to increase with climate change.

Super-Typhoon Haiyan and the "Unexpected Wilderness"

On November 8, 2013, the strongest typhoon ever recorded to hit land tore through Central Philippines. The super-typhoon Haiyan (locally named Yolanda) had, at landfall, an estimated one-minute sustained wind speed of 190–195 mph[4] (315 km/hr), based on the reading of the Joint Typhoon Warning Center.[5] As a point of comparison, Hurricane Katrina had a maximum one-minute sustained wind speed of 174 mph, or 21 mph slower. Haiyan's wind created an 8–16 foot (2.3–5m) storm surge that swept away almost everything in its path.[6] The scope of this super-typhoon covered a distance equivalent to that between Berlin and London. Fourteen provinces in the Philippines were hit. The number of recorded deaths has been pegged at 6,300 (the government stopped counting at this number), making it the deadliest natural disaster in the history of the Philippines; an additional 1,061 people were listed as missing. Typhoon-related injuries numbered 28,689;[7] the number of households damaged was 1.2 million; and by mid-January 2014, the number of people displaced reached 4.1 million.[8]

The unexpected wilderness was experienced in the disappearance of boundaries between the city and the Cancabato Bay, with the huge waves bringing in ships, on the one hand, and taking away people and houses, on the other. The storm surge, which (rather than the strong winds) caused most of the deaths, dissolved the physical boundaries between "civilization" and "nature." In its aftermath, there was as well the dissolution of boundaries between the living and the dead. As one of the survivors pointed out, the whole area became a graveyard.

Part of my data for this essay is based on eyewitness accounts and formal semistructured interviews,[9] conducted in January 2015 with thirty survivors (fifteen women and fifteen men) from three coastal barangays in Tacloban.[10] The interviews focused on, among other issues, shifts (if any) in their view of nature after experiencing the super-typhoon, as well as how they survived the disaster and showed resilience.[11]

All of the respondents' houses and communities were wiped out by Typhoon Haiyan. Among these survivors, four had immediate family members who died (husband, son/daughter);

two had immediate relatives who were seriously wounded. All of them had neighbors and friends who perished. They all saw dead bodies on the streets, many of which were swept to their shore from the areas that were wiped out across the bay; the bodies remained uncollected for weeks. Their communities have since been declared a "no build zone." However, because of the government's slow rehabilitation process, most of the survivors have gone back to rebuild their houses in the same area along the coast of Cancabato Bay.

Post-Wilderness Experience

Typhoon Haiyan was a traumatic event for the survivors. Though nature for them remains beautiful, and a blessing—they recognize that it is their main source of nourishment and that storms are a natural part of their life cycle—it is also true that many survivors continue to exhibit signs of posttraumatic stress.

A year and two months after the Typhoon Haiyan disaster, almost half (23 percent women and 18 percent men) of those I interviewed still feel afraid, "nervous," or "could not sleep" whenever there is strong wind or rain. Even the men express that they now have a "phobia" or "trauma" and they "panic" or "lose themselves" (*nawawala sa sarili*) whenever a storm comes. Some (3 percent women and 7 percent men) are now afraid to go to the sea to gather shells, catch fish, or even bathe. Jose, a community organizer who also lives along the coast, has not "made peace" with the sea yet: "At the moment, I am angry at the sea; I do not want to take a dip. I used to play in the sea when the tide is high. Now when I look at the sea, I remember the people it had taken. . . . The sea had snatched them from us." Osang, a fifty-two-year-old mother whose son remains missing, is also afraid to bathe in the sea. "I might see a skull and bones of humans . . . but if I see my son . . . I will embrace him."

Most of the interviewees observed, too, that the weather/climate is changing and has become more and more unpredictable. They used to just look at the sky or the waves and they already knew whether it would rain or not. After Haiyan, it seems that one moment everything looks fine—and then suddenly, the wind blows strong, or intense rains pour. In their perspective, typhoons last longer and have become more frequent and stronger.[12]

Climate Change and the Unexpected Wilderness

Although it is difficult for climatologists to show a direct correlation between climate change and specific extreme weather disturbances such as Typhoon Haiyan or Hurricane Katrina, these experiences of "unexpected wilderness" show what could happen when, due to global warming, extreme weather events occur in the future with greater frequency.[13]

The Intergovernmental Panel on Climate Change has established that indeed anthropogenic climate change is already producing severe effects in our environment, including more natural hazards.[14] Its 2013 report confirms the following about climate change:

> Warming of the climate system is unequivocal, and since the 1950s, many of the observed changes are unprecedented over decades to millennia. The atmosphere and ocean have warmed, the amounts of snow and ice have diminished, sea level has risen, and the concentrations of greenhouse gases have increased.[15]

> Human influence on the climate system is clear.[16]

> Cumulative emissions of $CO2$ largely determine global mean surface warming by the late twenty-first century and beyond. Most aspects of climate change will persist for many centuries even if emissions of $CO2$ are stopped.[17]

Climatologists confirm that models point to more intense, if not more frequent, tropical cyclones caused by global warming, especially toward the late twenty-first century and more prominently in the western North Pacific hit by Haiyan.[18]

People in the Philippines are among those already experiencing such unpredictable or more frequent extreme weather events. Keep in mind that Haiyan was the second super-typhoon to hit the country within less than a year, after Super-typhoon Bopha, which struck the southern regions in December 2012. A little more than a year after Haiyan, in the first week of December 2014, Super-typhoon Hagupit (which thankfully decreased in strength when it made landfall) threatened the eastern coast of the Philippines again. As of August, this current year (2015) has also been unusually active, with twenty-five storms forming in the Pacific by August, six of them reaching the maximum Category 5 status.[19]

Resilience as an Ecological Virtue

The unexpected wilderness that climate change brings about requires the development of virtues that can help us deal more adequately with this challenge. One ecological virtue, or character disposition, that this essay proposes is resilience. Being in a typhoon belt and the Pacific Ring of Fire, Filipinos are used to natural hazards, such as typhoons and earthquakes, and have thus developed a certain form of resilience. What does it mean to speak of resilience as a virtue, and in particular, as an ecological virtue? The goal of virtue ethics, according to Aristotle and Thomas Aquinas, is human flourishing. How can resilience contribute to human flourishing in the context of climate change's unexpected wilderness?

My methodology will proceed as follows. First, I will analyze discourses on resilience in various fields with particular attention to what they can contribute in understanding the significance of resilience as a character trait, or constellation of traits, especially in the context of climate change. Second, I will focus on rearticulating resilience as an ecological virtue, by distinguishing its similarity and difference from other resilience discourses; by comparing it with Thomas's concept of the virtue of fortitude and its relation to other virtues; and by providing examples of its manifestation among the Haiyan survivors and their communities.

Discourses on Resilience

In Ecology

In the 1970s, the Canadian ecologist Crawford Stanley Holling introduced the concept of resilience in ecology to refer to "the ability of a system to maintain its structure and patterns of behavior in the face of disturbance."[20] For example, organic matter coming from a variety of plants provides the carbon and nitrogen that are the main nutrients for crop growth. With intensive farming and use of herbicides that kill weeds, plant biodiversity is reduced—

and so too is the ability of the soil to replenish the nutrients. To be sustainable, the resilience of the land should be considered, and the input and output of organic matter should be monitored.

By the 1980s, this biological metaphor of resilience had migrated to other fields, including the social sciences.[21] Interdisciplinary discourses now speak of social ecology, as natural and human ecology are understood to be inseparable. The concept of resilience in social-ecological systems, however, has been criticized for not being sensitive to which individual creatures survive (a function of power relations), since it is the balance of the system that is valued.[22] Studies have also focused on what makes "resilient ecosystems" more than what constitutes resilience in peoples.

Resilience: A Principle in Climate Change Adaptation

By 2005, "building resilience" had been employed by the United Nations, donors and NGOs as an important principle in climate change adaptation.[23] With climate change, more extreme hazards are expected to occur, oftentimes in the same areas of the world where poverty and natural disasters already disproportionately affect people's lives (e.g., Southeast Asia, Pacific atolls, Africa); in such places, there is a clear need to build resilience, in order to reduce suffering and maximize people's resources for coping and overcoming crises.[24] The term "resilience," then, remains descriptive in the field of ecology, but in development circles, it has become a normative concept.

Also within the discourse of development, resilience has come to be regarded as a positive counterpart of the idea of vulnerability. Vulnerability, which was a key focus in the disaster sector in the 1990s and early 2000s,[25] identifies populations most at risk when exposed to hazards by looking at their marginality in society due to their social class, gender, race, disability, and so on. Resilience, in contrast with vulnerability, focuses instead on the strengths and potentials of the community.[26] Greg Bankoff, a social and environmental historian of Southeast Asia, argues for this need to go beyond vulnerability discourse: he points out that societies such as the Philippines, which are chronically exposed to hazards, can develop a culture of disaster. "Perhaps beyond the concept of a society's vulnerability lies that of a culture's adaptability; it is the measure of the two that ultimately determines its exposure to risk."[27] Resilience discourse thus complements vulnerability in its stress on the resources at hand, on patterns of coping, and on creative construction: all of these need to be considered when evaluating the risk a community faces.

In terms of practical impact, others would say that the term "resilience" has more attractive power and force than sustainability.[28] In 2013, after Superstorm Sandy[29] and other natural disasters during which electric power was lost for an extended period of time, the American Solar Energy Society in Baltimore advertised solar power as an effective backup that could provide resiliency in such situations. Resilience in this sense connotes something more positive—a "rebounding or springing back."[30]

In contrast, the idea of sustainability, which has been a slogan in environmental advocacies, often raises the question, "And how long can this be sustained?" Moreover, the term "sustainability" has been compared to the term "internetworking," which was not catchy and had slow acceptance. Resilience, on the other hand, is likened to the word "networking," which easily caught fire. Sustainability, however, need not be pitted against resilience as a principle for climate change adaptation. They can be viewed as two sides of the same coin, with different emphases (one focused on the future generations, the other on surviving in the immediate here and now). For those in agencies involved in disaster response, however, the concept of resilience needs to be further clarified, as it is not clear yet whether it makes sense to divert some resources to the building of resilience—a relatively long-term concern—as opposed to more immediate concerns after a disaster strikes.

Co-optation in Neoliberal Discourse

Despite its potential usefulness, the idea of resilience can also be used as an ideology to abdicate care, if it is framed as a belief that people can simply bounce back and self-correct without outside aid. This is not liberating for those people who lack the resources to do so.

Resilience discourse has been likewise employed to support what Naomi Klein calls "disaster capitalism."[31] Disaster capitalism makes use of catastrophe as an opportunity for private reconstruction and

investments that benefit only the "haves" and not the "have nots."
Klein links this approach to natural disasters to broader neoliberal
economic policies advocated by Milton Friedman and the Chicago
School, including the war on "big government" and the increasing
privatization of services that had long been the functions of the
state. In Klein's account, the rebuilding of Iraq was one example of
a disaster industry that has been tapped as well in the post-Katrina
and other disaster reconstructions. Disasters now are being greeted
with delight by this new form of private industry. Among these
opportunistic companies is Help Jet Bills, which advertises itself
as "the world's first hurricane escape plan that turns a hurricane
evacuation into a jet-setter vacation."[32] When there is a serious
storm, the company whisks the evacuees (who have reserved their
places long before) out on a luxury jet to five-star golf resorts,
spas, or Disneyland (with their cat or dog, important documents,
photo albums, and family heirlooms). Another form of disaster
capitalism is involved when coastlines are closed to rebuilding by,
for instance, Sri Lankan victims of the 2004 Asian tsunami, but
not for owners of tourism facilities.[33] Prime coastlands are being
taken over by private owners in the name of disaster prevention.

Social Equity as Fundamental to Climate-Resilient Development

Others negatively view the focus on resilience as a sort of
"surrender"; resilience here is understood to mean a refusal to
reverse our unsustainable practices, and instead simply adapt to
the climate-changed environment. A climate-resilient development
model, however, is founded on the very principle of sustainability;
it is "a socioeconomic trajectory that generates and sustains human
livelihoods in ways that both mitigate and adapt to global climate
change."[34] Such a model aims to maintain warming below 1.5–2
degrees centigrade, beyond which the effects would be catastrophic
for the planet. This necessitates economically developed countries
shifting to energy sources that are noncarbon, and economically
developing countries to at least low-carbon, if not renewable,
energy. For John Barry, author of *The Politics of Actually Existing
Unsustainability*, another feature of a climate-resilient development model is social resilience, meaning that the model fosters

social solidarity and equity.[35] Barry defines a resilient community as "one that has high levels of solidarity, low levels of socioeconomic inequality, and empowered citizens."[36] For him, the role of public and private sectors should also be emphasized in resilience discourse, especially in contexts where people or communities are constrained by structures and lack of resources to help themselves. Resilience thus integrates climate change adaptation, disaster risk reduction, and poverty reduction, with people's and communities' own strengths and potentials as the starting point.

Psychosocial Theories

In psychosocial theories,[37] resilience consists of the capacity to (1) cope with difficulties or adversities; (2) resist destruction of competencies on the physical, psychosocial, and spiritual dimensions, and on the personal, familial, and communal levels; and (3) adapt and develop new proficiencies on the personal and social domain.

Both positivist and humanistic psychology speak about resiliency. The emerging field of positive psychology focuses on positive dispositions and how society shapes these traits, thus resulting in an interest in resiliency. Positive psychology can be criticized, however, for judging resilience as a virtue in itself regardless of the context or circumstance.[38] Humanistic psychology, in contrast, adopts a more holistic perspective of resiliency, which considers how it is related to other virtues, as well as evaluating the circumstances that help in determining whether it is a virtue in a particular case or not. For example, Adolf Hitler's father was an illegitimate child. His younger brother and father died when he was young and left their mother in poverty. Adolf became homeless and later, his mother passed away as well at the young age of forty-seven. Despite all of this, he emerged to become a leader and an excellent orator. If one decontextualizes resilience from what Adolf Hitler did as dictator of Germany, one could consider him a resilient person. But Aristotle reminds us that a virtue that leads to malevolent and not benevolent ends cannot be considered a true virtue. "Virtue is that which makes its possessor good, and renders his work good."[39] Thus Hitler's ability to overcome adversity cannot be considered an instance of the virtue of resiliency.

Synthesis

Resilience as a buzzword has emerged in ecology as a descriptive concept, and has migrated to development circles as a normative principle in climate change adaptation. In psychosocial theories, it has been used to refer not only to the character trait of a system but also to an individual disposition, and even as a virtue. There are three elements basic in resilience as a trait or more accurately a combination of traits: the ability to (1) deal with vicissitudes; (2) maintain competencies—physical, psychosocial, and spiritual, on the personal, familial, and communal levels—despite stress; and (3) adapt creatively on the personal and social levels. While my focus in this essay is resilience as a virtue, it is my contention too that this virtue should lead to acts that promote climate-resilient development that strives for social equality.

Rearticulating Resilience within Ecological Virtue Ethics

Thomas Aquinas holds that, in order to become true virtue, a given virtue should interrelate with other virtues. In this section, we explore how resilience as a character disposition is linked to other virtues, such as hope, fortitude, justice/solidarity, and humility; how resilience is nourished; and how it can be a virtue in the context of the unexpected wilderness that climate change produces.

Resilience Nourished by Meaning, Life Goals, and Hope

For Viktor Frankl, who survived concentration camps in Nazi Germany and went on to found the school of psychotherapy known as logotherapy, finding meaning for one's life is central to building resilience in the face of traumatic events.[40] Each person, according to Frankl, ultimately has the freedom to choose how to respond to tragedy. The experience of loss can push one to search for meaning. Furthermore, finding meaning in itself is already a form of healing, without which the victim is led to despair.

To be able to construct a "coherent life story" in the search for meaning is important in trauma recovery, not only from climate-related disasters, but also from socioeconomic and other types of disruptions. In line with this, psychosocial theories identify as among the main strengths of resilience discourse its recognition of the importance of life goals. To find meaning and have a life goal especially helped the Haiyan survivors to rise up from their depression. Didith, whose husband and daughter were swept away by the waves, was initially too depressed to function: "I was just lying down and sleeping. Those beside me in the evacuation center were consoling and encouraging me reminding me that I have three other children whom I need to help to survive." This gave her the will to rise up and start working to be able to provide food for her children. Similarly, Gloria, whose husband perished, exclaimed: "I wanted to die as well. But I have a paralyzed son and a grand-child." At that time when the roads were hardly passable because of all the scattered debris, she walked several kilometers to the City Hall to ask for medicines for her son. Sylvia's husband, who sustained a serious wound while trying to save his mother from drowning, later died from an infection, as there was no doctor in the first three days after the super-typhoon. "I lost hope when my husband died, but I thought of my ten-year-old child." For these three women, the thought that they still needed to live for the sake of their children, their hope for the future, pulled them out of their depression and enabled them to overcome the tragedy-induced loss of their competencies.

Resilience and Fortitude

Fortitude[41] for Thomas (*fortitudo*) moderates fear arising from the awareness of one's vulnerability, the greatest of which is the fear of death. He acknowledges two acts of fortitude: *aggredi and sustinere*. *Aggredi* involves taking initiative and is similar to Aristotle's concept of fortitude, or *andreia*. Building on the model of a soldier in battle for the sake of the *polis*, Aristotle's *andreia* is focused on firmness to fight in the battlefield: "Fortitude is about fear and daring." [42] It is close to what Filipinos calls *lakas ng loob* (inner strength to take risk).

Sustinere, on the other hand, entails endurance. For Thomas, who is concerned with the courage of Christian martyrs, endurance is the principal act of fortitude.[43] He focuses on "private combat," where a person perseveres in acting righteously even in the face of threats. His concept of martyrdom includes those who "cleave to faith and justice" in the face of grave threats. *Fortitudo* for him need not involve confrontation or aggression, but entails firmly standing up for the truth in the face of overwhelming opposition or evil. It is roughly equivalent to the Filipino *tibay ng loob* (inner strength to stand firmly even in the face of danger, pain, or toil).[44]

Both endurance and initiative taking are important elements of resilience. *Sustinere* or endurance lies underneath patience and perseverance. The Haiyan survivors exhibited *sustinere* when they endured patiently three to five days without food, without aid, without even changing their clothes—and all this without resorting to violence.

Aggredi (risk taking) is another facet of resilience that is needed to survive disasters. *Aggredi* was manifest in the Haiyan survivors who risked walking several kilometers through two-story-high debris to get to where aid was available, or as with Gloria, to get medicines for her paralyzed son.

Resilience, Humility, and Creativity to Transform

A common image of resilience in Asia is the bamboo, which bends with the strong wind but is able to bounce back again. Resilience, however, is much more than going back to a former state. It involves creativity to transform and become better. This necessitates humility to recognize and correct one's mistakes.[45]

According to a scientific study of early warning efforts for the Super-typhoon Haiyan, 94 percent of the deaths in the three cities with the highest mortality (Tacloban among them), could have been prevented if the residents had been evacuated. While the government and media called on coastal residents to evacuate days before the typhoon, many people remained in their houses. It was a common practice in these coastal communities, when there were evacuation warnings, for the men to stay behind to guard their domestic belongings and animals from looters. Others also assumed that, as in previous warnings of storm surge, the water would reach only the shores. Thus only those living directly along the coasts evacuated, and even in these cases, many men and a few women stayed behind. However, whole families living in concrete houses on the side of the road (not directly on the coast) did not evacuate, believing that their homes could withstand the strong winds, and that the waters would not reach them. Many others did not understand what a storm surge is.

Most of the Haiyan survivors I interviewed indicated that they now immediately evacuate when there is a strong typhoon warning. Each community/barangay today has a designated relocation area, and an evacuation committee to help in the evacuation process. In the wake of the threat of another super-typhoon (Hagupit) in 2014, some survivors of Haiyan evacuated as soon as they heard warnings from the newscast, even before the government order came. The threat of Typhoon Hagupit led to the evacuation of more than a million people. Gregorio, who continues to live in a makeshift house, and like most of the other men lost his livelihood due to the devastation of Haiyan, spoke about finding a new mission in life in his work as a member of the evacuation committee, charged with looking for vehicles to transport people to the evacuation centers.

Resilience Nurtured by Sharing and Solidarity

The survivors recount many tales of sharing and solidarity among themselves, such as sharing food or their houses as evacuation centers during and after the typhoon. Those who left to temporarily go to relatives in other provinces allowed their neighbors to stay in their homes. There was sharing of what was scavenged from the wreckage: food, water, and clothing. Survivors engaged in *pintakasi*, or community self-help, to clear the streets of the debris.[46]

The aid given by the donor agencies and the church was a source of hope for the survivors. The Tzu Chi Foundation was among the first, if not the first group that arrived at the scene of the disaster. Many of my interviewees spoke about how the foundation, which was criticized by some sectors for its "dole outs," had given them hope in its cash-for-work program. From the perspective of the survivors, who were at first too shocked to respond well—some were even catatonic—the cash for work pushed them, at the very least, to rise up and register. And even if they could not work well, they still received the equivalent of twelve dollars at the end of each day.

Some Tzu Chi volunteers were actually victims of Typhoon Ketsana, which in 2009 poured the equivalent of a full month of rainfall into Metro Manila and nearby provinces in only six hours. They had also received help from the foundation and are now—in solidarity with the victims of Haiyan—paying that help forward.

Over and above the provision of basic needs, the Tzu Chi Foundation, which is a Buddhist group, helped rebuild Santo Niño, the Catholic church of Tacloban. Master Cheng Yen, their spiritual leader, said: "Most Taclobanons are Catholics. They need their faith and spirituality especially during this time of disaster. Your Church is the pillar in the city and should be restored soonest."[47] I think that this is interfaith solidarity at its best!

Resilience and Justice

Fortitude requires justice to be moral. Thomas, quoting Ambrose, says: "Fortitude without justice is an occasion of injustice; since the stronger a man is, the more ready is he to oppress the weaker."[48] Like fortitude, resilience too must be guided by social justice in order to be moral. Currently, the countries that are most resilient to the impact of climate change are those that historically emitted the most carbon dioxide into the earth's atmosphere, while those who contributed the least greenhouse gases are the most vulnerable to the impact of climate change. The resilience, then, of the global North is not founded on justice. The 1971 Synod of Bishops denounced this economic order in their document *Justice in the World*:

> It is impossible to see what right the richer nations have to keep up their claims to increase their own material demands, if the consequence is either that others remain in misery or that the danger of destroying the very physical foundations of life on earth is precipitated. Those who are already rich are bound to accept a less material way of life with less waste, in order to avoid the destruction of the heritage which they are obliged by absolute justice to share with all other members of the human race.[49]

More than four decades later, premised on the climate as common good, Pope Francis's encyclical *Laudato Si'* affirms the global North's ecological debt to the global South.[50] "The developed countries ought to help pay this debt by significantly limiting their consumption of nonrenewable energy and by assisting poorer countries to support policies and programs of sustainable development."[51] Climate justice advocates argue that countries which historically have produced the greatest carbon emissions because of industrialization in the past 150 to 200 years have exhausted their "fair share" of the earth's biocapacity. Their climate debt consists of both adaptation and emissions debt. [52] Adaptation debt is what these countries owe to the global South so the latter can adapt to the changing climate or in a sense become climate-resilient. Emissions debt is what the industrialized countries owe both to the global South and our common home. As they have used up their "fair share" of the atmospheric space, they would need to pursue a path of negative growth to prevent a further 1.5- to 2-degree centigrade rise in the earth's temperature, at which things will turn cataclysmic for all. If they cannot afford a negative growth rate, they could offset this debt by financing the shift to clean energy in developing countries. This will in turn allow the global South to exercise their right to develop without burning fossil fuels.

The path to ecological justice is not easy. Resilience as endurance is needed by ecological activists whose lives are threatened by unjust resource exploiters. According to the Global Witness report, over the years between 2002 and 2013, almost a thousand environmental activists opposing mining, deforestation, and so on, have been killed. The killing of environmental activists further increased 20 percent in 2014. Oliver Courtney of Global Witness remarked, "There can be few starker or more obvious symptoms of the global environmental crisis than a dramatic upturn in killings of ordinary people defending rights to their land or environment." [53]

On the local level, a year after Super-typhoon Haiyan, members of affected communities joined a climate walk for climate resilience, to call on the state to help rehabilitate people's livelihoods destroyed by the super-typhoon, and to "invest more in preparing for climate-related disasters." [54] A facilitating approach [55] by the government and other social institutions is necessary for resilience as a virtue to translate to climate-resilient communities. For instance, even if the people would now prefer to live in more strongly built houses in safer places, they are still not able to realize this because of lack of resources and government support. The survivors clamor for the government to build safe evacuation centers: They report that hotels in Tacloban dramatically raise their prices whenever a storm threatens to hit the area, since these are among the few buildings deemed to be structurally strong and safe enough to survive another super-typhoon.

Resilience Is a Virtue for Everyone

Moral resilience is a constellation of virtues of fortitude (endurance and risk taking), humility, creativity, sharing, solidarity, hope, and justice. As a term, it has the advantage of having a history of articulation with ecological issues, especially as a normative concept in development circles with respect to climate change.

If moral resilience is a virtue, what would constitute its deficiency and excess? Thomas underlines that "moral virtue is a habit of choosing the mean."[56] The mean is that which is between "doing or feeling too little and doing or feeling too much." If resilience as an ecological virtue is the mean, the extremes would be, on the one hand, indifference/passivity/fear in the face of ecological crisis or disaster and on the other hand, hubris in the form of wantonness/recklessness or "blind confidence in technical solutions,"[57] devoid of a corresponding conversion in humanity, lifestyle, and model of economic development.

Resilience is an ecological virtue not only for those who are the current victims of climate change. Resilience is required of activists both in the global North and South to move governments and corporations to shift to noncarbon or low-carbon energy resources. Resilience is needed by both individuals and nations in resisting a consumerist lifestyle and the superdevelopment[58] that generates this. As Pope Francis has affirmed, "Reducing greenhouse gases requires honesty, courage and responsibility, above all on the part of those countries which are more powerful and pollute the most."[59]

Working to contain climate change requires resilience's attitude of hope. The reports of the Intergovernmental Panel on Climate Change can be frightening and paralyzing. We need hope in order to persevere in the struggle even in the face of huge obstacles such as those posed by powerful deniers that climate change is anthropogenic.[60] "The failure of global summits on the environment," Pope Francis rightly noted, "make[s] it plain that our politics are subject to technology and finance."[61]

As more and more countries suffer from climate-related disasters, and more places are unexpectedly transformed into "wilderness," the more pressing it becomes to cultivate resilience as an ecological virtue.

Notes

[1] The WILD foundation defines wilderness as "the most intact, undisturbed wild natural areas left on our planet . . . that humans do not control and have not developed with roads, pipelines or other industrial infrastructure." "What Is a Wilderness Area?" WILD Foundation, http://www.wild.org.

[2] Cyril F. Kormos, *A Handbook on International Wilderness Law and Policy*, http://www.wild.org.

[3] The Wilderness Act of 1964, http://www.wilderness.net.

[4] Haiyan exceeded the strength of Hurricanes Camille (1969) and Allen (1980) in the North Atlantic Basin, and Super-typhoon Tip (1979) in the Western North Pacific. The next second strongest at landfall was Hurricane Camille, which hit Mississipi at 190 mph sustained winds (Mark Fischetti, November 12, 2013, "Was Typhoon Haiyan a Record Storm?" http://blogs.scientificamerican.com).

[5] Deutsche Gesellschaft für Internationale Zusammenarbeit (GIZ) GmbH report, "Assessment of Early Warning Efforts in Leyte for Typhoon Haiyan/Yolanda," 2014.

[6] Ibid.

[7] "NDRRMC: Yolanda Death Toll Hits 6,300 Mark Nearly 6 Months after Typhoon," April 17, 2014, http://www.gmanetwork.com.

[8] See "Disasters in the Philippines: Typhoon Haiyan," https://www.academia.edu.

[9] A semistructured interview is a mixture of questions that were set beforehand and are open-ended, thus allowing the interviewer to probe deeper into the answers or other issues. Because the questions prompt discussion, the interviewees can raise points not previously considered by the interviewer. The names of the respondents have been changed in this account. Content analysis was employed to categorize the responses. Secondary data were drawn from published news articles and other literature on Haiyan.

[10] A barangay is the smallest administrative unit in Philippine society.

[11] There is no exact translation of "resilience" in the local languages. I used *lakas ng loob, tibay ng loob*, and other related terms.

[12] Less than three months after Haiyan, on January 31, 2014, tropical storm Kajiki/Basyang placed Eastern Visayas under a storm signal no. 2; in March 2014 tropical storm Caloy/Chanchu placed Eastern Visayas under signal no. 1, March being a strange month to have a typhoon. A little more than a year after Haiyan, Super -typhoon Hagupit/Ruby, which thankfully decreased in strength when it made landfall, threatened the eastern coast of the Philippines in the first week of December 2014. Toward the end of the same month, Jangmi/Seniang brought incessant rains that led to landslides and flooding.

[13] "Coastal Systems and Low-lying Areas," www.ipcc.ch.

[14] IPCC, "Climate Change 2007: Synthesis Report," www.ipcc.ch. See also

Pope Francis, *Laudato Si': On Care for Our Common Home*, no. 23, www. w2.vatican.va, henceforth to be referred to as *LS*.

[15]IPCC, "Climate Change 2013: The Physical Science Basis," Summary for Policymakers. www.ipcc.ch.

[16]Ibid.

[17]Ibid.

[18]See, for instance, Kerry Emanuel, "Downscaling CMIP5 Climate Models Shows Increased Tropical Cyclone Activity over the 21st Century," http:// www.pnas.org.

[19]"Twin Typhoons Spin in the Pacific, Adding to Active Storm Season," www.smh.com.au.

[20]Crawford Stanley Holling, "The Resilience of Terrestrial Ecosystems: Local Surprise and Global Change," in *Sustainable Development of the Biosphere*, ed. William C. Clark and R. E. Munn (Cambridge: Cambridge University Press, 1986), 296. See also "Resilience and Vulnerability," Stockholm Environment Institute, www.gecafs.org. A good survey of the definitions of "resilience" in various domains (ecological, community, individual) is "Definitions of Community Resilience: An Analysis, A CARRI Report," Community and Regional Resilience Institute, www.resilientus.org.

[21]"Resilience and Vulnerability," 29.

[22]See also the critique of Susie O'Brien, "Resilient Virtue and the Virtues of Resilience: Post-Bhopal Ecology in Animal's People," *Kunapipi* 34, no. 2 (2012): 23–31; Michael Fabinyi, Louisa Evans, and Simon J. Foale, "Social-Ecological Systems, Social Diversity, and Power: Insights from Anthropology and Political Ecology," *Ecology and Society* 19, no. 4 (2014).

[23]Simone Levine, Adam Pain, Sarah Bailey, and Lilianne Fan, "The Relevance of 'Resilience'?" Humanitarian Policy Group Brief 49, http://www.odi.org.

[24]"Hyogo Framework for Action (2005–2015): Building the Resilience of Nations and Communities to Disasters," http://www.unisdr.org.

[25]François Grünewald and Jeroen Warner, "Resilience: Buzz Word or Critical Strategic Concept," http://www.urd.org.

[26]Ibid.

[27]Greg Bankoff, "Rendering the World Unsafe: 'Vulnerability' as a Western Discourse," *Disasters* 25, no. 1 (2001): 21. See also idem, "Living with Risk: Coping with Disasters: Hazard as a Frequent Life Experience in the Philippines," http://www2.hull.ac.uk.

[28]Carol Pierson Holding, "Will 'Resilience' Replace Sustainability?" CS-RHub.com.

[29]Hurricane Sandy swept through the Caribbean in October 2012.

[30]Holding, "Will 'Resilience' Replace Sustainability?"

[31]Naomi Klein, "Disaster Capitalism: The New Economy of Catastrophe," *Harper's Magazine*, October 2007.

[32]Naomi Klein, *The Shock Doctrine: The Rise of Disaster Capitalism* (New York: Metropolitan Books/Henry Holt, 2007), 525.

[33]Ibid., 463–87.

[34]Lyuba Zarsky, "Climate-Resilient Industrial Development Paths: Design Principles and Alternative Models," in *Towards New Developmentalism:*

Market as Means Rather than Master, ed. S. R. Khan and J. Christiansen (New York: Routledge, 2010).

[35]John Barry, *The Politics of Actually Existing Unsustainability: Human Flourishing in a Climate-Changed, Carbon Constrained World* (New York: Oxford University Press, 2012).

[36]Ibid., 27.

[37]Psychosocial sciences here refer to the aggregation of social sciences, evolutionary theory, psychology, and developmental theories. Craig Steven Titus, *Resilience and the Virtue of Fortitude: Aquinas in Dialogue with the Psychosocial Sciences* (Washington, DC: Catholic University of America Press, 2006).

[38]Brent Dean Robbins, Harris Friedman, et al., "Resiliency as a Virtue: Contributions from Humanistic and Positive Psychology," in *Continuity versus Creative Response to Challenge: The Primacy of Resilience and Resourcefulness in Life and Therapy,* ed. Marek J. Celinski and Kathryn M. Gow (Hauppauge, NY: Nova Science Publishers, 2011), 93–104.

[39]Aristotle, *Ethics*. ii, 6, cited by Thomas Aquinas, *Summa Theologica* II-II q.123, art. 1 "Whether Fortitude Is a Virtue?" *St. Thomas Aquinas Summa Theologica,* trans. English Dominican Province, vol. 3 (Westminster, MD: Christian Classics, 1981). *Summa Theologica* shall henceforth be referred to as *ST.*

[40]Maria Marshall and Edward Marshall, *Logotherapy Revisited: Review of the Tenets of Viktor E. Frankl's Logotherapy* (Ottawa: Ottawa Institute of Logotherapy, 2012).

[41]See Craig, *Resilience and the Virtue of Fortitude.*

[42]Aristotle, *Ethics* ii, 7; iii, 9, cited by Thomas, *ST* II-II, q. 123, art. 3, "Whether Fortitude Is about Fear and Daring?"

[43]"The principal act of fortitude is endurance to stand immovable in the midst of danger rather than attack them" (*ST* II-II, q 123. art. 6). See also Monica Jalandoni, "Fortitude in the Philippines: Impact on Women," in *Transformative Theological Ethics: East Asian Contexts,* ed. Agnes M. Brazal et al. (Quezon City: Ateneo de Manila University Press, 2010), 201–18.

[44]*ST* II-II, q. 123, art. 2.

[45]Thomas links fortitude to humility. "Now it belongs to fortitude of the mind . . . to acknowledge one's own infirmity, and this belongs to the perfection that is called humility" (*ST* II-II, q. 123, art. 1, "Whether Fortitude Is a Virtue?").

[46]Nancy J. Karlin, Sherilyn Marrow, Joyce Weil, Sara Baum, and Tara S. Spencer, "Social Support, Mood, and Resiliency Following a Peruvian Natural Disaster," *Journal of Loss and Trauma* 17 (2012): 470–88.

[47]"Cash for Work: A Kind of Business Continuity Plan," www.apecscmc.org.

[48]*ST* II-II, q. 123, art. 12.

[49]1971 Synod of Bishops, *Justice in the World* (70), www.shc.edu.

[50]Pope Francis, *Laudato Si'* (51), www.vatican.va.

[51]Ibid. (52).

[52]See Tim Jones and Sarah Edwards, "The Climate Debt Crisis: Why Paying Our Dues Is Essential for Tackling Climate Change," World Development Movement, November 2009, 7.

[53]"Sharp Rise in Environmental and Land Killings as Pressure on Planet's Resources Increases—Report," April 14, 2014, www.globalwitness.org.

[54]"One Year after Haiyan: Farmers, Fisherfolk Join Historic March Demanding for Climate Resilience," www.oxfamblogs.org.

[55]Grünewald and Warner, "Resilience: Buzz Word or Critical Strategic Concept."

[56]Aristotle, *Ethics* ii, 6, cited by Thomas, *ST* I-II, q. 64, art. 1. See also Aristotle, *The Nicomachean Ethics*, trans. Harris Rackham (Hertfordshire, UK: Wordsworth, 1996), 35.

[57]*Laudato Si'* (14).

[58]See *Laudato Si'* (109) and *Sollicitudo Rei Socialis* (28).

[59]*Laudato Si'* (169).

[60]"US Senate Refuses to Accept Humanity's Role in Global Climate Change, Again," www.theguardian.com.

[61]*Laudato Si'* (54).

"You Want to Get Religion, Go in the Wilderness"

Delores Williams and Hope in the Midst of Ecological Despair

Bridget E. O'Brien

If the human species has not already passed the final point at which it would be possible to prevent worldwide climate collapse, then we swiftly approach that marker. According to a February 2015 paper published in *Science,* our actions have pushed the Earth past four of nine "planetary boundaries" needed to remain a hospitable environment for human life, those boundaries being extinction rate, deforestation, level of carbon dioxide in the atmosphere, and oceanic nitrogen and phosphorus levels.[1] In 2014, the United Nations Intergovernmental Panel on Climate Change (IPCC) reported with "very high confidence" that anthropogenic climate change will lead to heat strokes, extreme storms, and water scarcity for urban human communities, and with "high confidence" that anthropogenic climate change will lead to decreased food security and water availability for rural human communities, around the globe.[2] The IPCC warns, "Continued emission of greenhouse gases will cause further warming and long-lasting changes in all components of the climate system, increasing the likelihood of severe, pervasive, and irreversible impacts for people and ecosystems."[3] Even if anthropogenic greenhouse gas emissions reached zero, the IPCC concludes that the impacts of human-driven climate change will nonetheless continue for centuries.[4]

In the face of such data, we cannot only ask how we are to

prevent environmental catastrophe; we must begin to ask how we can respond to the impossibility of preventing a catastrophe we know is coming. This question of how to find hope in the midst of ecological despair is a question for all persons of good will facing the environmental crisis. It is particularly pointed for Christian theologians who wish to engage in joint action with non-Christians, for the popular narrative of Christian interaction with the environmental movement often concludes that Christian hope poses an impediment to environmental action, rather than offering a positive contribution to broader ecological discourse.

Figures from journalist Bill Moyers to theologian Catherine Keller have attributed U.S. resistance to environmental protection legislation to Christian eschatological hopes.[5] Political scientists report that Evangelical Christian belief in the Second Coming corresponds to political resistance to governmental measures to curb climate change.[6] Lest theologians dissociate ourselves too strongly from popular eschatology, sources more familiar to Catholic and mainline Protestant thought, including Augustine, have also been linked to an environmentalism-inhibiting perspective that holds that, in Peter Phan's words, "Nature is not created for its own sake but to serve the needs of humans and hence does not possess an internal goodness and is not destined to share in eternal beatitude. It is fated to disappear or at best to perdure simply as an external environment for glorified humanity."[7]

I do not propose that these critiques accurately condemn the broad tradition of Christian eschatology. Still, we must be conscious that Christian involvement in the environmental movement falls under a shadow of suspicion generated by such associations of Christian hope with disregard for the physical world. Yet even in the face of this distrust, a robust theology of hope is one of the key distinctive contributions Christians can offer to the environmental movement. I suggest that Delores Williams, a founder of womanist theology, offers one of the best contemporary theological sources for such a robust theology of hope.

In her 1993 book *Sisters in the Wilderness*, Williams draws from the experiences of black women in the United States during and after slavery and the biblical narrative of Hagar. Seeing resonances between the narrative of this biblical African woman who is enslaved, raped, and abused and the experiences of African and African-descended women under the U.S. chattel slavery system, Williams reads the Genesis accounts from the perspective of Hagar, not her owners, Sarah and Abraham. Interpreting the Hagar story in light of African American women's experiences and vice versa, Williams articulates a theology that celebrates black women's cultivated artfulness at "making a way out of no way."[8] She repeatedly turns to this phrase, deeply rooted in African American experience and reflection, to describe black women's response to God's offer of hope where hope seems absurd.[9] This dynamic makes Williams a particularly rich source in articulating a Christian hope that leads us to act for our planet whether it is threatened or condemned: her work is centered on celebrating abundant resourcefulness where resources are forcibly removed. This resourcefulness, received as an empowering gift from God, sustains the individual who is faced with destruction and demands that she act creatively to sustain a community living under that same threat.

As related in Genesis 16:1–16 and 21:9–21, Hagar is an Egyptian woman, and Sarai's slave. Williams notes that Hagar "is introduced as the solution to a problem confronting a wealthy Hebrew slave-owning family."[10] As yet unable to conceive a child herself, Sarai suggests to her husband Abram, "Go into my slave-girl; it may be that I shall obtain children by her" (Gn 16:2). When Abram does this, Hagar becomes pregnant. After handing Hagar over to be raped by Abram, Sarai resents Hagar's response to her own pregnancy, and so, with Abram's permission, "Sarai dealt harshly with her"—and Hagar runs away to the wilderness. Williams notes that in escaping from slavery, "Hagar becomes the first female in the Bible to liberate herself from oppressive power structures."[11] But this self-liberation is not unambiguously positive: alone in the wilderness as a pregnant woman, Hagar has no way of providing herself with basic necessities for survival. While Williams names Hagar's liberation action as courageous, placing her "momentarily in control of her destiny," it also causes a crisis of what Williams terms survival and quality of life.[12] In the wilderness, no one is assured of water or food; there are threats from animals and from heat.

Thus far in Hagar's biblical narrative, the interactions have remained at the horizontal, human interpersonal level. It is Sarai who suggests Abram impregnate Hagar; it is Sarai who is offended by Hagar's response to her pregnancy; it is Abram who authorizes

Sarai to mistreat Hagar. But once Hagar flees to the wilderness, God enters into the scene, indicating, for Williams, that "the divinity is with Hagar in the midst of her personal suffering and destitution."[13] The angel of the Lord meets Hagar by a spring of water. Yet the interaction does not go as we might hope. God does invite Hagar to speak, and is thus the first actor in the narrative to show interest in Hagar's own history or desired plans: "The angel of the Lord found her by a spring of water in the wilderness, the spring on the way to Shur. And he said, 'Hagar, slave-girl of Sarai, where have you come from and where are going?' She said, 'I am running away from my mistress Sarai.' The angel of the Lord said to her, 'Return to your mistress, and submit to her' " (Gn 16:7–9).

Immediately after asking about Hagar's own wishes, then, God orders her to return to the place of oppression from which she has just liberated herself. Williams insists that we face the full difficulty of this passage, in which God seems to endorse slavery, sexual violence, and the harsh mistreatment of a vulnerable woman: "The angel of Yahweh is, in this passage, no liberator God."[14] Here, Williams develops one of the key distinctions between her womanist theology and black liberation theology: Williams insists that oppressed and marginalized persons do not always experience God's presence as liberating freedom from death-dealing systems. Instead, God's presence can be experienced as enabling survival and quality of life within those death-dealing systems. God does not guide Hagar through the wilderness, providing her with manna until she reaches a land flowing with milk and honey. God tells her to return to the nearest place that can provide the basic resources she needs to survive, where she is to use Abram's resources to keep herself and her unborn child alive.

If this were where God's interaction with Hagar ended, her wilderness experience would be a waste, and one might be tempted to conclude from this passage that dramatic human actions for salvation are destined to fail unless directly set in motion by God. But the angel of the Lord does not leave Hagar at this point. This is no painful lesson in the dangers of liberationist Pelagianism. Instead, the angel offers an ambiguous promise to Hagar: "I will so greatly multiply your offspring that they cannot be counted for multitude. . . . Now you have conceived and shall bear a son; you shall call him Ishmael, for the Lord has given heed to your affliction. He shall be a wild ass of a man, with his hand against everyone, and everyone's hand against him, and he shall live at odds with all his kin" (Gn 16:10–12).

Williams notes that it would be easy to read this promise as a curse, rather than a blessing. Yet she insists on contextualizing Ishmael's promised pugnacious nature within the life he will have: Ishmael and Hagar will make their lives in the wilderness, where they will face harsh conditions. The angel of the Lord offers Hagar a strategy for their survival. From this perspective, Ishmael's wild nature is not savagery that a better blessing would see civilized out of him, but the promise of a match between Hagar and Ishmael's wilderness environment and the skills needed to sustain life there.

Finally, Williams draws our attention to Hagar's words, which end this episode in the wilderness: "[Hagar] named the Lord who spoke to her, 'You are El-roi'; for she said, 'Have I really seen God and remained alive after seeing him?' Therefore, the well was called Beer-lahai-roi; it lies between Kadesh and Bered" (Gn 16:13–14). Hagar thus becomes the only person in the Bible to give God a name. Hagar's escape to the wilderness does not follow the Exodus-liberation account we might expect. Nor, however, is her act of self-liberation deemed pointless or arrogant. Instead, Hagar's courageous, risk-filled action for her own liberation is the necessary condition for Hagar's direct and intimate encounter with God, who promises her that, through her son, she will eventually have the resources needed to live in the currently unsurvivable wilderness. Without erasing the ambiguity of a theophany that returns Hagar to slavery, we must acknowledge the power of an enslaved woman naming God herself, and thus implicitly rebuking the misnaming of God at work in Abram and Sarai's simultaneous reliance on God and violence toward Hagar. In the Bible translation Williams uses, the meaning of the name El Roi is related to Hagar's saying, "Did I not go on seeing here, after him who sees me?"[15] Thus, Hagar's encounter with God ends with affirmation that God sees her, *and* that her sight—her self-understanding as someone other than Sarai and Abram's possession—is upheld, and will go on. God is not at work here as a liberator, but the resources God offers for Hagar's survival and quality of life include validating her own theological insight. God sends Hagar back into slavery so that she will have the resources to survive physically, but God does not send her back without awakening new spiritual resources which will help her survive Abram's household.

This affirmation of sight continues when Hagar returns to the wilderness in Genesis 21. This second time, she has not chosen to go to the wilderness, but is rather exiled along with her son following Sarah's demand that Abraham drive Hagar and Ishmael away, lest "this slave-girl's son" share the inheritance with Sarah's son Isaac. This time, it is Hagar and not God who questions her ability to survive in the wilderness. Having finished the last of her water, Hagar sets down her son under a bush, walks away so that she will not have to witness his death, and weeps. But God calls to her and tells her to pick up Ishmael, for God's wilderness promise to Hagar still stands. Finally, God opens Hagar's eyes, and she sees a well of water (Gn 21:18–19). In Williams's words, "God gave her new vision to see survival resources where she saw none before."[16] God empowers Hagar to make a way out of no way.

For Williams, this wilderness experience is shared by black women in the United States. She writes, "We can speak of Hagar and many African American women as sisters in the wilderness struggling for life, and by the help of their God coming to terms with situations that have destructive potential."[17] For enslaved black women and men, the wilderness was a positive symbol, "a free and friendly space where one received from Jesus the strength needed to rise above one's ailments."[18] As in the biblical story of Hagar and Ishmael, the wilderness was open to enslaved men and women alike, as shown by the inclusivity of spiritual lyrics: "You want to be a Christian, go in de wilderness,/ Go in de wilderness, go in de wilderness,/ Mournin' brudder, go in de wilderness/ You want to get religion, go in de wilderness,/ Go in de wilderness, go in de wilderness/ . . . / 'Flicted sister, go in de wilderness."[19] In the period of slavery, the wilderness experience offered a space of isolation from the slave environment, in which intense spiritual struggle led to the establishment of a healing and strengthening relationship with Jesus. Yet wilderness never became so purely a symbol that the challenges to survival posed by the wilderness were lost. And so, Williams notes, for the postslavery black community, "wilderness" was often used to describe the hostile world into which the individual had to sojourn to try to make a living for herself and her family.[20] While the antebellum black population was liberated from slavery, systemic economic violence and structural white supremacy mean that black women's struggle for survival and quality of life continues.

For Williams, then, the wilderness symbol is always complex: wilderness is a place where survival is threatened and received as gift; a place of attempted liberation and a place where liberation is deferred. What is consistent among these uses of wilderness is intense struggle, profound encounter with God, and the empowering gift to find resources for survival and quality of life. In Williams's words, "For many black Christian women today, 'wilderness' or 'wilderness-experience' is a symbolic term used to represent a near-destruction situation in which God gives personal direction to the believer and thereby helps her make a way out of what she thought was no way."[21]

White theologians should be cautious about appropriating black contextual theology for their own purposes, and we must not remove the womanist core from Williams's work. At present, all of humanity faces a near-destruction situation, but despite this universal fragility, we are immediately affected more or less depending on our social situation. At the global level, the nations which produce the most carbon are those least immediately affected by global climate change, and vice versa, as noted in *Laudato Si'* (51). If our response to the ecological crisis is to be a response of genuine hope, and not a naïve optimism about the power of technology to save us from the sins of industrialization, theological reflection must amplify the voices of those who will be most affected by global climate change.[22] The IPCC notes that in every country, regardless of its level of development, those who are poor will be the most severely affected by the ecological crisis.[23] Due to the gendered and racialized character of poverty in the United States, a disproportionate number of black women are included. But Williams offers theological resources for all who seek hope in the midst of ecological despair—hope where hope seems absurd. An account for Christian ecological hope developed by a white theologian in conversation with Delores Williams should not represent a decontextualizing appropriation of Williams's work, but a humble acknowledgement that black women should be central to our consideration of the victims of ecological collapse.

If our ecological hope is to qualify as genuinely Christian, rather than a secular optimism of the privileged, then our hope must contend with the genuine possibility of ecological collapse. It must not ignore the suffering of our brothers and sisters in order to maintain a conviction that everything will turn out all right. It must contend with the possibility that our acts of ecological self-liberation will fail or be found to be untimely, and it must make room for a discussion of survival and quality of life alongside liberation. It must inquire into how we are to survive and maintain quality of life in the midst of global ecological catastrophe. Johann Baptist Metz's turn to eschatology was driven by the insistence that Christian hope cannot exclude those who have already died, seemingly defeated by the sins of history's victors.[24] We find ourselves at a slightly different location: we are faced with the question of how to hope for those not yet born, yet potentially already doomed. The shape of our hope must join a faith in God's ultimate victory with a willingness to find sustenance in what is not yet victory, but only the ability to endure until tomorrow.

This willingness to see survival and quality of life as experiences of salvation must chasten us against any temptation toward political purity in our search for responses to the ecological crisis. Hagar is sent back to slavery so that she and her unborn son can survive, yet this does not affirm the goodness of slavery. We may have to form coalitions we find deeply objectionable in order to work for survival and quality of life for future generations. This does not mean we need to abandon commitments which place us in opposition to those with whom we work.

A Williams-rooted account of ecological hope should reject both a romanticized view of the natural and a neoliberal confidence in the triumph of "civilizing" technology. Williams's praise of black women's history of making ways out of no ways makes no essentializing or romanticized claims about the "natural" feminine gifts of black women. In analyzing the stories, language, and strategies that black women have used for survival in the wilderness of the world, she describes strategies that are representative of how God has empowered black women to "make a way out of no way," and names these as "arts" to draw attention to the finely honed skill black women have developed in response to crises of survival. Williams highlights four such strategies: cunning ("a wholesome shrewdness" to ensure individual and communal survival), encounter (discerning how and when to mobilize mass action, and how and when to encourage endurance), care (commitment to familial and communal relationships) and connecting (developing and deploying networks across personal and cultural differences to address community crises).[25]

Cunning, encounter, care, and connecting are not descriptive of black women's survival strategies because it is the nature of women in general or black women in particular to prize connection above analysis. Instead, Williams directs our attention to the ways black women have developed these skillful arts out of survival necessity and taught them to their daughters, sisters, nieces, and friends. Black women's history of struggling against forces which seek their destruction has taught them that arts that mobilize human connection are better survival strategies than technologies that isolate individuals from their communities.

Williams does not set us up for an optimism in the strength of human ingenuity, sent out to conquer the wilderness through neoliberal development. Instead, as in the case of Ishmael, survival strategies are matched to the environment; the environment is not remade or conquered by these strategies. Nor does Williams present the environment itself as purely good: throughout Williams's work, the wilderness environment remains a complex symbol. It is a place that threatens survival, yet also a place where survival is assured. Thus an ecological hope articulated in conversation with Williams will not embrace a Romantic nostalgia that ignores the challenges of the wilderness even prior to anthropogenic environmental collapse. Williams insists on the goodness of the wilderness and insists on the goodness of honed human cunning. Williams's theology does not take us into a gleaming technocratic future dominated by an Apple aesthetic, nor does it send us into a nostalgic retro-agrarianism unreachable by the urban poor. Instead, Williams's theology takes us into the wilderness, and then back—sometimes back to slavery, sometimes back to the liberated community, but always back to a commitment to deploy one's skills for the survival and quality of life of the community. And so, in this time of ecological despair, if we want to get hope, let us go in the wilderness.

Notes

[1]Will Steffen et al., "Planetary Boundaries: Guiding Human Development on a Changing Planet," *Science* 347, no. 6223 (February 2015), http://dx.doi.org/10.1126/science.1259855.

[2]R. K. Pachauri and L. A. Meyer, eds., *Climate Change 2014: Synthesis Report Summary for Policy Makers. Contribution of Working Groups I, II, and III to the Fifth Assessment Report of the Intergovernmental Panel on Climate Change* (Geneva: IPCC), 15–16.

[3]Ibid., 8.

[4]Ibid., 16.

[5]Bill Moyers, "Environmental Armageddon" (Lecture, Center for Health and the Global Environment, New York, December 1, 2004), https://www.beliefnet.com. Catherine Keller, *Apocalypse Now and Then: A Feminist Guide to the End of the World* (Minneapolis: Fortress Press, 1996), 4–5. While Lynn White focused his 1967 ecological critique of Christianity (Lynn White Jr., "The Historical Roots of Our Ecologic Crisis," *Science* 155, no. 3767 [March 1967]: 1203–7) on theologies of creation rather than eschatology, the view that Christian theologies pose the greatest roadblock to ecologically protective public policy may be traced back to White.

[6]David C. Barker and David H. Bearce, "End-Times Theology, the Shadow of the Future, and Public Resistance to Addressing Global Climate Change," *Political Research Quarterly* 66, no. 2 (June 2011).

[7]Peter Phan, "Eschatology and Ecology: The Environment in the End Times," *Dialogue & Alliance* 9, no. 2 (September 1995): 103.

[8]Delores S. Williams, *Sisters in the Wilderness: The Challenge of Womanist God-Talk* (Maryknoll, NY: Orbis Books, 1993), 236.

[9]Ibid., 57.

[10]Ibid., 15.

[11]Ibid., 19.

[12]Ibid., 20.

[13]Ibid.

[14]Ibid., 21.

[15]Ibid., 23.

[16]Ihid., 32.

[17]Ibid., 109.

[18]Ibid., 112.

[19]Quoted by Williams, *Sisters in the Wilderness*, 111.

[20]Williams, *Sisters in the Wilderness*, 117.

[21]Ibid., 108.

[22]See *Laudato Si'* (20): "Technology, which, linked to business interests, is presented as the only way of solving these problems, in fact proves incapable of seeing the mysterious network of relations between things and so sometimes solves one problem only to create others."

[23]Pachauri and Meyer, *Climate Change 2014*, 13.

[24]See Johann Baptist Metz, *Faith in History and Society: Toward a Practical Fundamental Theology*, trans. J. Matthew Ashley (New York: Crossroad, 2007), 84: "The hope that Christians have in the God of the living and the dead, in God's power to raise the dead, is the hope for a revolution on behalf of everyone, those who suffer unjustly, those long ago forgotten, even the dead."

[25]Williams, *Sisters in the Wilderness*, 236.

Good Chaos, Bad Chaos, and the Meaning of Integrity in Both

Nancy M. Rourke

What does integrity have to do with wilderness or with wildness? Integrity, as a virtue, seems to be about consistency, honesty, and staying the same despite changes and chaos—despite, that is, the threat of wildness. Thus wildness and integrity seem opposed, but this is not a simple nor straightforward opposition. Instead, integrity and wildness often intersect—and this paper finds, at the intersection of wildness and integrity, a harmony and a significant contribution to a Catholic environmental virtue ethic.

The wildness within which we live is a moral and existential necessity. We need it. In this paper, I will refer to wildness (unpredictability, violent conditions, privation, predation, threat) as chaos. Chaos includes the constant suffering, pain, need, and life-threatening unpredictability of our world. It includes creation's ways of opposing safety, security, basic needs, flourishing, meaning, and even survival. At the same time, such privation, unpredictability and threat often indicate not natural processes but injustice and moral wrongness. Therefore, in environmental ethics, chaos pulls our attention to the climate consequences of our lifestyles of consumption, blindness, and waste. In pursuit of wealth and convenience, we poison the skies—and others experience drought, flood, destruction, death, and extinction as a result. This is bad chaos. However, chaos also manifested in this world before and apart from anthropogenic climate change, and even before and apart from the existence of human beings. This nonanthropogenic chaos, I will argue, can be construed as good. To discuss chaos, then, one must first examine the differences between these two varieties of chaos.

Consider first anthropogenic chaos. "Man is suddenly becoming aware that by an ill-considered exploitation of nature he risks destroying it and becoming in his turn the victim of this degradation. Not only is the material environment becoming a permanent menace—pollution and refuse, new illness and absolute destructive capacity—but the human framework is no longer under man's control, thus creating an environment for tomorrow which may well be intolerable." This description of anthropogenic chaos comes not from Pope Francis's 2015 *Laudato Si'*, but from Pope Paul VI in his 1971 *Octogesima Adveniens*.[1] Forty-five years before *Laudato Si'*, short-sighted human practices—overwhelmingly those of Northern and Western lifestyles like my own—had already begun to poison creation. When we learned of our culpability, we continued to poison and even to increase our emission of carbon, accelerating the extinction of species, ecosystems,[2] and cultures.[3] The chaos threatening the poor and vulnerable begins with us. The definition of integrity with which I began, focused as it is on the value of consistency, would insist on staying the course despite these changes. Already we see that a different definition of integrity is needed.

Now consider nonanthropogenic chaos. If chaos is marked by suffering and pain, then a literal reading of Genesis would imply that there was no chaos in God's good creation before Adam and Eve sinned. Traditionally, Christianity identifies the Fall as the point at which the current conditions of creation began, and identifies Eden before that Fall as the world as God meant it to be. Did that world include chaos? Well, given an understanding of Adam and Eve as real people and the Fall as a historical event, the answer would be no. Yet with today's understanding of evolution, the answer is not so simple. We know that pain and suffering long predate the existence of creatures advanced enough to make conscious moral choices. To take a simple but powerful example, Norman Wirzba reminds us that there was eating before human beings existed, and this means that death was taking place. "Death is eating's steadfast accomplice."[4] Here life itself begins the cycle of creatures' need to take from outside of themselves, to destroy and consume, and in that way to power the fires of life with the death of the Other. This means that, if we take seriously both evolution and a historical-critical reading of Genesis, we must accept that the cycle of life and death is in fact part of

God's good creation. God saw the world as good, and we know that death is an inextricable part of this world. Somehow, then, despite how difficult it might seem, we must acknowledge that gratitude is the proper response to this cycle of death and life. To be grateful for death—! Sin does not explain all chaos; instead, evolution, a central fact of all existence, also includes chaotic chance and wildness—indeed, depends on it. Animals eat other animals; parasites prey; and chance circumstance often throws creatures into conditions which they cannot survive. Those that do survive, evolve; mutations and chance lead some to adaptation and others to extinction. This process continues today: it is a wild process, a chaotic process . . . and a process that creates new forms of life, complexity, and beauty. Evolution means that wildness, privation, unpredictability, threat, and chaos persist and cannot ultimately be regarded as entirely bad. Chaos is necessary to creation itself: hence, "good" chaos.

We (humans) do not normally find chaos to be good, but chaos, disorder, and unpredictability seem necessary for wonder, creativity and inspiration. As a light-hearted illustration of this, innumerable cross-stitch patterns note that a messy house is a sign of great creativity. More tellingly, fertile soil is soil full of death and decay. In addition, Dale Jamieson identifies "fear, dread, pain and terror"[5] as necessary for the experience of the sublime. Catherine Keller exegetes this chaos or *tehom*, finding in it "the potential for good or ill."[6] Chaos can be anthropogenic and nonanthropogenic (as Keller's *tehom*). Whether *tehomic* or orchestrated against creation, or born of a mix of both, chaos exists, persisting regardless of its origins, and a responsible Christian ethic must take it seriously.

The experience of chaos—of death, pain, deprivation, anxiety, and meaningless suffering—redoubles on itself. When a human recognizes that a situation is descending into chaos, a feedback loop of suffering and dread begins.[7] We become overwhelmed. There are, however, strategies available to us that help us manage chaos. One of these is scale: when chaos descends, we can change our scale of observation. Zooming in or out during crisis lets us find hope, rest, or encouragement. For example, changing the temporal scale of our focus can make a life-threatening chaos resemble a temporary disruption of meaning or of safety, or a period of difficulty for a greater good, or a stage of recovery from worse to better. Changing the scale of our perception lets us make meaning of chaos. This is what we mean when we console by saying that things will get better, that the sun will come up tomorrow. This is what we are often (but not always) doing when we turn to the eschatological perspective in order to find hope in the midst of terrifying "signs of the times."

But changing our scale-focus does not eliminate chaos. We cannot eliminate chaos. It is evident deep within the patterns of creation. Fractal geometry, representing a phenomenon that many other disciplines have discovered, teaches us that chaos across different scales is quite well ordered. In fact, chaos iterates across scales. And if chaos is a characteristic of creation, then God has called it good. When we change the scale of our perception, we are not denying a truth or entering into a lie. We are only choosing to look differently. The chaos remains. We are left to conclude both that chaos works against our survival, and that if we are to survive, then we must survive in cooperation with chaos. Now we can bring this paradox to virtue ethics. Let us do this with a focus on the virtue most likely to cause problems with the idea that we must cooperate with chaos: the virtue of integrity.

Pope Francis's encyclical *Laudato Si'* charges us to think about integral ecology, repeatedly pointing to what ecology knows: everything is connected. Moral character demonstrates this interconnectedness, so I will consider integrity within the context of the whole moral character. The whole moral character can be understood as the "place" where integrity happens. Elsewhere this has been called a virtues ecology, or an examination of a virtues ecosystem.[8] Here the system of interactions among the virtues matters more than the definition of any one virtue.[9] Integrity is a trait of an entire moral character—a normative and descriptive characteristic of a moral character's functioning. It is a virtue *of* a moral character rather than a virtue *belonging to* a moral character. It is a metavirtue.

But what, exactly, is integrity? In order to define the term, we need first to look at a moral character ecologically. In a virtues ecology, a moral character is like a bioregion. It looks at the functions that happen within a moral character (for example, virtues *balance, strengthen, govern, inform*; the will *chooses*; the intellect *reasons*) and at these functions' interactions. Like all systems of interrelated interrelationalities, ecological systems follow certain rules.[10] We can use these rules to interpret the interactivities of a moral character. Here are some of these rules:

1. An individual can never do only one thing. (Everything we do leads to many other changes.)
2. Species exhibit universal individuation. (All species are unique, as are all individuals.)
3. Weak and diffuse causality matters.
4. All ecosystems are open systems with porous boundaries.
5. All ecosystems are *nested*.

Each of these rules has implications for a virtues ecology. I will limit my focus to the last rule: nestedness.[11] A moral character is nested within biological, geographic, social, economic, and ecological systems. Nested within a moral character are further ecosystems: mental, anatomic, moral, emotional, and social systems, to name a few. Systems of interrelationality exist between moral agents and within moral agents, and between and within a moral character's constituent "parts." Pope Francis echoes this, noting the "interrelation between ecosystems and between the various spheres of social interaction."[12]

Each ecosystem influences and is influenced by its neighboring ecosystems, and all of these function as participants in a larger region's ecosystems (recall rule #4 on porous boundaries). Each system is also a subsystem, a participant in a larger set of systems. This brings us back to thinking about scale. A virtues ecology lets us look at metaethics on the scale of a moral agent's internal worlds.[13] When we do this, though, we are still seeing the larger scales of observation (society, family, politics). Responsive integrity exists across and between the scales. They do not merely exist within one another; they are *nested* within each other. This means that a moral character is constantly responsive to the character of its contexts, and that it is never entirely distinguishable from the moral character of the moral agent's societies. Persons absorb and reinforce the virtues of our societies, internalize and perpetuate the values of surrounding social structures. We do this in many ways: deliberately, nonvoluntarily and involuntarily, carefully, casually, and unconsciously. Because a moral character has porous and imprecise boundaries, the lines delineating an individual's moral character are never precisely definable. At the same time, the porous boundaries *within* a moral character, between the virtues, explain why it is difficult to identify where one virtue ends and another begins, and why strengthening one virtue always means strengthening others.

With this understanding of a moral character, let's reapproach the virtue of integrity. Environmental ethicists who speak of integrity generally view it as a characteristic of a bioregion. Many deem it a fundamental ecological principle (especially Laura Westra).[14] But we want to define integrity as a virtue. Here, integrity is the habit, capability, and tendency of a human person *to participate in* ecological integrity, without and within. Leonardo Boff has described this, calling it mental ecology: "Mental ecology strives to achieve a psychic integration of human persons so as to make them gentler in their relationships with the natural and social environment and to bring them into a more lasting harmony with the universe in reverence and balance."[15] In other words, integrity is a good responsiveness across and between scales. It must reflect a moral agent's nestedness. A moral agent is integrated into the systems of her contexts, and her internal worlds are likewise integrated within her self. The systems of her virtues' interactivities are integrated in her home, work, country, village, family, and these systems are integrated into and within her self. A moral agent with integrity is responsive, inside and out, above, below, past, future, "laterally, frontward, backward and inwardly."[16] Heightened awareness of this nestedness can help us recognize the relationships between our world's many issues of injustice, as Boff has done.

This means that integrity is not so much a component *part* of a moral character as it is simply that character's fractal reproducibility. Integrity is a skill, partially infused by the nature of our existence within creation. An individual with no integrity catapults out of the Earth into the vacuum of space. She or he disintegrates. So the characteristic of integrity is both normative and descriptive. It describes how we are and asks that we act in accordance with our true nature—that is, beings with internal worlds, nested within "external" worlds.

This definition of integrity calls to mind weaker definitions of solidarity which name not a way we ought to be but a way we are—interconnected—and then function as a moral mandate by asking that we simply acknowledge this reality and live in accordance with it. Such definitions of solidarity seem to describe what I call integrity. Stronger definitions of solidarity require us to move from a recognition of interconnectivity to a choice to thrust ourselves out of our current place of power and wealth and protection into danger, deprivation, threat, hunger, exposure. A well-formed (stronger) virtue of integrity brings a moral agent in our context from the idea to a practice of solidarity. One might even say that integrity is a gateway virtue.

Integrity, as a resonating between the scales of a moral agent's worlds, requires the virtue of attunement (which I've defined elsewhere as a function of prudence[17]) to perceive truths of these worlds, without and within. A moral agent with integrity has a character that integrates these truths by means of her own self.

This point about truth brings the theological virtues into view. For a Catholic definition of integrity, of course, Christian cosmology is essential. First among the scales within which we aim to resonate is the eschatological scale of truth. Integrity for a Christian means resonating in response to both Christianity's "already" and "not-yet" reality. No moral agent can fit seamlessly with both these at once, so integrity is best imagined as a vacillation, a restless resonating between the *telos* of creation and the worlds of our sinful denials and fears. An individual with integrity stands in the middle of many concentric (and concentric-ish) spheres, quivering to bring them into alignment or at least harmony. Integrity can do this by propelling the moral character to respond to prudence's attunement to the theological virtues.

So Christian integrity is an integrity with the whole and the parts, from heart to yard to bioregion to globe to eschatological future, from seed to branch to tree to cross. But the heart is divided, the yard is a mess, and the tree has problems, so this cannot be a linear, orderly project. This brings us to the relationship between chaos and character. Integrity with respect to creation requires us to take in creation's chaos, good and bad.

Taking chaos into the moral character is good in several ways. One: It nurtures creativity. Two: It prevents a sanitized teleology. Three: It (helpfully) muddies our theological anthropology and our moral categories.

First: Valuing chaos in a moral character is a way to recognize the importance of imagination—of newness. Many theologians, environmental ethicists and philosophers have noted that imagination's role in moral formation has not been sufficiently recognized.[18] Unpredictability, complexity beyond human comprehension, and an appreciation of chaos help the cultivation of virtue. After all, pristine soil—simple soil, soil without death—is in the end soil without life. Such soil allows nothing to grow. Fertile soil, in contrast, is a complex mixture of living, dying, and dead elements. As rich, fertile soil requires the chaos of death and decomposition in order to bring forth new life, so too does human moral character need complexity and chaos to grow. Dirt should be dirty; character should encompass chaos.

Second: Valuing chaos in a moral character prevents a sanitizing of teleology. Defining flourishing is notoriously difficult for virtue ethics and for ecologists. In our efforts to identify what is and is not flourishing, we can easily reach for control, systematization, predictability. A *telos* with no room for chaos can lead to a bleached, still, static "flourishing" that is narrow in scope and oblivious to its global implications. A sanitized "flourishing" strengthens patriarchy, stifles complexity, and finds itself threatened by difference. It exacerbates xenophobia, racism, and classist presumptions. It is a lifeless *eudaimonia*, an ultimate idolatry of human reason.

Finally: taking chaos into the moral character helps us grow past a theological anthropology that imagines an individual atomistic self, with blurry edges, as the central focus of ethics. It nourishes a theological anthropology that is instead centrally focused on the webs of our interactivities. Recognizing the role of chaos in moral character also helps metaethics muddy our traditional moral categories. For example, our very sharp view of autonomous moral agency overlooks virtue ethics' view of character formation as habituation. This view implies a degree of inevitability from moral character to action, and from action to habit to moral character. Virtue theory sees a snowball effect toward perfection of virtues (and formation of vices). There is a shaded, dusky corner in this region of moral agency. Moral agents have will and deliberate, but we also have temperaments and act from habit.[19] The line between human moral agency and divine agency is also porous and imprecise. God's agency, God's grace, operates in the depths of our choices, in the mechanics our deciding, perhaps to a greater degree than we often understand.[20]

External input into a moral character is continual, to the degree that we can hardly call it "external" at all. Integrity—responsiveness across and between scales—requires us to acknowledge this lack of clarity. Here is a point at which Catholic theology might seek partnerships with reformed theology and with process theology. Environmental ethicist and theologian Willis Jenkins has said: "Global ethics should take up . . . questions . . . without attempting to integrate them all into a comprehensive worldview. That would undermine the diversity of moral worlds and the mutual accountability they have wrought."[21] This describes a theology done with integrity, taking in the chaos.

Notes

[1]Pope Paul VI, *Octogesima Adveniens* (1971), para. 21.

[2]Marten Scheffer, *Critical Transitions in Nature and Society* (Princeton, NJ: Princeton University Press, 2009).

[3]For example, see Jennifer Redfearn, dir., *Sun Come Up*, documentary (2011).

[4]"Eating . . . is the means of life itself—but also death. For any creature to live, countless seen and unseen others must die, often by being eaten themselves. Life as we know it depends on death, needs death, which means that death is not simply the cessation of life but its precondition" (Norman Wirzba, *Food and Faith: A Theology of Eating* [New York: Cambridge University Press, 2011], 1).

[5]Dale Jamieson, *Reason in a Dark Time: Why the Struggle against Climate Change Failed—and What It Means for Our Future* (Oxford: Oxford University Press, 2014), 190.

[6]Catherine Keller, *Face of the Deep: A Theology of Becoming* (New York: Routledge, 2003), 80– 81 and throughout.

[7]Note Elaine Scarry, *The Body in Pain: The Making and Unmaking of the World* (New York: Oxford University Press, 1985), and Eric J. Cassell, *The Nature of Suffering and the Goals of Medicine* (New York: Oxford University Press, 1991).

[8]See Nancy M. Rourke, "A Catholic Virtues Ecology," in *Just Sustainability: Ecology, Technology and Resource Extraction,* ed. Christiana Peppard and Andrea Vicini, SJ, Catholic Theological Ethics in the World Church Series, vol. 3 (Maryknoll, NY: Orbis Books, 2015), 194–204; and Nancy M. Rourke, "Prudence Gone Wild," *Environmental Ethics* 33 (Fall 2011), 249–66. This is in accordance with Leonardo Boff's observation, "There is an internal ecology just as surely as there is an external ecology, and they mutually condition each other" (Leonardo Boff, *Cry of the Earth, Cry of the Poor: Ecology and Justice* [Maryknoll, NY: Orbis Books, 1997], 6). See also Pope Benedict XVI, "Message for the Celebration of the World Day of Peace 2007" (January 1, 2007), para. 8, and *Caritas in Veritate* (June 29, 2009), para. 51, and his "Mes-

sage to the Brazilian Bishops for the 2011 Lenten Ecumenical Brotherhood Campaign in Brazil" (February 16, 2011), all available at www.vatican.va.

[9]I'm following the lead here of many environmental virtue ethics philosophers, including Phil Cafaro, Ronald Sandler, Geoffrey Frasz, and especially Louke van Wensveen, whose book *Dirty Virtues: The Emergence of Ecological Virtue Ethics* (Amherst, NY: Humanity Books, 2000) offers a good overview of this area.

[10]See Howard T. Odum, *Environment, Power, and Society for the Twenty-first Century: The Hierarchy of Energy* (New York: Columbia University Press, 2007); Holmes Rolston III, *Environmental Ethics: Duties to and Values in the Natural World* (Philadelphia: Temple University Press, 1988), especially page 180; Douglas W. Larson, *Cliff Ecology: Pattern and Process in Cliff Ecosystems*, Cambridge Studies in Ecology (Cambridge: Cambridge University Press, 2000); Edward T. Wimberley, *Nested Ecology: The Place of Humans in the Ecological Hierarchy* (Baltimore: Johns Hopkins University Press, 2009); Lawrence B. Slobodkin, *A Citizen's Guide to Ecology* (New York: Oxford University Press, 2003); Richard Karban, *How to Do Ecology: A Concise Handbook* (Princeton, NJ: Princeton University Press, 2006); and Frank R. Spellman, *Ecology for Nonecologists* (Lanham, MD: Government Institutes, 2008).

[11]Systems "such as seas, cities and savannahs have structures and processes that blend into adjacent nature, often without discontinuities and only rarely with distinct boundaries" (Howard T. Odum, *Systems Ecology* [New York: Wiley, 1983], 3). See also Odum, *Environment, Power, and Society,* 59.

[12]Pope Francis, *Laudato Si'* (2015), para. 141.

[13]Kevin O'Brien has described the trade-off between scale and resolution. For more, see his excellent chapter on scale (chap. 4) in Kevin O'Brien, *An Ethics of Biodiversity: Christianity, Ecology, and the Variety of Life* (Washington, DC: Georgetown University Press, 2010), 79–80. For a discussion of how ecologists make this choice see Larson, *Cliff Ecology,* 1–17.

[14]See Laura Westra, *An Environmental Proposal for Ethics: The Principle of Integrity* (Lanham, MD: Rowman and Littlefield, 1994), and Laura Westra and John Lemons, eds., *Perspectives on Ecological Integrity* (Dordrecht, The Netherlands: Kluwer Academic, 1995).

[15]Boff, *Cry of the Earth,* 6–7.

[16]Ibid., 4. Boff also notes that science calls for a "spirituality of integration," and his own political and ethical theology demonstrates the complexity of attentions required for this kind of integrity (Boff, *Ecology and Liberation: A New Paradigm* [Maryknoll, NY: Orbis Books, 1995], 38). Boff's influence on *Laudato Si'* is strong in this respect.

[17]Rourke, "Prudence Gone Wild."

[18]A recent book focusing on the cultivation of virtue repeatedly praises messiness and complexity as important for foundations of good moral growth (Nancy E. Snow, ed., *Cultivating Virtue: Perspectives from Philosophy, Theology and Psychology* [Oxford: Oxford University Press, 2015]). See also Willis Jenkins, *The Future of Ethics: Sustainability, Social Justice, and Religious Creativity* (Washington, DC: Georgetown University Press, 2013), 288;

Jonathan Gosling and Peter Case, "Social Dreaming and Ecocentric Ethics: Sources of Non-Rational Insight in the Face of Climate Change Catastrophe," *Organization* 20, no. 5 (September 1, 2013): 705–21; Louke van Wensveen, "The Cultivation of Virtue" (February 2012) at the Garrison Institute.

[19]In Snow, *Cultivating Virtue*, see Daniel C. Russell, "Aristotle on Cultivating Virtue," 36, and Dan McAdams, "Psychological Science and the *Nicomachean Ethics*: Virtuous Actors, Agents, and Authors," 318.

[20]"Jesus is not for the Christian tradition simply an example of good character, but is also a source of power to emulate that example. Christians speak not simply of imitating Jesus, but of assimilation to Christ, conformity with Christ— terms that place a question mark over independent human agency." In Snow, *Cultivating Virtue,* see Jennifer Herdt, "Frailty, Fragmentation, and Social Dependency in the Cultivation of Christian Virtue," 229.

[21]Jenkins, *Future of Ethics*, 120.

PART III

SPIRITUAL PRACTICES
FOR A CHANGING EARTH

Spirituality for a Suffering Earth

Death, Grief, and Transformation

Julia Brumbaugh

This essay initiates an exploration of the role of grief in the current ecological crisis, and suggests some of the elements of a spirituality or spiritualities that might help human beings who are trying to live well, with and for the life on our fragile and fierce planet. Our dominant culture needs to be profoundly reordered when it comes to the role of grief in our lives, to learn to experience grief through an understanding of human beings as profoundly connected to the rest of planetary life, and to be willing to dwell in, rather than avoid, suffering and grief.

Let me begin by situating this essay (and thereby myself) in a place that I love: in Portland, Oregon, at a spot overlooking the Willamette River that is known at the University of Portland simply as the Bluff. My parents met at this place, the University of Portland; I was born twelve years later in a hospital just up the Willamette River, and I was brought to a home just across the Columbia. I grew up across that mighty river and upstream a bit, near the mouth of the Columbia River gorge.

I don't live in this place anymore, and I haven't for a long time, but I still know it as part of my own body—these waters, these trees, this ground. When I breathe the air—the air scented by the Willamette and Columbia rivers, with a hint of sea tang if the wind is right; when my eyes take in the light, saturated by the mystical blue-green of Douglas firs, cedars, and hemlocks, when the dampness of this earth touches my skin—I know that I am home, and I can feel my body adjust to the recognition of its own belonging. Breathing is easier, and the muscles of my back and shoulders release. No other place on earth binds me to itself like this one. In this place, I hope to come close to the love, knowledge, and personal experience that Steven Bouma-Prediger argues is the foundation of our ability to really care for, and to act for the well-being of, our planet.[1] He writes: "We care for only what we love. We love only what we know. We truly know only what we experience. If we do not know our place—know it in more than a passing, cursory way, know it intimately and personally—then we are destined to use and abuse it."[2] Of course, my intimacy with this river valley, which is nestled between the low mountains of the Coast Range and the high mountains of the Cascades, means that no other place pierces me with sorrow quite like this place. The missing wetlands, the stripped hillsides, the miles and miles of pavement, the giant air-conditioned houses, and the strip malls covering over strawberry fields, cattail ponds, and coyote hunting grounds that used to be here always strike me painfully. The losses are personal and they cut to the quick. They are a grief to me—and yet, I don't how to grieve them. Pushing Bouma-Prediger's thought a bit further, if I do not really know how to grieve *this* place and its wounds, deaths, and empty silences, how can I possibly confront and grieve the losses we currently face on our planet and how can I respond to them? How can any of us?

It seems to me, though, that notwithstanding the significant resources for grieving that we might learn from other cultures the world over, many of us living within the dominant US market-driven culture are not particularly good at *any* grieving. Popular culture gives us very little help, and what help it does give comes frequently in the form of platitudes like "that which does not kill you makes you stronger"; "God never gives us more than we can handle"; and "everything happens for a reason." These all carry the implication that some good that wouldn't otherwise be depends on this loss, often with a pious sense that God is bringing these things about, so we should be able to move through them easily. Of course, part of the mystery of suffering is that, in the words of M. Shawn Copeland, "From some women and men, suffering coaxes real freedom and growth" or "squeezes a delicious ironic spirit and tough laughter."[3] While from others, she adds, "suffering extracts a bitter venom."[4] For Copeland, reading the stories of Black Women under slavery, it is clear that the path to freedom, growth, or tough laughter is a long one that individuals and communities reach, if ever, only through long wrestling and no small amount of creativity and love. But when mourners at funerals I have attended promise the mother of a dead child that it all means something, or when a spouse is expected to be back to work and fully functional within weeks of his partner's burial, something deeply unwise is at work, a folly that serves to console the consoler, not the griever, and which supports productivity and business as usual, but not healing and transformation.

Why does this matter for the wilderness of our changing planet? I suspect that clichés like "everything happens for a reason" spoken in the face of terrible suffering are clumsy attempts to refer both to divine care of the world and to dodge the frightening and destabilizing reality of another person's, and even one's own, loss(es), especially when they seem particularly meaningless, and to put everything back on track to make sense and back to "normal." The trouble is that the assumptions about human beings and God embedded in these clichés, as problematic as they are for interhuman suffering, translate in even more problematic ways when applied to the world and its travails. If I am right that many of our default cultural responses to devastating losses are to try to explain them away as meaningful and even as part of some good plan of God's, then, when confronted with the intimate and enormous losses to planetary life, we won't face the destabilizing, but very real possibility that current planetary changes will be without any meaning we can see, and lead to no good end, for humans and for our planetary kin. If we don't learn to grieve all that is lost, which often involves confronting our own responsibility for these losses, neither will we resist the forces bringing those losses about, nor creatively allow something new to be born in us and in the world.

To address questions about how our ability to grieve might limit or, alternatively, provide a basis for new ways of being in the world that are more open for life and renewal, I want to bring insights into the conversations from two very different scholars. First, work by Judith Butler interrogates the experience of grief, reaching as she does so for the anthropological insight that part of what is so staggering and disorienting about grief is how the loss of another can imply a loss of one's self. Second, David Abram's work on the sensuous self, our animal being, confirms and extends

Butler's insight in profoundly helpful ways by connecting our animal bodies to the sensual world to which we belong. Taking these two together, I hope to find insights and recourses for grieving the losses of our shared planetary life.

First, Judith Butler. In an essay called "Violence, Mourning, Politics," Butler explores the links among these realities in the context of the US response to the terror attacks of September 11, 2001.[5] In this essay, she addresses three questions to the reader that can help us here. First, who is grievable? Second, what does grief reveal about who the griever is? And, third, is there something to be gained from "tarrying with grief, from remaining exposed to its unbearability and not endeavoring to seek a resolution for grief through violence?"[6]

Butler's concern in asking the question "Who is grievable?" is human-centered and political, rightly asking why we don't grieve for the victims of our national violence. But in our context of a mass extinction and countless other forms of planetary deaths, we must, as the environmental ethicist Ashlee Cunsolo Willox argues, extend this question to other-than-human beings.[7] Why don't we grieve more, and particularly publicly and politically, for these tremendous and devastating losses of animal and plant life, and of the integrity of our soil, air, and water? There are, of course, the same kinds of political reasons that prevent us from raising laments for Afghani and Iraqi children preventing us from crying out and finding ourselves upended and disoriented by, for example, the catastrophe of the clear-cutting of old growth forests between Portland and Seattle, catastrophes repeated the world over. But for the purposes of this essay, I want to focus on a more intimate reason Butler's thinking invites—that those lives, human, but also animal and vegetable, do not consciously form for us an essential part of the community, the "we," that we belong to. Thus in order to grieve these lives, we need to expand our sense of *to whom we belong.*

Butler takes this insight further by examining what happens to us when we do grieve the loss of someone, which is part of her answer to her second question, who is the griever? In her analysis of the experience of grief, Butler describes the way that grieving is ecstatic insofar as it takes us outside of ourselves. In that bewildering space of grief, we find ourselves wondering not only about the one we have lost, the one who has died, but about who I have become in the other's absence. She writes:

> But maybe when we undergo what we do [in grief], something about who we are is revealed, something that delineates the ties we have to others, that shows us that these ties constitute what we are, ties or bonds that compose us. It is not as if an "I" exists independently over here and then simply loses a "you" over there, especially if the attachment to "you" is part of what composes who "I" am. If I lose you, under these conditions, then I not only mourn the loss, but I become inscrutable to myself. Who "am" I, without you? When we lose some of these ties by which we are constituted, we do not know who we are or what to do. On one level, I think I have lost "you" only to discover that "I" have gone missing as well. At another level, perhaps what I have lost "in" you, that for which I have no ready vocabulary, is a relationality that is composed neither exclusively of myself nor you, but is to be conceived as the tie by which those terms are differentiated and related.[8]

So, in the context of what Butler is exploring, the lack of grief for those not within my community signals a lack of ties that bind with those others, a lack that might itself be something to grieve. But it also reveals something positive about human beings—I am not just myself, but when I grieve you, I can tell, if I am attentive, that I am in you and you are in me, and without you, I have to become someone new. I don't think this is news, the observation that we need a more richly interrelational account of human beings. But adding the insights of David Abram to Butler's invites us to think—or better, to *feel*—the ways that this constituting relationality Butler describes exists among each of us with the world, with our friends and neighbors the blue jay, the salmon, and the mountain lion, and with trees and grasses, even the soil, the water and the stones of this earth.

David Abram is an ecologist, anthropologist, and philosopher, whose work in books like *The Spell of the Sensuous* and *Becoming Animal* investigates human being in the larger world, particularly examining the way literacy and technology and other "civilizing" forces have strained human relations with the "natural world."[9] He argues that much modern life teaches us to barricade ourselves from the natural world and to believe that we are not really of the earth, when in fact we are. In a poignant image from a recent interview, for example, Abram describes the poverty of our self-understanding through a reflection on *eros*, which much of modern Western culture tends to reduce to human sexuality. He says:

> I am trying to open an erotic relationship to—well—to everything. . . . Otherwise, we're stuck trying to satisfy all of our craving for otherness—our organism's ancient need for sensuous contact and interchange with the more-than-human earth—we're stuck trying to satisfy that deep longing entirely through our human relationships. Which, I think, blows apart so many marriages, and indeed makes all of our human relationships very brittle. 'Cause we're trading all of this intense, erotic energy around entirely among ourselves, forgetting its ancestral source and spark in the broader interchange between the human animal and foragers in a thoroughly animistic context, negotiating rich and often difficult relationships with myriad facets of the multiplicitous surroundings. It's only very recently that we've been born into a civilization that denies the rest of nature as a set of inanimate objects and determinate, mechanical processes. Which blocks the possibility of relationship with those things.[10]

Abram, then, invites us to be in the world differently, where our animal bodies are in relationship with the animate world, where we belong to and are porous—both materially and pneumatically—to everything else. Abram's work reminds us that we are already porous to the world, with every breath, every bite of food, every sip of water, every moment we are touched—as we are every minute of every day of our lives, by air and water. We move within the world and the world moves in and through us. We are, in a sense akin to Butler's sense of relationality, constituted by these relationships.

With Butler and Abram's combined help, I can begin to approach an answer to Butler's second question, "What does grief reveal about the griever?" more substantively regarding human grief for the other-than-human world. The reason the clear-cuts cut me is because they do, in fact cut me. Maybe I usually live without attention to my fellow creatures and their travails, but I am bound to them whether or no. And sometimes the field of stumps and piles of branches littering the ground where there once was a tall forest does hurt me. And maybe it is not mere sentimentality or nostalgia, but rather because I am cut down, too, with the forest, because I was in it, and it—with all its abundant life—was in me. Who am I—who are we—without the forest?

This, then, leads us to think about Butler's third question: "What can we gain by tarrying with grief?" What do we gain undertaking the long, slow work of mourning for the forest? The work of grief resulting from death and destruction is precisely this: to tarry in the grief and rage, and, as often as not, the shame and fear that accompany death. Doing so will, as grieving does, take us out of ourselves. The annihilation of species and ecosystems is materially and spiritually tearing us apart from the inside as well as from the outside, even if many of us do not know how to recognize or face it. The task is to rebuild, to renew with the pieces that remain, but it is grievous work, work that the dominant culture's failures regarding grief (and shame) amplify immeasurably, precisely because they rush us quickly past the disorientation, the fear, and the emptiness that seem to consume the griever, toward an easy, but likely superficial, "moving on."

We must learn to tarry, as an alternative to quickly passing over grief, because it is one of the conditions of healing and transformation. Part of the terrible freedom of those moments lived in the wake of another's death, particularly one marked by senselessness, is that what we might rebuild from the fragments that remain may be hard and isolated, spitting venom at others, or it might be soft and open, producing laughter and tears, binding us closer to each other and creating pathways of connection. It is important, therefore, that we build up spaces and practices to support each other when it is necessary to tarry in the bewildering wilderness of grief. We must learn to feel through the fearful, disorienting discovery of the interconnection of our lives with all the life around us, and experience that the loss of others, whether human or animal or plant or even mineral, is always going to take time, creativity, and courage if the fragile chance for the transformations Copeland and others describe might be possible. Traditions like the Jewish practice of sitting shiva, Buddhist mindfulness, and Christian grave-tending can all give us hints about how to provide shelter for the grieved and wounded spirit so that something new might be born in time. Those of us with thin grieving resources, whether for interhuman losses or for losses in the planetary community, will also have to learn from traditions that have deeper wisdom here, as well as to create and retrieve a sense of self that honors our connections to all that is, as well as practices that help us inhabit spaces we'd rather avoid.

For Christians, hope in the Crucified and Risen One invites us to trust that the willingness to go toward suffering, here and now, toward the suffering of the earth itself, and to tarry in that suffering while it lasts, will serve our ability to participate in the earth's healing, and our healing with it.

Notes

[1]Steven Bouma-Prediger, *For the Beauty of the Earth: A Christian Vision of Creation Care*, 2nd ed. (Grand Rapids, MI: Baker Academic, 2010).

[2]Ibid., 21.

[3]M. Shawn Copeland, "'Wading through Many Sorrows': Toward a Theology of Suffering in Womanist Perspective," in *A Troubling in My Soul: Womanist Perspectives on Evil and Suffering*, ed. Emilie M. Townes (Maryknoll, NY: Orbis Books, 1993), 109.

[4]Ibid.

[5]Judith Butler, "Violence, Mourning, Politics," in *Precarious Life: The Powers of Mourning and Violence* (New York: Verso, 2004), 19–49.

[6]Ibid., 30.

[7]Ashlee Cunsolo Willox, "Climate Change as the Work of Mourning," *Ethics and the Environment* 17, no. 2 (2012): 137–64.

[8]Butler, "Violence, Mourning, Politics," 22.

[9]David Abram, *The Spell of the Sensuous: Perception and Language in a More-Than-Human World* (New York: Pantheon, 1996), and *Becoming Animal: An Earthly Cosmology* (New York: Pantheon, 2010).

[10]Patricia Damery, "The Environmental Crisis and the Psyche: A Conversation with David Abram and Patricia Damery," *Jung Journal: Culture and Psyche* 7, no. 1 (2013): 116–17.

From Tourists to Pilgrims and Monks

The Need to Cultivate a Spirituality of Rootedness

Katherine A. Greiner

In 2014, my parents remodeled the house they have lived in for the past twenty-five years. For the better part of four months, they lived out of suitcases, staying in friends' guest rooms or in local hotels. This itinerant lifestyle took a bit of a toll on my father. "This experience is showing me," he ruefully quipped, "that I am much more of an Emily Dickinson than I am a Rick Steves." The tone of his voice indicated that he interpreted his desire to be at home as a fault or a limitation. After all, true living consists of adventure and travel, right? His self-observation highlights the common cultural lure and lore that "real" experience must happen away from one's home. Think of the caricatures: homebodies are portrayed as narrow-minded, conservative, and stuck, while travelers and explorers are portrayed as adventurous, worldly, open, progressive, and well-rounded.[1] In our contemporary, first-world society, mobility in the form of tourism has become something of a status symbol, a valuable expression of one's autonomy and freedom. This tends to spread the problematic myth on which consumerism depends—what we have is not enough and where we are is not where we should be.

Certain models of Christian discipleship can inadvertently participate in cultivating this tourist orientation. Christian discipleship is often depicted as a journey, requiring one to leave the safety and comforts of home to go and serve in distant and unknown places.[2] We see this manifested today in the growing popularity of short-term mission and service trips organized by church groups,

parishes, and both secondary and postsecondary education institutions. I do not wish to undermine the positive impact service
immersion trips have, particularly on adolescents and traditional-
age college students. Recent sociological studies do suggest that
serving in other global and cultural contexts can increase civic and
community involvement and create more culturally, racially, and
ethnically sensitive individuals.[3] But because of the increasingly
mobile and disconnected culture we live in today, service and
mission trips risk becoming opportunities for "voluntourism," a
potentially exploitive way to interact with people and places in
dire need for the sake of making ourselves feel better. Certainly,
this is not what Christian discipleship should look like, even if
discipleship does require some sort of journey. Discipleship, William T. Cavanaugh argues, cannot be embodied by tourists, but
by pilgrims. The church must seek to cultivate pilgrims, whose
journey remains steadily centered in God and not self.[4]

But as much as we need to cultivate the capacity for moving out
into the world to the geographic frontiers and the peripheries, we
also need to help cultivate a capacity for belonging, so people can
learn to stay committed to knowing and loving particular places
and people. Our current lack of commitment to and knowledge of
the world around us is so severe that many have linked the ecological crises we face to how disconnected most people are from the
local places that provide their food, water, and resources. Breaking
the tourist orientation for that of the pilgrim will require a radical
paradigm shift in our collective imagination. It will require thinking of discipleship not only in terms of journey, but also in terms
of dwelling. Developmental psychologist Sharon Parks states:

> If we are to be faithful stewards of our planet, our tradi-
> tions, and our future, we need to restore the balance between
> transcendence and immanence in our common discourse, in
> our economic-political-theological vision, and in our spiritual
> practice. . . . In other words we will not find the wholeness
> we seek until the imagery of home, homesteading, dwell-
> ing, and abiding is restored to a place of centrality in the
> contemporary imagination.[5]

The emphasis on service and discipleship occurring "out there"
needs to be counterbalanced with what I call a spirituality of

lived rootedness, a way of being that nurtures and tends to the human yearning to belong, to be home. Cultivating a spirituality of rootedness can help develop a much-needed commitment to tend to local lands, ecosystems, and communities. It can also help curb the frenetic, status-seeking need to be on the move, while at the same time helping those truly called to journeying to become pilgrims instead of tourists.

In order to illustrate our cultural need for a spirituality of rootedness, this essay will first outline Cavanaugh's assessment of the problem of the tourist orientation and the need for pilgrims and monks. Next, using the insights of Sharon Parks, this essay will argue that the archetype of the monk and the images of dwelling and home need to be emphasized as authentic expressions of discipleship. Last, this essay will show how poets and cultural critics Wendell Berry and bell hooks both embody this spirituality of rootedness and how their writings about belonging and commitment to place can help us reimagine discipleship embodied in the practices of homesteading and homecoming.

Moving from Tourists to Pilgrims

In his article "Migrant, Tourist, Pilgrim, Monk: Mobility and Identity in a Global Age," the theologian William T. Cavanaugh criticizes the notion that increasing mobility signifies the end of national borders and the beginning of a utopian global village. He does so by highlighting the prevalent role borders continue to play in the global market economy and how they continue to form the identities of migrants and tourists. While the migrant crosses borders to survive, the tourist crosses borders to be entertained. Migrants are forced to cross borders as a matter of survival, usually to escape oppressive governments and to find work. Because the global market depends on these displaced peoples as a cheap labor source, migrants are dehumanized with stigmas such as "illegal" and "undocumented." Unable to claim a new national identity and unable to return home, migrants are forced to remain uprooted and adrift. Tourists, on the other hand, remain protected by their citizenship and are thus free to move from place to place, unencumbered by borders. But this does not do away with borders, Cavanaugh argues, for borders ensure a tourist's ability to "experience" exotic and wild places. Cavanaugh laments this growing "tourist orientation," a self-centered imperialistic desire for amusement and diversion that exploits local lands and eco-systems as well as local communities.[6]

Cavanaugh claims that Christians must challenge this tourist orientation by adopting the medieval archetype of pilgrim. Rather than seeking escape or transcendence for the sake of self, pilgrims move to empty the self and are always in search of God. Seeking the kenotic, communal, humble, transformative, and eschatological, pilgrims challenge the social divisions of the status quo. While the pilgrim orientation is one of self-emptying, the tourist orientation is one of self-fulfillment.[7] What the pilgrim makes holy, the tourist slowly desecrates. "The presence of pilgrims hallows a particular place; the presence of tourists hollows it out."[8]

Pilgrimage is a popular and an evocative ecclesial image. As the documents of Vatican II emphasize, we are a pilgrim people, journeying together in eschatological hope toward the reign of God.[9] There is no question that people who participate in service immersion trips or other forms of community service must learn to cultivate the pilgrim orientation: a humble, vulnerable stance that allows participants to witness, to be surprised, and to learn and grow, rather than to observe, as a tourist, with a sort of voyeuristic tendency. How best to educate people toward this pilgrim orientation is a critical question—certainly one that continues to be addressed by innovative and creative pedagogical approaches in service learning.[10]

A Need for Both Pilgrims and Monks

Yet if all disciples are on pilgrimage, who learns to stay in place? Toward the end of the article, Cavanaugh shows that the pilgrim depends on the hospitality and stability of the monks. In medieval times, monks provided safe lodging and nourishing provisions for those on pilgrimage. In fact, extending hospitality to pilgrims is one of the central pillars of the monastic Rule.[11]

As two different manifestations of Christian discipleship, the pilgrim and the monk depend on each other. The monk represents the human need for belonging and home, while the pilgrim represents the human need for autonomy and mobility. They also share common traits. Both the pilgrim and the monk are centered on

God and others, rather than self. Detached from their own desires and expectations, they are open to knowing and loving others intimately and humbly, one along the journey, going out into the world, the other staying rooted in place offering hospitality to those along the road. Thus, both orientations focus on forming right relationship with places and people. The monk tends to the home fires while the pilgrim journeys out in the world. Both are exemplars of Christian discipleship.

Sharon Parks shows that at one time, these images of dwelling and journey were "intimately linked."[12] Yet over the course of the Enlightenment and the industrial revolution, these faith images have been disconnected, and the image of journey now dominates in our modern discipleship discourse.[13] This cultural bias for journey, and its concomitant emphasis on the need to develop personal autonomy, ignores a crucial component of human experience: our need for home, for connection, and for being in right relationship not only with our human community but also with the entire community of creation.

Furthermore, this bias toward journey over dwelling reflects the ways gender dichotomies still shape our collective imagination. We associate the human yearning for homemaking and dwelling as "feminine" values and, therefore, see them as somehow less important than yearning for journey and pilgrimage. Paradoxically, in the attempt to create "equal rights" between men and women, the ways women had traditionally been educated in homemaking and home economics were left by the wayside.[14] The bias indicates that we need to reconnect the images of home and pilgrimage. Parks observes:

> At this pivotal, dangerous, and promising moment in history, the formation of adequate forms of meaning and faith—and perhaps the future of our small planet home—is dependent, in part, upon the liberation, reappropriation, and renewed companionship of the metaphors of detachment *and* connection, pilgrims *and* homemakers, journeying *and* homesteading.[15]

"Renewing the companionship" between journeying and homesteading both in our communities and in our personal lives is a critical step in combating the culturally dominant tourist orientation. But given how much of an emphasis is placed on authentic discipleship as journeying outside one's own neighborhood, renewing this companionship requires attending to the neglected capacity for homemaking. It is developing the skills and capacity for belonging to place that will help reconnect these two manifestations of discipleship.

Homesteading and Homecoming: Practices of Rootedness

Wendell Berry has become one of the most important prophets of our time, speaking out against the disastrous effects of industrialization and the need for agricultural and educational reform. He is a poet, an essayist, a novelist, and an activist. But most important, Berry is a fourth-generation farmer in rural Kentucky. He returned home in the early 1960s, and there he has stayed for the past fifty years. He made a conscious choice to write and work in and from this place. What makes him a unique voice in the cacophony of commentators on environmental reform movements is his devotion to his small bit of earth, his farm in Port Royal. He knows and loves that place with a fierce intimacy that I suspect few of us have witnessed or experienced. And it is this intimacy that gives him the credibility of a prophet and wisdom figure. He rarely leaves his home anymore, commenting, "As I grow older, I grieve over every moment I'm gone from this place, because it is inexhaustibly interesting to me."[16]

While Berry is certainly a homebody, no one could accuse him of being narrow-minded. In 2012, he was invited to deliver the 41st Jefferson Lecture of the National Endowment of the Humanities. The title and central theme of his lecture, *It All Turns on Affection*, stands as a summation of his lifetime's work as a writer, an activist, and a farmer. In this lecture Berry emphasizes that it is *love* and *affection* for place and the people of place that are our only hope for survival. When human beings forget their interdependency with the rest of the earth, when we only understand our relationship with creation in terms of monetary value, we will destroy ourselves—perhaps but not necessarily before we destroy everything else. He claims that affection—not some moral imperative—must be the primary stance for sustainability, for affection guarantees care and care guarantees living within our limits. He writes:

I do not believe . . . that morality, even religious morality, is an adequate motive for good care of the land-community. The primary motive for good care and good use is always going to be affection, because affection involves us entirely . . . without this informed, practical, and *practiced* affection, the nation and its economy will conquer and destroy the country.[17]

One of his most pointed critiques is of the demise of the local economies and settlement. Mobility, Berry argues, is misconstrued as advancement. Without local economies, we cannot hope to cultivate any sense of affection for place. But, as he rightly notes, our educational system, as a product of the industrial revolution, does not encourage people to stay in place. "Our educational system," he writes, "has educated least of all for settlement, or for what Wes Jackson calls homecoming."[18] Without settlement, we cannot develop authentic practiced affection. Without affection, we cannot adequately understand our relationship with the land and the people closest to us. Thus, through his writings, we enter a monastery that both comforts and challenges us to contemplate our own connection to home and to the place where our deep commitments lie.

Berry's affection for the land and his community is reflected in and sustained by his practices of homesteading. Through his work as a farmer, he has developed the ability to observe and articulate the intricate interdependency human beings have with each microscopic organism. His care for his land and community makes him an honest critic and qualified diagnostician of that which is killing the planet. At the same time, he is honest about his own struggles. Homesteading and farming should never be conceived as idyllic, pie-in-the-sky escapism. It is hard, risky work that makes human beings vulnerable to the reality of how much we depend on the land and how much we are part of it. His practice of homesteading is primarily an act of vulnerable love and commitment to his community—no matter the cost.

If Wendell Berry exemplifies the practice of homesteading, bell hooks exemplifies the practice of homecoming. After a decadeslong illustrious academic career at a variety of prestigious universities, she returned to her home state of Kentucky and took a teaching position in Appalachian Studies at Berea College. In her

2008 book *Belonging: A Culture of Place,* hooks discusses what drew her back to Kentucky and the ways in which disconnection and separation from the land are linked to racism, sexism, and classism. Her narrative speaks to her courage in going back to places of past pain in order to transform that pain into a sense of belonging:

> Again and again as I travel around I am stunned by how many citizens in our nation feel lost, feel bereft of a sense of direction, feeling as though they cannot see where our journeys lead, that they cannot know where they are going. Many folks feel no sense of place. What they know, what they have is a sense of crisis, of impending doom. Even the old, the elders, who have lived from decade to decade and beyond say life is different in this time "way strange" that our world today is a world of "too much"—that this too muchness creates a wilderness of spirit, the everyday anguish that shapes the habits of being for those who are lost, wandering, searching.[19]

Hooks shows the role displacement has played in our collective loss of belonging. Displacement of peoples from rural communities, including the slow displacement of the black population from the agrarian south, erases the collective memory and wisdom of entire communities who have so much to teach us about right relationship within communities and with the land. Rural brain drain may be lamented, yet it is often depicted as just an inevitable consequence of human progress. But displacement—whether it is on the ranches and farms of the Columbia Plateau in Oregon or in the mountains of Appalachia—does not signal progress, but demise. Returning to and recommitting one's self to these places can restore and transform the pain and separation displacement causes. The practice of homecoming can serve as a source of ecological and community healing. Hooks explains this in the context of the black experience.

> More than ever before in our nation's history black folks must collectively renew our relationship to the earth, to our agrarian roots. For when we are forgetful and participate in the destruction and exploitation of dark earth, we collude

with the domination of earth's dark people, both here and globally. Reclaiming our relationship to nature, to farming in America, and proclaiming the humanizing restorative of living in harmony with nature so that earth can be our witness is meaningful resistance.[20]

Thus, hooks's personal narrative shows us that homecoming can be an act of critical consciousness-raising and a powerful, if quiet, revolutionary act.

Hooks's personal narrative of homecoming is not romantic or sappy. It is a painful, honest, and complex act of resistance against the racist and classist systems that alienated and displaced so many people from the land. Ultimately her return home gave her an opportunity to participate in the healing of her own sense of humble connectedness and cultivate a sense of wholeness.

> Although I come from a long line of Kentucky country folk . . . I am having to learn my stewardship. I do not have the longed-for green thumb but with a little help from my community, I am doing the work of self-healing, of earth healing, of reveling in this piecing together of my world in such a way that I can be whole and holy.[21]

Berry and hooks's practices of homesteading and homecoming are practices of a spirituality of rootedness. Their writings serve as metaphorical monasteries where pilgrims can encounter their hospitality, humility, sense of community, and compassionate connectedness to the land. Prophets of place, like Berry and hooks, can help reorient us toward the sacredness of our home places and communities.

Cultivating a spirituality of lived rootedness must have implications for how we think about and educate for discipleship. I think Berry and hooks can help us. Creating a culture that honors both the pilgrim and the monk's approach to discipleship requires intentional changes in our institutional and ecclesial cultures. What would happen if we encouraged people to ask not "Where do you feel called?" but "Where do you come from?" What if we helped people imagine discipleship in terms of moving back as well as moving out?

For I am convinced, along with Cavanaugh, Parks, Berry, and

hooks, that all of our conversations about and actions toward developing practices of ecological justice, sustainability and stewardship, or conservation and preservation will come to little fruition if we do not spend energy learning how to love the places we are from—wherever they might be. And learning to love comes through the act of vulnerable, intimate, and connected knowing. Just as loving our fellow human beings requires commitment and intimacy and vulnerability, so too does loving the ground beneath our feet, the rivers and streams that sustain us, the trees that provide our oxygen and the intricate ecosystems that we do not even fully understand. It is in this stance of love and deep affection that we can acknowledge the fatal wounds our kind has inflicted on the body of the Earth and begin to reconcile ourselves to begin the healing process. It is in this relationship that we begin to acknowledge and respect not our rights but our responsibilities to the land-community. But this takes time. It takes effort. It requires a patient ability to attentively notice and learn about place. And it takes strong commitment to then stay and serve in place, discerning carefully any restless wanderlust that seems to dominate the modern conception of true living. When cultivated, the lived rootedness of the monk can help reorient us to develop the right relationship with the ground beneath our feet as we continue on our collective pilgrimage.

Notes

[1]Margaret E. Guider, OSF, "The Dwelling and the Journey—The Early Franciscan Experience of Mission," Annual Federation Council Conference Proceedings (Pittsburgh: Franciscan Federation, 1988), 21–30.

[2]Over the course of his pontificate, Pope Francis has often alluded to discipleship as journey, particularly in his appeal for Christians to "go to the frontiers." However, as author Chris Lowney points out, Francis's references to the frontiers have less to do with geography and more about paying attention to groups and individuals that remain relegated to the peripheries of our own communities. Chris Lowney, "Francis Challenges Us to Take Dusty Paths to New Frontiers," National Catholic Reporter, September 27, 2013, www.ncronline.org.

[3]In the past decade, more sociological and ethnographic research has been done on the impact that mission and service trips have both on the beneficiaries and the participants themselves. Results are mixed, with many researchers concluding that mission trips can have a lasting impact on the participants' giving, volunteering, and civic engagement if the participants are given op-

portunities for ongoing reflection and appropriation of the experience. See, for example, LiErin Probasco, "Giving Time, Not Money: Long-term Impacts of Short-term Mission Trips," *Missiology: An International Review* 41, no. 2 (2013): 202–24.

[4]Cultivating pilgrim orientation requires more than participation in service and mission trips. In his research on short-term missions (STMs), Kurt Alan Ver Beek argues that in order for an STM to bring about any significant positive behavioral change in the lifestyle of participants, an STM must be seen as just "one piece of a structure that also includes support and accountability before and after the trip." In other words, the travel by itself does not necessarily bring about lasting conversion or a pilgrim orientation; this requires ongoing nurturing and practice (Kurt Alan Ver Beek, "The Impact of Short-Term Missions: A Case Study of House Construction in Honduras after Hurricane Mitch," *Missiology: An International Review* 34, no. 4 [2006]: 478).

[5]Sharon Daloz Parks, "Home and Pilgrimage: Companion Metaphors for Personal and Social Transformation," *Soundings* 72, no. 2/3 (1989): 303.

[6]William T. Cavanaugh, "Migrant, Tourist, Pilgrim, Monk: Mobility and Identity in a Global Age," *Theological Studies* 69 (2008): 341–49.

[7]Ibid., 349.

[8]Ibid., 350–51.

[9]*Dogmatic Constitution on the Church (Lumen Gentium)*, 48, www.vatican.va.

[10]For example, Boston College runs a service immersion program called the Arrupe program. Not only do the carefully selected students go to serve in various countries throughout South and Central America and the Caribbean, they spend time in group prayer, discernment, and educational instruction before, during, and after the trips.

[11]Cavanaugh, "Migrant, Tourist, Pilgrim, Monk," 353–55.

[12]Parks, "Home and Pilgrimage," 305.

[13]The Christian spiritual life is often depicted as a journey through images of "the way," the road, and the ascent, and little attention is given to the images of dwelling and home. See, for example, "The Spiritual Journey," chapter 3 of *Christian Spirituality: Themes from the Tradition*, by Lawrence S. Cunningham and Keith J. Egan (New York: Paulist Press, 1996), 47–65.

[14]Jane Roland Martin, *Reclaiming a Conversation: The Ideal of the Educated Woman* (New Haven: Yale University, 1985), 190. Berry also blames the role industrial farming plays in separating people from husbandry.

[15]Parks, "Home and Pilgrimage," 301.

[16]Wendell Berry, "Landsman," in *It All Turns on Affection* (Berkeley, CA: Counterpoint, 2012), 53.

[17]Berry, "It All Turns on Affection," in *It All Turns on Affection*, 32–33.

[18]Berry, "Starting from Loss," in *It All Turns on Affection*, 69.

[19]bell hooks, *Belonging: A Culture of Place* (New York: Routledge, 2009), 1.

[20]Ibid., 119.

[21]Ibid., 68.

"Preach Good News to All Creation"

Mark 16:15

Regina A. Boisclair

I live and teach in Alaska, the state that identifies itself as "the last frontier." This last frontier is also a canary to the worldwide ecological crisis. The villages of Kivalena, Shishmaref, Shaktoolik, Unalakleet, Koyukuk, and Newtok are threatened if not yet irreparably destroyed. In thirty to fifty years, almost two hundred other Alaskan Native Bush Villages will have to move or disband—their present locations will be uninhabitable. And it is not only human habitation that is threatened: more and more frequently, polar bears are drowning for lack of arctic ice.

This last frontier was the location of the *Exxon Valdez* disaster that ravaged the waters, marine life, and economic foundation of Prince William Sound; it is also home to an oil-based economy promoted by loud powerful voices that discard the reams of scientific evidence supporting ecological concerns. Presently Pac Rim, an "outside" company, seeks to establish a coal mine and de-water a fork in the Chuitna River where all five kinds of salmon return to spawn.[1] There is also the projected Pebble Mine—designed to extract a huge deposit of gold, copper, and molybdenum—situated in the headwaters of two of the rivers that feed Bristol Bay. If built, Pebble would have a high risk of polluting the world's most productive source of wild salmon. Yes, scientific and technological knowledge as well as industrialization have greatly enhanced human comforts, but these come at "the price of unexpected consequences that have proved increasingly disastrous for the rest of creation as well as ourselves."[2] Disputes over natural resources have ever played a large role in human history, but if we fail to fully address and successfully arrest ecological degradation, eventually there will be no resources at all.

In this essay, I explore some Christian responses to ecological concerns. I am especially interested in how the Bible has been used to foster ecological awareness, and so I examine two significant issues in this area. First, I identify four approaches to ecological hermeneutics and offer a simplified alternative. The theory and practice of biblical interpretation, however, do not have the same capacity to move minds and hearts as does the choice of which biblical texts to proclaim in public worship. Thus, second, I discuss a proposed change in the three-year Sunday lectionaries (Catholic and Revised Common) that would foster greater sense of ecological responsibility.

Ecological Hermeneutics

The contemporary ecological movement emerged in response to Rachel Carson's study *Silent Spring,* published in September of 1962; ecological concerns entered Christian discourse in response to Lynn White's 1967 article, "The Historical Roots of Our Ecologic Crisis."[3] That article continues to be cited; it is often reproduced in textbooks and is enormously popular with post-Christian secular students. Today, almost fifty years later, Christian scholars are still responding to White's challenge.

If White's understanding of Christianity was flawed by an assumption that some of Calvin's perspectives permeate every branch of Christianity, his claim that Christian anthropocentrism deeply influenced a Western ideology that ignored the well-being of the natural world is valid. Over the past twenty-five years, the larger topics of ecology have become important in Christian, ecumenical, and interreligious discourse.[4] More recently, Pope Francis has placed ecological issues front and center in Catholic concerns.[5] While White's charge was founded on his understanding of Genesis 1:27–28, a response to White can also be found in the Bible itself.

While Genesis 1:27–28 reports that God created humankind, male and female, in his image and likeness, and instructed them to "fill the earth and subdue it; and have dominion" over the whole created order, those who challenge White while fostering an ecological ethic do so by finding in other biblical texts alternatives to *dominion* and *subdue.*

Scholars engage in hermeneutics when they seek to determine the meaning of biblical texts for contemporary readers and communities that are far different and distanced from the original authors, as well as communities and readers for whom these texts were intended.[6] Just as recognition of the patriarchal premises in biblical texts led to feminist hermeneutics, and recognition of biblical passages that support domination according to race, class, culture, and education led to postcolonial interpretation, the recognition that anthropocentrism has dominated Christianity and biblical interpretation catalyzed the emergence of ecological hermeneutics. In exploring how the Bible has been recently applied to environmental concerns, I have identified four approaches but propose to move beyond these to a simpler alternative and overriding principle.

The first approach is that of *The Green Bible*, published in 2008. *The Green Bible* prints passages concerned with nature in green letters to signify how "God saw everything he had made and indeed it was very good" (Gn 1:31).[7] However, a number of relevant passages do not appear in green letters,[8] and some passages in green letters celebrate the destruction of nature by human violence. In addition, some green verses have no clear relationship to the natural world.[9] In sum, the effort is disappointing; there is no sense that there is any coherent, overarching principle that determined how the passages printed in green lettering were identified and selected. One reviewer notes, "*The Green Bible* isn't even a reference Bible that trains readers to see its agenda in Scripture. It leaves readers on their own to figure out the relevance of passages both green and black."[10] The Green Bible does attempt some theoretical discussion: eleven articles placed before the biblical texts in *The Green Bible* identify various Jewish and Christian ecological perspectives. I consider the strongest of these articles to be the message by Pope John Paul II, "Peace with God the Creator, Peace with All Creation," and an essay by N. T. Wright, "Jesus Is Coming—Plant a Tree."

The second approach, a more coherent hermeneutical approach than that of *The Green Bible*, is that of the Evangelical Environmental Network. Although it is true that significant numbers of Evangelical Christians consider environmental concerns "misconceived and misplaced"[11] since they are convinced the natural world will be totally destroyed and replaced by new heavens and a new earth (2 Peter 3:11–13) as part of Christ's imminent second coming, it is also true that growing numbers of Evangelicals are convinced that a time of divine wrath approaches "for destroying those who destroy the earth."[12] The Evangelical Environmental Network brings together biblical texts to foster efforts to moderate climate change, to conserve land, to prevent water and chemical pollution, and to assist the poor. This network's mission statements are punctuated with biblical citations to proof-text their premises. For example:

Declare the Lordship of Christ over all creation.
"He is the firstborn over all creation. For by him all things were created. All things were created by him and for him. He is before all things, and in him all things hold together." (Colossians 1:15b; 16a, c; 17, John 1:1–3)

Deepen our walk with the Lord that God's will
"be done on earth as it is in heaven." (Matthew 6:10)[13]

The Evangelical Environmental Network interprets scripture with scripture. In an article describing "Green Millennialism," Harry O. Maier considers its mission premises, arguing that this is

a skillful application of Evangelical biblical hermeneutics. . . . Foregrounding one set of texts over another here makes room for re-reading an apocalyptic biblical tradition that *prima facie* is less friendly to environmental considerations, such as those more disjunctive visions of ecological disaster found in Revelation and elsewhere (Rev. 8.16 and 2 Pet 3.10). Such foregrounding also strategically counters a heavy emphasis on the Fall, the curse of the earth of Gen 3.17 and notions of depravity favored especially in the Reformed theological systems out of which Evangelicalism traditionally emerges.[14]

A third and still more sophisticated hermeneutical strategy is found in the six ecojustice principles devised by the Earth Bible Project. Initiated in Australia, sponsored by the Society of Biblical Literature, and edited by Norman Habel, the Earth Bible Project articulates principles that seek to give a voice to the earth from biblical texts. These six principles are:

> *The principle of intrinsic worth:* the universe, Earth and all its components have intrinsic worth/value.
>
> *The principle of interconnectedness:* Earth is a community of interconnected living things that are mutually dependent on each other for life and survival.
>
> *The principle of voice:* Earth is a subject capable of raising its voice in celebration and against injustice.
>
> *The principle of purpose:* the universe, Earth and all its components are part of a dynamic cosmic design within which each piece has a place in the overall goal of that design.
>
> *The principle of mutual custodianship:* Earth is a balanced and diverse domain where responsible custodians can function as partners with, rather than rulers over, Earth to sustain its balance and a diverse Earth community.
>
> *The principle of resistance:* Earth and its components not only suffer from human injustices but actively resist them in the struggle for justice.[15]

Yet, what is missing in these principles is God! Ernst M. Conradie, a South African scholar and participant in the University of Exeter, UK, project concerning uses of the Bible in environmental ethics, observes that Earth Bible principles seem designed to impress the secular world—but "abandon the attempt to be persuasive within the traditions that have kept the reading of these texts alive."[16]

Conradie then suggests what I identify as a fourth approach to ecological hermeneutics: using the "Household of God" – *oikos*—as a Christian ecological hermeneutical principle. He considers *oikos* "as the root of ecojustice, ecological sustainability and ecumenical fellowship that integrates the social agenda of the churches as the whole work of God (creation, providence, redemption, recreation) as the economy of God." Conradie considers household (*oikos*) an apt Christian image for identifying passages that bring together

1. an ecological doctrine of creation within which God's Spirit abides;

2. an anthropology of human stewardship as care for the created order;
3. an ecclesiology of membership in "the household of God" (Eph 2:19–22,) as sojourners of "the way";
4. an appreciation of the Eucharist as a table of fellowship where God's Word is spoken; and
5. an eschatology of hope that the earth, home of humanity, will also be home to God.[17]

Although there is much to commend this idea, I find the theological considerations in Conradie's Household of God more complex than useful. Instead, I offer a simplified alternative: just as feminist hermeneutics resolved that scripture texts were to be assessed by their compatibility with Galatians 3:28 ("There is neither Jew nor Greek, there is neither slave nor free person, there is neither male nor female for you are all one in Christ Jesus"), I would propose that biblical texts should be assessed by their compatibility with Genesis 1:31 ("God looked at everything he made and found it very good") while also recognizing that Romans 8:19–22 is the apt description of everything God made today. Indeed, Romans 8:22 is the first biblical citation in Pope Francis's *Laudato Si'*,[18] with referential emphasis on the observation that "creation has been groaning." When one examines the passages quoted or cited in *Laudato Si'*, Genesis 1:31 is easily identified as the hermeneutic operating in this document.[19]

Clearly when Paul wrote "creation is groaning" (Rom 8:22), he was not speaking of climate change, greenhouse gases, or species extinction; I consider Paul to be claiming that creation longs for humanity to be free from the bondage he considers behaviors of the flesh—behaviors that in our time include various forms of ecological harm. It was not the disobedience of Eve and Adam that disordered creation; it was not even God's curse of the earth (Gn 3:17). Rather, it was the inclination to sinfulness that theology attributes to Eve and Adam, aspects of which errancy led humanity to wanton consumption and domination (Gn 1:28) at the expense of the environment rather than to a pattern for living that cherishes an operative of "cultivate and care" (Gn 2:15).

To be led by the Spirit as children of God and the body of Christ is to realize that through the incarnation the Word of God, the agent of creation (Jn 1:1–3, Col 1:15–16) itself entered his own creation as a human being (Jn 1:4), and in so doing sanctified the cosmos. In addition, in his teachings Jesus used nature (earth, water, plants, flowers, seeds, birds, animals, and fish) to illustrate his message.

Ecological Responsibility and the Sunday Lectionary

Studies and hermeneutical theories on the part of biblical scholars have a limited influence. Though they have the capacity to influence other scholars and various national denominational and local policies, they do not move the minds and hearts of most Christians. Even papal encyclicals have a limited influence—although many hope that *Laudato Si'* will be different. I sense the biblical texts proclaimed and preached have the capacity to promote ecological consciousness. In the Catholic and mainline Anglican and Protestant churches, these texts are assigned by lectionaries. I do not sense it a coincidence that the encyclical *Laudato Si'* was issued during the week between two Sundays when some of the readings assigned in the Catholic lectionary foster awe for the natural world.[20]

Two studies, one by Lawrence Mick, a Catholic, another by Lisa Dahill, a Protestant, identified passages relevant to ecological concerns; Mick for the Catholic three-year lectionary[21] and Dahill for the three-year Revised Common Lectionary.[22] From these studies we can see that over a three-year period the Roman Missal Lectionary assigns relevant readings from the Old Testament to forty-six occasions, relevant psalms to ninety-one, and relevant epistles or selections from the Book of Revelation to fourteen. The Revised Common Lectionary assigns many identical passages—in addition to other relevant readings from the Old Testament—to sixty-four occasions, related psalms to one hundred seven occasions, and, as well, fourteen second readings from the epistles or the Book of Revelation. Both Lectionaries also appoint sixteen relevant gospels. While some of the occasions to which these passages are appointed do not lend themselves to stressing the need to foster the earth, the animals, and the air that sustains us,[23] many of these readings do and thereby offer an important concern for Christian conduct.

Norman Habel, a Lutheran pastor and the leading voice for the Earth Bible Project, devised a special Season of Creation, suited to fit into the three-year lectionaries for the four Sundays in September that precede the Feast of St. Francis of Assisi on October 4. Each of these four Sundays offers a collection of readings that foster a particular theme related to the natural world as the focus for each of the Sundays.

Year A: The Spirit of Creation

Forest Sunday	Gn 2:4b–22	Ps 139:13–16	Acts 17:22–28	Jn 3:1–16
Land Sunday	Gn 3:14–19; 4:8–16	Ps 139:7–12	Rom 5:12–17	Mt 12:38–40
Wilderness Sunday	Jl 1:8–10, 17–20	Ps 18:1–19	Rom 8:18–27	Mt 3:13–41 or Mk 1:9–13
River Sunday	Gn 8:20–22; 9:12–17	Ps 104:27–33	Rv 22:1–5	Mt 28:1–10

Year B: The Word in Creation

Earth Sunday	Gn 1:1–25	Ps 33:1–9	Rom 1:18–23	Jn 1:1–14
Humanity Sunday	Gn 1:26–28	Ps 8	Phil 2:1–8	Mk 10:41–45
Sky Sunday	Jer 4:23–28	Ps 19:1–6	Phil 2:14–18	Mk 15:33–39
Mountain Sunday	Is 65:17–25	Ps 48:1–11	Rom 8:28–39	Mk 16:14–18

Year C: Wisdom in Creation

Ocean Sunday	Jb 38:1–18	Ps 104:1–9, 24–26	Eph 1:3–10	Lk 5:1–11
Fauna Sunday	Jb 39:1–8, 26–30	Ps 104:14–23	1 Cor 1:10–23	Lk 12:22–31
Storm Sunday	Jb 28:20–27	Ps 29	1 Cor 1:21–31	Lk 8:22–25
Cosmos Sunday	Prv 8:22–31	Ps 148	Col 1:15–20	Jn 6:41–53

Every year these Sundays are followed by a Sunday devoted to the Blessing of Animals that has become associated with the Feast of St. Francis of Assisi. The readings assigned to that observance are: Gn 2:18–25, Ps 148, Rv 5:11–14, and Mt 6:25–29.[24]

Lutherans in Australia introduced the Season of Creation in 2000. By 2005 it was adopted by the Uniting Church of Australia and was endorsed by the Evangelical Lutheran Church of America and the National Council of Churches in the United States. The Season of Creation is now also celebrated in South Africa, Europe, and Canada. It has been strongly endorsed by the Catholic St. Columban Missionary Society and the Catholic Bishops of the Philippines. The Season of Creation has gained ecumenical support in fostering a Christian reverence for the cosmic order within worshiping assemblies.

Arguably this Season of Creation has merit; *nothing* in the appointed readings or liturgical prayers, suggested hymns, and other materials provided for each occasion suggests nature worship or alternative "New Age" variances from Christian orthodoxy. However, Lisa Dahill, who identified the relevant readings in the Revised Common Lectionary, voiced significant reservations concerning the introduction of a Season of Creation:

> As a deviation from the ecumenical calendar and lectionary, the proposed Season of Creation requires churches that wish to celebrate the gift of creation and deepen their ecological concern to step out of their broad communion with other Christian churches into a special and separate "season" of creation not well integrated into the flow of the rest of the church year. Such a proposal reinforces the misperception that Christianity, the church year and ordinary Christian worship in and of themselves are *not* creation-oriented, so that we have to exit these realities and just for these four weeks, proclaim this connection otherwise more or less absent from our worship.[25]

In a previous study on this topic I agreed with Dahill and questioned the introduction of a new season into the traditional church year with assigned readings devised, without dialogue, by *one* scholar.[26] (In contrast, considerable effort and many voices

devised both the Catholic and Revised Common Lectionaries.)
However, I have subsequently come to believe that it would be
advisable to introduce a dedicated segment of the church year to
ensure the message is heard. In light of the severity of our ecological realities, it is essential that the churches make full use of the
biblical witness to move minds and hearts. A Season of Creation
would be a way to underscore the severity of the problem and the
moral imperative that we change our life patterns of exploitation.

The changes we must incorporate call for serious *metanoia*.
Religions, far more than the sciences, have the capacity to mobilize humanity.[27] Today, in light of all that presently threatens
the stability of this planet our home and our lives, religions must
begin or continue even more to foster among their adherents a
commitment to care of the earth, of both its elements and its nonhuman creatures. For Christians this attention—and its ensuing
intentions—would fulfill the counsel of the Risen Lord: "Preach
Good News to all creation" (Mk 16:15).

Such preaching and such attention would, in the words of
Pope Benedict, recall us to the hope that animates Christian faith
in the living God: "The justified concern about threats to the
environment present in so many parts of the world is reinforced
by Christian hope, which commits us to working responsibly for
the protection of creation."[28] And working responsibly for the
protection of creation is, in the end, not simply a duty associated
with human "dominion" over creation, but instead is a profound
recognition that human beings are part of the "universal family"
of creation, joined in a "sublime communion" to all that God
has created:

> The created things of this world are not free of ownership:
> "For they are yours, O Lord, who love the living (Wis 11:26).
> This is the basis of our conviction that, as part of the uni-
> verse, called into being by one Father, all of us are linked by
> unseen bonds and together form a kind of universal family, a
> sublime communion which fills us with a sacred, affectionate
> and humble respect. Here I would reiterate that "God has
> joined us so closely to the world around us that we can feel
> the desertification of the soil almost as a physical ailment,
> and the extinction of a species as a painful disfigurement."[29]

Notes

[1]Shannyn Moore, "Perspective," *Alaska Dispatch News,* June 21, 2015, sec. B:9.

[2]Richard Bauckham, *Bible and Ecology: Rediscovering the Community of Creation* (Waco, TX: Baylor University Press, 2010), 170.

[3]Lynn White Jr., "The Historical Roots of Our Ecologic Crisis," *Science,* new series 155, no. 3767 (March 10, 1967): 1206ff. See also www.uvm.edu.

[4]Seminal studies include Thomas Berry, *Dream of the Earth* (San Francisco: Sierra Club, 1988), and the volumes produced following the ten Harvard Conferences on World Religions and Ecology, spearheaded between 1996 and 1998 by Mary Evelyn Tucker and John Grim. Official statements identifying concerns and protocols for fostering nature and nonhuman life issued by religious bodies throughout the world are posted on the Yale Forum on Religion and Ecology (http://fore.yale.edu).

[5]Robin Darling Young, "Does the Earth Have Rights? What to Expect—And Hope for—In the Pope's Next Encyclical." *Commonweal* 142, no. 9 (May 15, 2015): 8–10.

[6]Stephen J. Binz, "Contextual and Transformative Interpretation," in *Anselm Academic Study Bible: New American Bible Revised Edition,* ed. Carolyn Osiek (Winona, MN: Anselm Academic, 2013), 105.

[7]*The Green Bible: NRSV,* ed. Michael G. Maudlin and Marlene Baer (New York: HarperCollins, 2008).

[8]For example, although much of God's answer to Job (Jb 38–41) is printed in green letters, the description of the ostrich is not. It may be a dumb bird, but it is one of God's creatures and part of the natural world.

[9]E.g., Mark 10:45 is an important soteriological statement, but I fail to see how it has relevance to the Green Bible project.

[10]Telford Work, "Meager Harvest: The Green Bible Promises to Grow Our Understanding of Creation Care. Unfortunately, Its Results Don't Satisfy," *Christianity Today,* February 2009, 28+. Student Resources in Context. Web. May 23, 2015.

[11]Harry O. Maier, "Green Millennialism: American Evangelicals, Environmentalism and the Book of Revelation," in *Ecological Hermeneutics: Biblical, Historical and Theological Perspectives,* ed. David G. Horrell et al. (London: T & T Clark International, 2010), 247.

[12]Ibid., 255, from www.creationcare.org.

[13]www.creationcare.org.

[14]Maier, "Green Millennialism," 256.

[15]Listed in many places, such as *The Earth Bible,* vol. 2: *Earth Story in Genesis,* ed. Norman C. Habel and Shirley Wurst (Sheffield, Eng.: Sheffield Academic Press, 2000), 20. An analytical explanation of these principles is found in *The Earth Bible,* vol. 1: *Readings from the Perspective of Earth* (Sheffield, Eng,: Sheffield Academic Press, 2000), chap. 2.

[16]Ernst M. Conradie, "What on Earth Is Ecological Hermeneutics? Some

Broad Parameters," in *Ecological Hermeneutics*, ed. Horrell et al., 308–9 (my emphasis).

[17]Ibid., 310.

[18]*Laudato Si'* (2), www.vatican.va.

[19]Ibid.

[20]Eleventh Sunday, Year B: Ez 17:22–24, Ps 92:2–3,13–16, Mk 3:20–35; 12th Sunday, Year B: Jb 38:1, 8–11, Ps 107:23–31, Mk 4:35–41.

[21]Lawrence E. Mick, *Liturgy and Ecology in Dialogue* (Collegeville, MN: Liturgical Press, 1997).

[22]Lisa Dahill, "New Creation: The Revised Common Lectionary and the Earth's Paschal Life," *Liturgy* 27, no. 2 (January 2012): 3–16.

[23]E.g., Christmas and the Easter Vigil.

[24]http://seasonofcreation.com.

[25]Dahill, "New Creation," 4.

[26]Regina A. Boisclair, "Lectionary Reflections and Ecological Concerns: A Contribution to Dialogue," *Journal of Ecumenical Studies* 50, no. 1 (Winter 2015): 77–84.

[27]Testimony to this reality is found in John Grim and Mary Evelyn Tucker, *Ecology and Religion* (Washington, DC: Island Press, 2014).

[28]Benedict XVI, *Sacramentum Caritatis* (apostolic exhortation), 92, www.vatican.va.

[29]*Laudato Si'*, 89, with citation from apostolic exhortation *Evangelii Gaudium* (2013), 215, www.vatican.va.

PART IV

THE HUMAN PERSON
IN THE COMMUNITY OF CREATION

A Celebration of the Life and Work of Father Thomas Berry, CP

His Contribution to a Creation Theology for an Ecological Age

David Gentry-Akin

Wise and deeply joyful, strong and yet very gentle, Thomas Berry, a great soul, died on June 1, 2009, at the age of ninety-four, in the same place in which he was born, Greensboro, North Carolina, a place he deeply loved and one that nurtured his sense of nature mysticism from the time of his youth.

Berry was a historian of world cultures and religions, who eventually developed into a historian of the Earth and its evolutionary processes and thus came to describe himself as a "geologian." He received his PhD in European intellectual history with a thesis on Giambattista Vico's philosophy of history. Widely read in Western history, he also spent many years studying the cultural history of Asia. He lived in China and traveled to other parts of Asia. He authored two books on Asian religions, *Buddhism* and *Religions of India*.

For two decades, he directed the Riverdale Center of Religious Research along the Hudson River. During this period he taught at Fordham University, where he chaired the history of religions program and directed twenty-five doctoral theses. His major contributions to the discussion on the environment are in his books *The Dream of the Earth* (1988), *The Great Work: Our Way into the Future* (1999), and, with Brian Swimme, *The Universe Story* (1992). The last collection of essays published during his lifetime is *Evening Thoughts: Reflecting on Earth as Sacred Community*

(2006), and in August 2009, just a few months after his death, two more collections were published posthumously: *The Sacred Universe* and *The Christian Future and the Fate of Earth*.

A deeply committed Roman Catholic and a Passionist priest who regularly celebrated Mass for his family and friends well into the last months of his long life, Berry rarely mentions the name of God in his writings. My sense is that he came to feel that "God-talk" was so overly anthropocentric that it needed to be given a break, that what many people heard when the word "God" was uttered was not at all worthy of the name:

> We have come to know so much about God from our scriptures and our theological and religious traditions that somehow we have lost our sense of wonder. It seemed that we had control of God. God became reduced to our ideas of God, and belief in God became a sterile commitment on our part.[1]

And yet anyone who ever had an opportunity to meet or converse with Thomas Berry even for a short while would come away with a sense that one had had an encounter with a man of profound faith, that this man's faith in God was anything but a sterile commitment.

His urgent concern was with the exclusive and excessive anthropocentric focus of late Western history, culture, and religion, a focus that he believed was not only harmful to the Earth but impoverishing for the human soul. In many of his writings he makes the point that "we need the outer world in order to activate the inner world of the human," and that "the wonder and beauty of the natural world is the only way that we can save ourselves."[2] He writes:

> Just now we are losing our world of meaning through our destruction of the natural world wherein the divine speaks to us. The more we are absorbed into our own selves, the less competent we become in our patterns of communication with the outer world. So too the more shriveled we are in our inner world.[3]

As a truly Catholic thinker, Berry believed that analogy was the key to all human communion with the nonhuman, whether the divine or the natural world. The divine, he believed, has ways of speaking that are not human ways, just as natural phenomena have ways of speaking that are not human language. The task for us humans is to learn to read and interpret the scriptures of the universe as skillfully as we have learned to read and interpret the scriptures of the Bible. Berry writes:

> The effort to reduce all wisdom to a univocal language is a primary error or failure of our times. To think that the various natural phenomena, such as stars, do not speak to us is also an error. . . . This sense of human/nonhuman language goes back to the fact that the divine communicates to us primarily through the languages of the natural world. Not to hear the natural world is not to hear the divine.[4]

His critique of anthropocentrism runs throughout the corpus of his work. Berry argues that part of the difficulty of hearing the language of the natural world is that we have limited our understanding of speech to human speech alone. We foolishly allow ourselves to think that "persons speak; [but] nature does not." We restrict personhood solely to living human organisms, and do not extend the category of personhood to nonhuman animals, much less to inanimate realities. For Berry, this anthropocentric approach leads to a severely impoverished grasp of reality, to a diminishment of language itself:

> By denying that birds and other animals have their own modes of communication, by insisting that the river has no real voice and that the ground itself is mute, we stifle our direct experience. We cut ourselves off from the deep meaning in many of our words, severing our language from that which supports and sustains it. We then wonder why we are so often unable to communicate even among ourselves.[5]

The Story of the Universe:
The Reconciliation of Myth and Knowledge

Berry writes about the need for a new universe story, for what he calls a "functional cosmology":

The universe story is the quintessence of reality. We perceive the story. We put it in our language, the birds put it in theirs, and the trees put it in theirs. We can read the story of the universe in the trees. Everything tells the story of the universe. The winds tell the story, literally, not just imaginatively. The story has its imprint everywhere, and that is why it is so important to know the story. If you do not know the story, in a certain sense you do not know yourself; you do not know anything.[6]

Notice that the "story" of which Berry speaks entails an embrace of reality, not an escape from it. More than a fanciful story, the story of the universe represents a new moment in history in which scientific fact and cultural myth—in the sense of a story of the origin of the cosmos and of humankind—converge. Such a convergence may at first seem far-fetched, but in fact scientists themselves have come to realize what Berry calls the "trans-scientific implications of science."[7] By this, Berry means that, at the edges of scientific inquiry, there is a belief element. Science can prove a great many things, but ultimately further scientific progress depends on an intuitive element that is very similar to faith in that science eventually comes up against mysteries with which it cannot deal adequately. Berry gives gravitation as an example of this phenomenon: we experience it and we can subject some aspects of it to empirical verification, but ultimately it remains a mystery for us.

The universe story about which Berry writes appears to make possible a return to reality and a return to myth at the same time. This appears to be achieved in Berry's thought through a reconciliation of the dualism between the immanent and the transcendent principles of divinity. Our theology has emphasized transcendence to such an extent that we are left with a desacralized reality and what is for many only a fanciful and irrelevant notion of divinity. Reality and myth are so far removed from one another that they no longer have any point of contact. "God" then appears as nothing more than a wishful human projection. What is needed is to bring reality and myth back into relationship so that the myth can once again become "functional": so that it can be enlisted in helping to resacralize reality.

Berry is careful to note that he is not arguing for the return of myth understood in an ahistorical way. The understanding of the universe he seeks to advance "is different from many previous understandings. It is historical, rather than metaphysical, time."[8] In this sense, it is discontinuous with the mythologies of the primal peoples and even with the mythologies of some of the established world religions such as Hinduism, which understand time cyclically. It is continuous with biblical revelation in the sense that it is time-developmental. However, it is continuous with primal mythologies in the sense that it is a cosmological story, a story in which the whole cosmos provides the context and the human is understood within that larger context. It is discontinuous with traditional interpretations of salvation history in that it transcends salvation history's anthropocentrism. Berry's story of the universe holds forth the possibility of the rebirth of myth in Western culture, but a myth—a "functional cosmology" is Berry's term—which does not contradict science but rather coincides with it.

Radical Expansion of the Self and Resacralization of the Universe

Berry rejects notions of classical theism that posit the existence of a God who is entirely external to creation, arguing instead that "there is no God without creation and there is no creation without God."[9] As noted earlier, Berry is sparing in his use of the term "God" because he feels it has become too domesticated through overuse: we are too quick to think that we know what we mean when we talk about God. Our domestication of the term robs the term of the sense of mystery which is, in fact, integral to its meaning. However, one might venture to suggest that the deeper reason for Berry's sparing use of the term "God" is because of its long association with Platonic dualism. In Nietzschean terms, the word-concept "God" must be allowed to die, to lie fallow for a while, as we strive to construct a cosmology that moves beyond all of the problems we have identified with Platonic dualism, a new cosmology that is based on realism rather than idealism. Once this is done, we can begin to construct a notion of the divine that is consistent with that cosmology, keeping in mind the Thomistic dictum that a mistake about nature always results in a mistake about God.

Nevertheless, Berry's philosophy is anything but atheistic. His concern is with a resacralization of the universe. In Berry's view, classical theism cannot help us with this project. For him, "The term 'God' refers to the ultimate mystery of things, something beyond that which we can understand adequately."[10]

The problem, as Berry sees it, is that the biblical religions have drawn the primal notions of all-pervasive divine presence together and constellated them into a single, transcendent creator who is thought to exist apart from the universe.[11] Gradually, everything in human experience is subjected to rational scrutiny and found to be lacking any inherent sacral character. The only antidote to this problem is a radical one in the sense that nothing will solve the problem short of a resacralization of absolutely everything. In our late modern predicament we come against the choice of deciding that either *everything* is sacred, or *absolutely nothing* is: "The universe is a community of subjects, not a collection of objects."[12] Berry argues, not for the end of the self, but for a radical expansion of the self:

> There are always two modes of any being, its microphase mode and its macrophase mode[;] in other words, its particular mode and its universal mode. We are not ourselves without everything else. We have many selves: our personal self, our family self, and our community self. We are never really apart from ourselves. . . . We do things for our family self as well as our personal self because these are identified. We exist for our human self, our community self, our Earth self, our universe self.
>
> In this sense, we are not simply genetically cousin to everything else but we have a certain identity with everything else. We cannot save ourselves without saving everything and everybody else. Unless we are activated by some other person, we cannot be our true selves. We depend on each other to give us ourselves. We become a self by giving ourselves and receiving ourselves.[13]

Berry's language is entirely nonanthropocentric: the "self" of which Berry writes encompasses the entire universe, and individual human selves become themselves most fully through their participation in that larger self. Sacrifice, when it is called for, is not so much a matter of "self-sacrifice" as it is a matter of choosing the larger self, of recognizing one's individual self in the larger self. At

nthropocentrism has been deeply harmful to the
erry argues, while at the same time it has been
technological advances that now make the human
to the continuation of life itself. We need to shift,
m anthropocentrism to biocentrism and geocen-
theless, the human role in the future of life on Earth
cal than at any time in history. In the Cenozoic era,
absolutely no role in the direction of the life process,
the emerging Ecozoic era, humans will be a condition
everything that happens.[29] This is why it is so crucial that
e to a deeper understanding of our role within the greater
"We cannot make a blade of grass but there is liable not to
lade of grass unless we accept it, defend it, and foster it."[30]
Berry sees it, humans are not on the Earth to change it or
ect it, and certainly not to destroy it. We are here to appreciate
o be grateful for it. Gratitude is the heart of authentic religion:

Why do we have such a wonderful idea of God? Because we
live in such a gorgeous world. We wonder at the magnificence
of whatever it is that brought the world into being. This
leads to a sense of adoration. We have a sense of immense
gratitude that we participate in such a beautiful world. This
adoration, this gratitude, we call religion.[31]

This gratitude should move humans to respond to the creativity
of the divine with joy, celebration, and expressions of their own
creativity. For Berry, a sense of joy in the world is essential.[32]
The universe itself is a celebration: "Throughout the vast extent
of space and the total sequence of transformations of time, [the
universe] is a single, multiform, celebratory event."[33] Humans
become fully what they are called to be when they respond in
kind. Berry uses the aboriginal people of Australia as an example,
noting that every person is an artist, a poet, a craftsperson. In the
West, we have so specialized the arts that most people are made
to feel incapable of creative expression, and yet this is what makes
us most human.[34] Conceptual language alone fails us as a means
for giving expression to our response to the divine:

People generally experience an awesome, stupendous presence
that cannot be expressed adequately in human words. Since

the same time, it is just as likely that choosing the larger self will
at times entail the courage to assert the individual self—a willingness to claim individual uniqueness and difference—in order to
contribute to the well-being of the larger self:[14]

We are venturing into a truly new type [of] experience. It
requires a great deal of us. We did not choose to be here.
Once we are here, we must be willing to fulfill the destiny
assigned to us; that is our grandeur, that is our blessedness,
that is our joy, that is our peace. That is our gift to the great
community of existence that is making [this] journey as a
single sacred community.[15]

Communion takes place among all the creatures of the Earth,
and humans learn the story of the universe literally by "reading
the Earth."

For Berry, the key to the resacralization of the universe is the
telling of "the new story." This story gives us "a new sense of the
universe, one that had a precise beginning and has gone through
a sequence of differentiating transformations leading from lesser
to greater complexity and greater modes of consciousness."[16] The
beginning of the universe involved what Berry calls "articulated
energy constellations bound together in an inseparable unity. The
various parts of the universe are outwardly differentiated, inwardly
articulated, and bonded together in a comprehensive intimacy
of every particle with every other particle."[17] Understanding the
beginning of the universe in this way, Berry argues, is revelatory
of the divine, because, in studying the beginning of the universe,
we learn something about the nature of the powers that brought
the universe into being.

In a later development of his thought, Berry and his colleague
Brian Swimme refer to this trinitarian structure as the "cosmogenetic principle," which states that the evolution of the universe is
characterized by differentiation, autopoiesis, and communion.[18]
Berry and Swimme suggest some synonyms for how these terms
are to be understood:

Some synonyms for differentiation are diversity, complexity,
variation, disparity, multiform nature, heterogeneity, articulation. Different words that point to the second feature [of

autopoeisis are] subjectivity, self-manifestation, sentience, self-organization, dynamic centers of experience, presence, identity, inner principle of being, voice, interiority. And for the third feature, communion, [other terms would include] interrelatedness, interdependence, kinship, mutuality, internal relatedness, reciprocity, complementarity, interconnectivity, and affiliation.[19]

Berry and Swimme's "cosmogenetic principle" seems to be a way of allowing for difference, subjectivity, and communion within the same reality. It appears to be a contemporary philosophical attempt to deal with the classical problem of the One and the Many in a way that is also consistent with the findings of contemporary science. These are central ordering tendencies that have shaped the sequence of events in the universe in such a way that these events have become a coherent story.[20]

Invoking Aquinas, Berry tells us that the reason for "difference" in the world is because God cannot communicate Godself totally to any one being. Therefore, God "creates this array of beings so that the perfection lacking in one would be supplied by the other, and the total universe of things would manifest and participate in the divine more than any single being."[21] God's primary concern is with the totality, but differentiation constitutes the grandeur of the totality of things. Within the primary election of the universe, everything is elected, each in its own modality. Individuals are to be concerned with the greater whole because they derive their being from their participation in it, but each in its own unique way. Each being brings something to the whole that is irreplaceable, that no other being could bring. Without the contribution of each unique being, the whole would not *be* the whole: "The universe must be what it is universally for us to be what we are individually, because everything that happened in the whole course of the universe is present in each one of us, just like every atom is in contact with and affects every other atom of the universe."[22] This is why notions such as "objectivity" must now be abandoned. When a being comes into contact with another being, something changes in both of the beings: "We do not really know things in themselves in their objective reality, but rather by an intercommunion."[23]

The Role of

As Berry ex[
present at the beg[
into being shortly a[
radiation. This was fol[
that pulled things toget[
tion.[24] These two forces—[
the curvature of the universe,[
that neither of the forces overca[

If the rate of emergence had been [
faster or a trillionth of a fraction slo[
have either exploded or collapsed. It ha[
trillion trillionth of a margin. Why? Beca[
of the universe had to be such that the uni[
tinue expanding and yet neither explode nor c[
have a universe held together, but not held so [
its expansion or its creativity would be stifled. If th[
tion overcame the expansion, it would collapse. Bu[
expansion overcame the attraction, then it would explo[

This curve Berry refers to as "the compassionate curve th[
embraces the universe."[26] Human beings, for Berry, constitute the self-reflexivity of the universe because, in us, the universe reflects on itself. This reflection is nothing more than the expression, through human intelligence, of the curvature of the universe coming back upon itself. Human *re*-flection results from the curvature; human *af*-fection results from gravitational attraction. The human, in Berry's scheme, is in fact not *apart from*, but rather *a part of*, the universe:

The human is that being in whom the universe reflects on and celebrates itself and its numinous origin in its own, unique mode of conscious self-awareness. All living beings do this in their own way, but in the human, this becomes a dominant mode of functioning. It is not that we think on the universe; the universe, rather, thinks itself, in us and through us.[27]

136

Our excessive a[
human psyche, [
accompanied by[
species a threa[
Berry says, f[
trism.[28] Nev[
is more crit[
humans ha[
whereas i[
for almo[
we com[
whole[
be a [
A[
per[
it,[

it cannot be expressed in language, people often dance this experience, they express it in music, in art, in the pervasive of the beautiful throughout the whole of daily life, in the laughter of children, in the taste of bread, in the sweetness of an apple. At every moment we are experiencing the overwhelming mystery of existence.[35]

Berry's Work as an Important Resource for the Healing of the Environment and the Renewal of Theology

I believe that Thomas Berry's work is an important resource, both for the healing of the environment, and perhaps even more, for the renewal of theology. As my remarks make clear, Berry is certainly one who was urgently concerned about the fate of the environment, but his larger project was clearly a spiritual and theological one in that he felt that humans and their cultures and religious traditions were severely impoverished by their adoption of an instrumental way of viewing creation, as if it, and we, were here only as a "testing ground" for something better that was to come in the future, or, even worse, as if the earth were here only for human exploitation and consumption. His core insight, that "the universe is a communion of subjects, not a collection of objects," is the essential starting point for a revisioning of the God/human/earth relationship so that we can educate ourselves and our children to once again discern the presence of the Creator in all of creation. The gradual consignment, in modernity, of the sacred to a place and time thought to exist beyond the here and now has fostered an attitude of desacralization and consequent instrumentalization, first, of the earth and its resources—mineral, plant, and animal—and more recently, even of the human itself. Our Holy Father Francis's recent encyclical, *Laudato Si'*, captures the choice that lies before us when he writes:

> In this universe, shaped by open and intercommunicating systems, we can discern countless forms of relationship and participation. This leads us to think of the whole as open to God's transcendence, within which it develops. Faith allows us to interpret the meaning and the mysterious beauty of what is unfolding. We are free to apply our intelligence towards things evolving positively, or towards adding new

ills, new causes of suffering and real setbacks. This is what makes for the excitement and drama of human history, in which freedom, growth, salvation and love can blossom, or lead towards decadence and mutual destruction.[36]

Thank God for Father Thomas Berry, CP, for the gift that he was to theology and to Mother Earth. May we take his work more seriously and mine it for the rich insights and resources it offers us in the crucial moment in Earth and human history. I close with a wonderful poem written for Berry at the time of his death by Drew Dellinger.[37]

Carolina Prophet: Poem for Thomas Berry

we were dreamed
in the cores
of the stars.
like the stars,
we were meant to unfold

we were dreamed in the depths
of the undulating ocean.
like the waves,
we were meant to unfold

like bursting supernovas, birthing elements,
which crucibles give rise to creativity?

the world makes us
its instrument.

Father Thomas,
speaking for stars, in a voice
old as wind: "origin moments
are supremely important"

what are the origins
of a prophet?

found in syllables of Sanskrit,
or Chinese characters?
in a decade of midnight prayer?

in childhood epiphanies
rising like heat?

blue Carolina sky;
dark pines;
crickets;
birds;
sunlight
on the lilies,
in the meadow,
across the creek.

born in Carolina
on the eve of the Great War,
Saturn conjoining Pluto in the sky.
raised in a world of wires and wheels,
watching dirt roads turn to pavement.

brooding intensity,
measuring loss
when others could see only progress.

white hair communing with angels of Earth

Father Thomas, reminding us
we are constantly bathed in shimmering memories
of originating radiance

we are constantly bathed in shimmering memories
of originating radiance

the psychic stars:
the conscious soil:

this thin film of atmosphere;

and only gravity
holding the sea from the stars.

when a vision of the universe takes hold
in your mind, your soul becomes vast as the cosmos.

when the mind is silent,
everything is sacred.

like the spiral
like the lotus
like the waves
like the trees
like the stars,

we were meant to unfold.

—©2016 drew dellinger

Notes

[1]Thomas Berry, *The Sacred Universe: Earth, Spirituality, and Religion in the Twenty-First Century* (New York: Columbia University Press, 2009), 150.
[2]Ibid., 146.
[3]Ibid.
[4]Ibid., 145.
[5]Ibid., 145–46.
[6]Thomas Berry with Thomas Clarke, *Befriending the Earth: A Theology of Reconciliation between Humans and the Earth* (New London, CT: Twenty-Third Publications, 1991), 7.
[7]Ibid., 8.
[8]Ibid., 12.
[9]Ibid., 10.
[10]Ibid., 11.
[11]Ibid., 18.
[12]Ibid., 20.
[13]Ibid., 22.
[14]Ibid., 135–38.
[15]Ibid., 132.
[16]Ibid., 13.
[17]Ibid.
[18]Thomas Berry and Brian Swimme, *The Universe Story: From the Primordial Flaring Forth to the Ecozoic Era—A Celebration of the Unfolding of the Cosmos* (San Francisco: HarperSanFrancisco, 1992), 71.

[19]Ibid., 71–72.

[20]Ibid., 72.

[21]Berry, *Befriending the Earth*, 17.

[22]Ibid., 78.

[23]Ibid., 26.

[24]Ibid., 13.

[25]Ibid., 14.

[26]Ibid.

[27]Ibid., 21. The affinity between Nietzsche's doctrine of the will to power, understood as a cosmic force, and Berry's notion that the human is the universe's mode of conscious awareness should be noted by the reader.

[28]Ibid., 42.

[29]The terms "cenozoic" and "ecozoic" are based on the scientific tradition that divides Earth history into "eras." The Phanerozoic Eon (the eon characterized by evidence of reproductive activity) consists of the Paleozoic, the Mesozoic, and the Cenozoic eras. The Cenozoic era refers to the past 65 million years of geologic history that has been marked by the rapid evolution of mammals, birds, grasses, shrubs, and the higher flowering plants. The Ecozoic era is Berry's term for what he considers to be the emerging period of life following the end of the Cenozoic era. This era will be characterized, Berry believes, by mutually enhancing human-Earth relations.

[30]Berry, *Befriending the Earth*, 42.

[31]Ibid., 9.

[32]Ibid., 110.

[33]Ibid.

[34]Ibid., 104.

[35]Ibid., 11.

[36]Francis, *Laudato Si'* encyclical letter, §79. Issued May 24, 2015. www.vatican.va.

[37]Drew Dellinger, *Carolina Prophet: Poem for Thomas Berry*, http://drewdellinger.org.

The Cry of the Poor in the Amazon

Boff, Sobrino, Stang, and *Laudato Si'*

John Thiede, SJ

Leonardo Boff's work tying stewardship of the environment to a more robust understanding of our own humanity affirms that we are integrally tied not just to our own embodied selves but also to the earth on which we live. In his 1995 book, *Cry of the Earth, Cry of the Poor*, Boff argues that justice for creation is intimately tied to justice for humanity, thus challenging the notion that human beings are the center of spirituality and our world. This essay will articulate a significant link between, on the one hand, Boff's re-visioning of our human relationship to the environment, and on the other, the categories of the "crucified people" (as defined by Ignacio Ellacuría) and the "martyred people" (as defined by Jon Sobrino). This link will be exhibited concretely in the examples of the life and work of Chico Mendes and Sister Dorothy Stang, whose deaths remind us that those who work with rural farmers, indigenous peoples, and other marginalized groups do so at the risk of their own lives. The creation spirituality employed by Dorothy Stang and others can teach all of us, whether in the rain forest or in urban areas, how we might better defend the environment, while striving for justice for the crucified and the martyred peoples. This is an auspicious year to turn our attention to the poor of the Amazon, given the recent release of Pope Francis's environmental encyclical *Laudato Si'*, and that 2015 marks ten years since the death of Sr. Dorothy Stang, whose missionary work for justice in the Amazon led to her violent death.

Leonardo Boff: *Cry of the Earth, Cry of the Poor*

In his landmark 1995 book, *Cry of the Earth, Cry of the Poor*, Boff strives for a stronger bridge between theology and ecology.[1] The book presupposes many of the important tenets of liberation theology: the preferential option for the poor; fighting for justice for those on the margins; and solidarity; but it proves unique in the way it meshes liberation theology with the protection of an even greater good, what Boff calls Gaia, Pachamama, or what we might call Mother Earth. Boff subverts the traditional reading of the creation story (Gn 1:28–30), fighting against those who take this story as a mandate for humanity to dominate the earth. He even goes beyond the more moderate position of stewardship for creation. In a very real sense, he evokes a vision more like that of Teilhard de Chardin: the idea that we as men and women are but a speck in creation, and even Mother Earth is a small part of the fabric of the universe. In these broader terms, then, we must care for the earth because it is part of something greater, a whole that even modern-day science does not completely understand.

Boff insists that we have something to learn from those on the margins, those who live in rural areas, and specifically he points to the indigenous peoples who have lived in the Amazon river basin for centuries. These indigenous groups, such as the Tucano in the Upper Rio Negro, are famous for knowing the name of every type of tree, every plant, and every animal, big or small, in the ecosystem in which they live. Boff notes that one group utilizes 78 percent of the trees for a variety of sources, from herbal remedies to home building and religious ceremonies.[2] They do so without clear-cutting and without burning. In fact, they have an intricate system for farming that utilizes local resources so that farmers increase, rather than decrease, the number of resources in the area. They never outfish any portion of the river nor overharvest any particular type of plant or flower. In short, they live in a symbiotic relationship with the world around them. Further, they do this out of a sense of the sacredness of the world around them. Each being forms part of the fabric that God created. The Tucano might not know the doctrine of the Trinity or have any desire to debate the intricacies of transubstantiation, but they do know how to give thanks for what they have been given. When they kill any creature, they give thanks for that animal's gift of life: they recognize that animals die so that the people may live. They have dances for the harvest, for the change of seasons, for the summer solstice. They share a common bond with many indigenous groups when they give thanks to the creator God every day for providing for them through nature. This vision of the world seems to correspond more closely to what we might imagine the Garden of Eden to have been, rather than to Western visions of dominating power that we use to construct or in many cases destroy the Earth.

Beyond his similarities with many liberation theologians who want to defend the poor or fight for justice, Boff insists that we must also reclaim the sacredness of creation. The earth itself has dignity. He affirms that "all beings in nature are citizens, have rights and deserve respect and reverence."[3] Human beings must learn to live together in and with the Pachamama, the world around them. Human beings and nature must overlap, come together, and live sustainably. While some might have science fiction fantasies that there are places where no one has gone before in our universe, and to which we might escape if our world is destroyed, at this point we really only have one Earth, one Gaia, one Pachamama in which to live. If this is a common good for all to enjoy, then how can we not protect it, conserve it, and even give back to it?

Boff goes further in constructing his argument, comparing the presence of God in all things to a kind of "Theosphere." After recalling the Aristotelian idea of being, and that God is named in thousands of ways and manners, Boff asks how God might be named in a new ecological paradigm.[4] He writes, "The answer will have to emerge in a natural way from within our overall holistic experience of the universe and of ourselves in it."[5] In sum, he asks, how do we speak of the earth in terms of the sacred? If God is a part of everything that moves and has breath and being, then how can we acknowledge the presence of God in our urban environment, in our mountains, in our forests?[6]

Boff's consideration of indigenous populations in his native Brazil may open us to the possibility of appreciating the insights of our own indigenous population here in the United States. The Lakota Nation in South Dakota have a phrase worth noting: "*Mitakuye Oyasin*," or "We are all related." Certainly for the Lakota this means that all peoples are related, but there is also a deeper mystical sense in the term. The Lakota gives thanks for the seeds he takes from the prairie dog, the deer he kills, the tapestries she weaves, the child she births. We are all related, and all is given to us from Tunkashila, or Grandfather God. This idea resonates with what Boff presents about indigenous ideas from Brazil and shows us that we have something to learn from our own First Nations.[7]

But we need not always look elsewhere for such spiritual insights. Boff concludes his book by utilizing the Franciscan ideal of cardinal ecological virtues.[8] Boff's point is clear: St. Francis had a broader understanding of the created world than many of us do today.[9] St. Francis saw the world as a web of interconnectedness, in which all created beings live together in harmony with the world, with Gaia, with Pachamama. Mountain stream and valley, man, woman, animal: all form part of the created world. Francis, in his own mystical way, saw the world in the same way as our indigenous brothers and sisters: "We are all related," all part of the same spiritual and social fabric.

The Crucified People as a Lens for Reading Boff

Although Boff makes the significant move of linking justice and ecology, thereby calling us to hear the cry of the earth, his project could be deepened by introducing Jon Sobrino's terminology of "the crucified people" and "the martyred people." This would sharpen his focus on the cry of the poor. Although he does say that we need to empower the poor, to see a church of the poor, and to fight for justice for the poor, he does not go far enough in *Cry of the Earth, Cry of the Poor*.[10] He may have presumed his reader's knowledge of his many works in liberation theology from the 1970s and 1980s, in which he contextualizes liberation theology in his own country of Brazil. But Sobrino's two terms, which he derives from his experience in El Salvador, might usefully supplement Boff's 1995 text. Sobrino borrows the first term, "the crucified people," from fellow Jesuit Ignacio Ellacuría. Stated simply, the crucified people are the suffering and economically poor who face not only poverty but death. Sobrino and Ellacuría identify them as the historical continuation of Jesus' suffering on the Cross. Like Jesus, they are despised and rejected by others.[11] They evoke the mystery of the Cross and allow us to acknowledge that mystery in the reality we see around us.

The statistics Boff cites about people in the global South emphasize this suffering:

> 79% of humankind lives in the immense and poor South; 1
> billion people live in the state of absolute poverty; 3 billion
> do not have enough to eat; 60 million die in hunger every
> year; and 14 million young people under 15 years of age
> die each year as a result of hunger-caused diseases. There is
> practically no solidarity among human beings for dealing
> with this dramatic situation.[12]

These are the crucified people, those with whom we need to stand
in solidarity at the foot of the Cross. Sobrino elaborates the idea
of the crucified people to include all those who die a slow and
torturous death, not on a cross, but day in and day out, over
months or years, with inadequate potable water, food, shelter,
work, etc. With this thick description of the lives of too many
people today, Sobrino creates a new category of those who suffer.[13] These crucified people know that they must get up each and
every day to battle the elements, to find food, water, shelter, etc.
Significantly, their dilemma is not unrelated to the plight of the
earth. Boff cites statistics that can only lead to the conclusion that
humanity has contributed to a "death machine."[14] He points out
that between the years 1500 and 1850, approximately one species
was wiped out every ten years. But "since 1990 a species a day is
disappearing. At this rate, by the year 2000 one species per hour
will be disappearing."[15] We might stretch the image to say that
now in the year 2015 we have not only a crucified people, but a
crucified world. If Jesus as incarnate Word is always present and
the Ruah hovered over the waters at the dawn of creation, then
how must they weep as they look at the earth today.[16]

Sobrino: The Martyred People

After the death of the Jesuits at the UCA in 1989, Sobrino expanded the idea of the crucified people even further, and coined
a new term, "the martyred people." Without tracing in depth all
of his work in *Jesus the Liberator* and the 1995 Concilium essay
in *Martyrdom Today*, suffice it to say that Sobrino links today's
martyrs to Jesus Christ. He borrows the early Patristic idea that

Jesus was the protomartyr, and thus all Christian martyrs die as a martyr like Jesus. But as Sobrino reflects on the cross and martyrs today he gives us a new paradigm for what it means to be a martyr in our present context, describing first a "Jesus martyr" and later what he terms a "Jesuanic martyr." These modern martyrs do not die for their faith in the same way that the early Christian martyrs did: they do not die because of hatred of the faith. Rather, they die because of hatred of justice. Sobrino cites as examples Rutilio Grande, a Jesuit and the first native Salvadoran priest killed in the buildup to the Salvadoran civil war;[17] the US churchwomen killed in 1980;[18] his Jesuit brothers and two laywomen killed in 1989;[19] and the recently beatified Monseñor Oscar Romero, the San Salvadoran archbishop assassinated in 1980.[20] These exemplary martyrs prove very important for Sobrino's understanding of martyrdom today, but there are also those martyrs who die an anonymous death. They die unknown, even though their deaths, too, were caused by their work for justice. Some remain unknown outside their own country or even town, like many lay catechists killed in El Salvador, Rwandan Christians killed for hiding their Tutsi brothers in the Rwandan genocide, or numerous other examples. These martyrs, unnamed and unremembered, are still part of the great cloud of witnesses. Their personal witness is not diminished by their anonymity, and their deaths require the expansion of our understanding of the crucified people to that of a martyred people. It would be interesting to see how Boff would make use of this category of the martyred people, with its potential parallel to a martyred earth.

Pachamama and the Martyrs

In *Cry of the Earth, Cry of the Poor*, Leonardo Boff provides an example of an exemplary "martyr," labor leader and environmental activist Chico Mendes, and I will add a second name, that of Dorothy Stang.[21] Stang's story is widely known, but the life and death of Chico Mendes is likely unfamiliar to most North Americans today. Mendes was a union activist who was gunned down in December of 1988. He was actively working on a forest restoration campaign in northern Brazil. He had received numerous death threats from landowners who wanted to clear forest for minerals, logging, and ranching. He is often remembered as one who fought for environmental justice, but it is just as significant that he advocated for the poor, the rural farmer, and the indigenous peoples who had lived in that area, some for centuries. He was killed fighting for justice. Boff calls him "a martyr of the ecological struggle in the Amazon," but he could also fit Sobrino's category of a martyr for justice.[22] He fought for the environment, certainly, but also for the common person who lived in the Amazon.

Similarly, Dorothy Stang, a North American nun and a long-time missionary in Brazil, was killed in northern Brazil in 2005. She taught in schools, formed leaders for Christian base communities, taught catechism classes, and led communion services in far-reaching indigenous Amazon communities where no priests would go. Was she killed as a martyr for justice? As one of the martyred people, or as a Jesuanic martyr? Or did she die for the environment, as what some would term an eco-martyr? One could argue that she saw this Amazon forest as a place of the sacred and thus died for the land. Yet as she formed cooperative farming initiatives and fought for preserves that sustained the land, she also showed a great love and compassion for the common person living there. Stang provided a voice for those voiceless who found their rights trampled in the name of progress and development. She died because of her work for both people and land, which raises the question: Is this yet another new kind of martyr for today? We cannot avoid this question. Is Gaia, the Pachamama, Mother Earth, worth dying for? Is it possible to have a martyr for the good of creation?

In this short essay, I hope to evoke these questions. Certainly, Boff argues that we need to understand ourselves as part of the fabric of creation. We are part of Mother Earth; we are one species among many. Although perhaps we can steward creation, we cannot be separated from it, and our indigenous brothers and sisters have much to teach us in this regard. Although we have the technology to build a better world, most do not enjoy its advantages. Although we destroy acres of pristine rain forest, we may also be destroying new herbal remedies, new medicines, better ways to steward our world. These crucified indigenous peoples have also been martyred. They have sometimes died standing within the same confines of the rain forest where their ancestors thrived. They die along with the trees, the flowers, the fish, the birds, and all of God's created beauty. Are they also a martyred people? Do they show us a better way to live together, related as one community, as brothers and sisters in Gaia, in Christ?

Laudato Si'

One can see the hand of Leonardo Boff, and certainly the issues for justice for the earth and for the poor, in this latest papal encyclical, *Laudato Si'*. Although space does not permit engaging all the implications of this beautifully crafted document, let me briefly mention three areas pertinent to this essay's treatment of Boff. First, Boff expressly titles his book *Cry of the Earth, Cry of the Poor* and we find that exact phrase in the encyclical.[23] Although it is not directly attributed to Boff, it is notable that Boff utilizes the phrase and many ideas in the encyclical as early as twenty years ago. This theme is interwoven throughout the document and in a number of its concrete examples. As a former Franciscan, Boff would certainly approve of the document, which invokes the name and work of St. Francis, "the patron saint of all who study and work in the area of ecology. . . . He was particularly concerned for God's creation and for the poor and outcast."[24] The earth and the poor cry out together, or in the words of *Laudato Si'*, "These situations have caused sister earth, along with all the abandoned of our world, to cry out, pleading that we take another course."[25] Second, Pope Francis explicitly mentions the poor as those most harmed by the damage to the environment. In the introductory section we find this express concern: "Exposure to atmospheric pollutants produces a broad spectrum of health hazards, especially for the poor, and causes millions of premature deaths."[26] This phrase echoes Boff, Sobrino, and even the most recent conference of Latin American bishops at Aparecida.[27] The problem of potable water as a crisis especially for the poor gets explicit mention: "One particularly serious problem is the quality of water available to the poor. Every day, unsafe water results in many deaths and the spread of water-related diseases, including those caused by microorganisms and chemical substances. Dysentery and cholera, linked to inadequate hygiene and water supplies, are a significant cause of suffering and of infant mortality."[28]

Finally, *Laudato Si'* affirms numerous times that we are all related, an intuition we find in many indigenous tribes and peoples but specifically the Lakota nation in South Dakota. *Laudato Si'* approaches this by starting with the biblical narratives of the Pentateuch, specifically in Genesis: "After the creation of man and woman, 'God saw everything that he had made, and behold it was very good' (Gn 1:31). The Bible teaches that every man and woman is created out of love and made in God's image and likeness (cf. Gn 1:26). This shows us the immense dignity of each person, 'who is not just something, but someone. He is capable of self-knowledge, of self-possession and of freely giving himself and entering into communion with other persons.'"[29] And later, in the second chapter of the document, Pope Francis affirms, "Everything is related, and we human beings are united as brothers and sisters on a wonderful pilgrimage, woven together by the love God has for each of his creatures and which also unites us in fond affection with brother sun, sister moon, brother river and mother earth."[30] *Laudato Si'* ends with two prayers, and I would like to end this essay with the part of the first which encapsulates all three ideas: the cry of the earth, the cry of the poor, and our relationship with all of creation.

> O God of the poor,
> help us to rescue the abandoned
> and forgotten of this earth,
> so precious in your eyes.
> Bring healing to our lives,
> that we may protect the world and not prey on it,
> that we may sow beauty,
> not pollution and destruction.
> Touch the hearts
> of those who look only for gain
> at the expense of the poor and the earth.
> Teach us to discover the worth of each thing,
> to be filled with awe and contemplation,
> to recognize that we are profoundly united
> with every creature
> as we journey towards your infinite light.[31]
> Amen.

Notes

[1] The recent encyclical italicizes Boff's title though it does not directly cite it: "Today, however, we have to realize that a true ecological approach

always becomes a social approach; it must integrate questions of justice in debates on the environment, so as to hear *both the cry of the earth and the cry of the poor*" (*Laudato Si': On Care for Our Common Home*, Encyclical Letter of the Holy Father Francis [Rome: Vatican Press, May 24, 2015], 49), www.vatican.va.

²Leonardo Boff, *Cry of the Earth, Cry of the Poor*, trans. Phillip Berryman (Maryknoll, NY: Orbis Books, 1997), 124. He refers here to indigenous communities in Brazil and Venezuela.

³Ibid., 133.

⁴Ibid., 140.

⁵Ibid.

⁶One can find another parallel in *Laudato Si'* here: "The bishops of Brazil have pointed out that nature as a whole not only manifests God but is also a locus of his presence. The Spirit of life dwells in every living creature and calls us to enter into relationship with him. Discovering this presence leads us to cultivate the 'ecological virtues' " (no. 66). See National Conference of the Bishops of Brazil, *A igreja e a questão ecológica* (1992), 53–54; *Laudato Si'*, 88.

⁷We find similar meaning in *Laudato Si'*: "This is the basis of our conviction that, as part of the universe, called into being by one Father, all of us are linked by unseen bonds and together form a kind of universal family, a sublime communion which fills us with a sacred, affectionate and humble respect" (89).

⁸Boff, *Cry of the Earth*, 203. Chapter 11 is titled "Cardinal Ecological Virtues."

⁹As we saw in note 6, interestingly, *Laudato Si'* makes mention of the ecological virtues; see especially *Laudato Si'*, 88.

¹⁰Granted, Boff has other works that stress the preferential option for the poor, but even as recently as 2009 his emphasis remains focused on Gaia and Mother Earth as our common home; "Earth as Gaia: An Ethical and Spiritual Challenge," in *Eco-Theology*, ed. Elaine Wainwright, Luiz C. Susin, and Felix Wilfred, *Concilium*, vol. 3 (London: SCM Press, 2009).

¹¹Jon Sobrino, *Jesus the Liberator* (Maryknoll, NY: Orbis Books, 1994). See esp. chap. 10, pp. 254–71.

¹²As a reminder, the statistics that Boff cites are from 1995, and in many Latin American countries these statistics have gotten worse, not better! Boff, *Cry of the Earth*, 1.

¹³Again, it is clear that Sobrino borrows this term from Ellacuría but expands on the idea especially after Ellacuría's death in 1989.

¹⁴Boff, *Cry of the Earth*, 1.

¹⁵Ibid.

¹⁶Pope Francis gives us a negative example when he invokes the Cain and Abel story: "Disregard for the duty to cultivate and maintain a proper relationship with my neighbour, for whose care and custody I am responsible, ruins my relationship with my own self, with others, with God and with the earth. When all these relationships are neglected, when justice no longer dwells in the land, the Bible tells us that life itself is endangered" (*Laudato Si'*, 70).

¹⁷Tom Kelly's new book documents Grande's life and eventual death in

1977: *As a Gospel Grows Feet: Rutilio Grande, SJ, and the Church of El Salvador* (Maryknoll, NY: Orbis Books, 2014).

[18]There are numerous biographies of sisters Dorothy Kazel, Ita Ford, and Maura Clarke, and Maryknoll lay missionary Jean Donovan.

[19]Jon Sobrino, ed., *Companions of Jesus: The Jesuit Martyrs of El Salvador* (Maryknoll, NY: Orbis Books, 1990). Sobrino gives a heartfelt look at the murdered Jesuits in his community.

[20]One could consult a myriad of biographies, but the recent documentary film produced by Bob Pelton, CSC, gives a heartfelt look from the Salvadoran perspective (*Monseñor: The Last Journey of Oscar Romero*, a film by Ana Carrigan and Juliet Weber and produced by the Kellogg Institute at the University of Notre Dame, 2011).

[21]Boff, *Cry of the Earth*, 102.

[22]Ibid., 87.

[23]*Laudato Si'*, 49.

[24]Ibid., 10.

[25]Ibid., 53.

[26]Ibid., 20.

[27]Ibid., 38.

[28]Ibid., 29.

[29]*Laudato Si'*, 65; the quote within the text is from the *Catechism of the Catholic Church*, 357. This section also quotes the prophet Jeremiah that God knew us before we were formed in the womb, and the conclusion drawn from that text by Pope Benedict XVI that each of us is necessary and loved.

[30]Ibid., 92.

[31]Ibid., 246.

Wilderness in Public Theology

A Dialogical Approach

Mary Doak and Thomas Hughson, SJ

This essay is co-written so that the authors can bring into explicit dialogue their distinct approaches to a public theology of
wilderness. While differing in gender, generation, and theological
formation, we share a commitment to inserting critical theology
into US public life. We also share a concern that scholars currently working in public theology are not sufficiently responding
to each other's work. Even though theologians have increasingly
claimed the term and the tasks of "public theology," the recipro-
cal engagement among these theologians that would develop the
field of public theology (as well as each public theologian's own
work) has been neglected.

To contribute to the desired critical discourse among public
theologians, the topic of wilderness will be addressed here in a
dialogical format in which the authors' perspectives are mutually
informing. Mary Doak's work in public theology thus far focuses
on attention to the role of the narrative imagination in public
life, whereas Thomas Hughson has emphasized a Christological
grounding for Christian social consciousness in the public sphere.
In this essay, in the first part, "Wilderness as a Topic for Public
Theology," Doak will defend the importance of wilderness as a
topic central to any adequate American public theology. In the
second part, "Respect for Wilderness," Hughson will analyze the
concept of "wilderness" in American cultural history. In the third
part, "Wilderness and American Exceptionalism," Doak will then
discuss the concept of wilderness as it has informed the develop-

ment of American exceptionalism. Hughson will conclude in
"Wilderness as Eviction: A Critical Public Theology" by further
exploring the role of an ideology of wilderness in the construction of the public sphere. Together these distinct approaches
seek to demonstrate that the concept of wilderness is integral to
Euro-American political ideals and so must be interrogated in US
public theology.

Wilderness as a Topic for Public Theology (Mary Doak)

Public theology (as understood here) is the branch of theology
that is explicitly committed to engaging American public life. As
such, public theology undertakes a mutually critical correlation
between aspects of politics, culture, and society in the United
States, on the one hand, and religious beliefs and practices, on
the other.[1] Surely, wilderness (whether as the "unexpected wilderness" of global climate change or simply wilderness itself) is an
apt topic for such a public theology. US environmental policies
are affected by how society understands and values wilderness,
an understanding that is informed by religious (though not necessarily theistic) beliefs about the goodness of nature and the role
of humanity on earth.

Yet public theology has other reasons to be concerned with
wilderness, reasons that go beyond the relevance of wilderness
for environmental policies or support for nature preserves. Public
theology should address wilderness also—and especially—because an adequate public theology must attend to the narratives
through which people comprehend themselves and the sociopolitical issues they face. How we envision our collective social and
national projects, including how we understand the inheritance
and the debts of our past and what we hope to contribute to the
future, is integral to how we think about and make judgments
regarding specific public issues.[2] In the United States, especially
for Euro-Americans, this narrative self-understanding has been
deeply informed by the concept of wilderness, and particularly
by the early colonial commitment to transforming that wilderness
into garden or city.[3] In short, we misunderstand integral aspects
of the political imagination as it functions in the United States
when we ignore the influence of wilderness on Euro-American
political goals.

A further reason for serious theological engagement with wilderness is that thinking about the natural environment interrupts the tendency of much political theology (including American public theology) to value history and time as the arena of freedom, while dismissing nature and space as theologically insignificant constraints. Thinking about wilderness requires that we reflect on our spatial location, whether that be in "civilization," in "wilderness," or in some combination thereof. Paying attention to the public's location and relation to nature curbs the tendency toward an abstract or disembodied public theology that considers human actions as though they occur in a vacuum. There is a stubborn—and valuable—facticity in a shared place and in the presence of others with whom we share that place. America is not merely a historical project, after all, but also a place, a shared land (both cultivated and uncultivated).

Exploring the public significance of wilderness, then, engages an aspect of Euro-American experience that has deeply informed the dominant forms of political imagination in the United States. Reflecting on wilderness further highlights the complicated—and often toxic—relationship of Euro-Americans to their natural environment and to those often overlooked people who, though relegated to the margins of US history and culture, nevertheless share this land and the effects of US public policies.

Respect for Wilderness (Thomas Hughson, SJ)

Most English colonists in North America saw wilderness as an unruly, hostile, cursed, heathenish antiparadise to be converted into tilled field, cultivated garden, orchard, and pasture. Later, eighteenth-century American Christianity, influenced by science, the French Enlightenment, the Romantic movement, and H. D. Thoreau, altered that evaluation from combative to appreciative. In his magisterial *Wilderness and the American Mind,* Roderick Frazier Nash remarked, "The concept of wilderness as a church, as a place to find and worship God, helped launch the intellectual revolution that led to wilderness appreciation."[4] Territories beyond the frontiers were still other, but now with a touch of transcendence. Accordingly, public debates about the fate of "wilderness" to the west in the nineteenth and twentieth centuries embraced a positive view of wilderness.[5]

At the same time, forests and mountains in westward territories obviously housed vast stores of raw materials such as timber and ore. The plains offered space for expansion of agriculture. Through the nineteenth century, canals, railroads, westward trails, and eventually roads opened passage through lands European Americans had not settled. Wilderness also beckoned well-educated urban denizens of New York, Boston, and San Francisco to temporary respite from what they felt to be relentless and overcivilized striving. Camping allowed them to reclaim, as they saw it, their more elemental humanity, sometimes praised as a vigorous "manhood" [*sic*].

The American gaze toward continent-wide territory including wilderness, and not just the new republic's political structures of democratic self-governance, belonged to a distinctive, developing, national self-understanding. In Gertrude Stein's view, "In the United States there is more space where nobody is than where anybody is. That is what makes America what it is."[6] And, mused famed ecologist Aldo Leopold, "of what avail are forty freedoms without a blank space on the map?"[7] Of course, indigenous peoples inhabited places where "nobody is," those "blank spaces" on Euro-American maps.

In a Socratic spirit, though, what do we mean by the "wilderness" everyone speaks about? Nash pointed out that the concept of "wilderness" divides the natural world into two realms.[8] There is what agriculture or the stamp of organized human presence has domesticated, and then there is the rest of nature. This unmanaged remainder is "wilderness." Hebrew terms in the Scriptures, *midbar*, *arabah*, and *jeshimon* transmitted this meaning of wilderness. The Septuagint translated them into Greek as *eremos*, both a noun and an adjective. The Latin Vulgate carried the meaning in the word, *desertum*, translated into English as "wilderness."

A prehistoric layer is the base of biblical, classical, and Christian meanings of a wild, scarcely inhabited place. Noted but not examined by Nash, that deepest layer gained meaning from a protracted historical event in human history. About 8500 BCE the beginnings of agriculture appeared in the Fertile Crescent, in China between 8000 BCE and 7500 BCE, in Meso-America ca. 7000 BCE, and in North America ca. 5000 BCE.[9] Wilderness or equivalent terms and ideas referred to the mostly unmanaged nature hitherto the everyday environment, left largely unbent to human purposes by hunter-gatherers. The concept of "wilderness" was not possible before the transition from foraging to farming.

Recent and current research no longer conceives the transition as an agricultural revolution. Instead, scarcity bit by bit backed foragers in propitious surroundings into a millennia-long, multifactorial process that eventually became ubiquitous.[10] Food production gradually demanded stable villages in which people performed regular tasks in view of future benefits. Agricultural settlements changed the way hunter-gatherers had related with nonhuman nature, even if they already lived in pre-agricultural villages like Eynan-Mallaha in modern Israel. Whereas most research has assumed that foragers scratched out a means to survival under pressure from hunger, a small school of thought now contests that assumption. Ian Hodder, Jacques Cauvin, and Barbara Bender point to, respectively, antecedent symbolic, religious, and social factors that incited the ancient transition.[11]

Of potential theological interest, Cauvin acknowledges that the Fertile Crescent enjoyed favorable climatic, ecological, and biological conditions when Neolithic agriculture emerged after 9000 BCE.[12] But he argues that such external factors were conditions permitting, not causing, agriculture, since they also let hunter-gatherers flourish. Cauvin concludes that agriculture originated as an invention of the mind and imagination: he argues from archaeological evidence of changes in religious symbols that a religious change toward reverence for Mother Earth triggered the momentous shift.[13]

Lacking a contrast with agriculture, foragers like our ancient ancestors and most Native American tribes at the time of Columbus did not live in an environing nature they saw as a wilderness. To the contrary, observed Chief Standing Bear of the Oglala Sioux, "only to the white man was nature a wilderness." His people "did not think of the great open plains, the beautiful rolling hills and the winding streams as 'wild.' "[14] That fact stirs a major suspicion about land that Euro-Americans called "wilderness."

Nonetheless, Thoreau, Muir, and Leopold, along with many scientists, have extolled wilderness as creation on its own biotic terms in a pre-agricultural, nonindustrialized condition. What's not for public theology to like and support in the interpretative concept and praxis of "wilderness"? Ought not public theology bring theological substance into public arguments on behalf of the agenda of the Wilderness Society, and the Sierra Club (of which I am a dues-paying member)?

That wilderness is a public issue follows from the fact that the status of lands held in the US public domain presupposes a nation-state's original title to all land within its boundaries legally prior to parcels available to private ownership. Federal and state decisions determine which acreage will be incorporated into the 5 percent of public lands designated wilderness in the United States, including Alaska, or the 2 percent in the lower forty-eight states.[15] Since the Wilderness Act of 1964 about 110 million acres of public land have received the designation. Designation as wilderness means no roads, no vehicles, no permanent structures. Approximately 100 million acres of federal wildlands not yet officially designated as wilderness are at present risk of commercial development.

Wilderness and American Exceptionalism (Mary Doak)

As Hughson reminds us, wilderness is a theoretical construct in which an undomesticated and so wild (or "self-willed") nature is defined as distinct from the rural and urban landscapes shaped by and for humans. This concept of wilderness has been especially formative of the Euro-American sociopolitical imagination since colonial times, when settlers from Europe struggled to create a new society in what they saw as an untamed natural environment. Their Calvinist faith gave an initial meaning to this engagement with wilderness as a necessary stage in the journey to the promised land, the society they would establish in faith and justice.[16] Having completed their transatlantic exodus from Europe, how could they not interpret this wilderness as their own prelude to a land flowing with milk and honey, destined (some hoped) to be the shining city of perfect harmony promised at the end of the Book of Revelation?

Since the biblical pattern suggests that wilderness is integral to the achievement of the promised land, wilderness is not merely a negative stage, to be avoided or passed through as quickly as possible. Interpreted through a biblical lens, the wilderness is a place not only of danger and temptation but also of clarification, purification, and reorientation, as it was for the Israelites in their exodus from slavery and for Jesus in his wilderness retreat before his public ministry. As David Williams has shown in his analysis of American literature, wilderness has continued to function in the Euro-American imagination as a metaphor for the liminal state in which the self or society sheds an established identity in order to begin anew.[17] Wilderness is thus a place of freedom and creativity as well as of perilous chaos.

It is not surprising, then, that when Euro-Americans sought to define a distinct national identity, they turned to their wilderness, as Hughson notes above. Unable to compete culturally with Europe, the newly founded United States could, and did, celebrate instead the "unspoiled" beauty of its vast wilderness. Indeed, the exceptionalism by which the United States and its people claim to be unique among nations is rooted (for good and ill) in this possession of (by European standards) exceptional wilderness, a rich natural source of personal and social renewal as well as of beauty. Americans think of themselves as exceptional in large part because they had (and, as long as there is sufficient wilderness, continue to have) a rare opportunity to begin afresh, to construct a new society and new selves untainted with the accumulated corruptions of centuries of civilization.[18]

Even while this exceptionalism supports creative and reformist initiatives to improve self, society, and land, American exceptionalism has negative implications. There is a dangerous tendency in American exceptionalism to believe that the ideal has already been achieved.[19] If we have already gone through the wilderness and emerged into the long-awaited shining city or garden/paradise, then there is no need for further reform (and perhaps then no need to preserve the wilderness). Hence American exceptionalism recurs in public life as the arrogant assumption that the people and institutions of the United States are morally superior to others.

Conversely, in those times when imperfections are acknowledged in US society, exceptionalism can encourage an irresponsible ahistoricism. Why take seriously the past (and the moral debts we have incurred) if we can simply begin again, return to the wilderness and create ourselves and our society anew? When a new self and a new nation are always possible, one can ignore the horrors of history, the hard work of reconciliation, and the just demands for restitution.

There is a great deal of hubris, then, as well as a spirit of initiative in the exceptionalism that understands the American project as one of converting its wilderness into a more perfect society.

However, the wilderness that is valued as the basis of transformation also has ways of resisting such hubris. Venturing into areas of wilderness, one quickly learns that nature is less malleable to human goals and new beginnings than American exceptionalism often assumes. There is, after all, a degree of the unexpected in all wilderness, precisely because it is wilderness—nature that is not controlled by humans. Nature is ultimately not only the source but also the limit of all human projects of civilization, a point that global climate change is making quite clear.

A very good example of characteristically Euro-American attitudes toward the wilderness—and the wilderness's defiance of our hubris—can be found in the history of Death Valley National Park in southern California. Perhaps some of the attraction of Death Valley is that, like much of Euro-American culture, it tends to extremes. Holding the official record for the hottest temperature ever recorded, Death Valley is also incredibly dry, hostile to life, and stunningly beautiful.

Over 95 percent of Death Valley is designated wilderness, and in any case it is a place where nature remains 100 percent dangerous and undomesticated. Death Valley continues to live up to its name, as still today (and despite the roads, park rangers, and a few hotels) people die in the extreme heat and dryness there. The flora and fauna on the valley floor survive only because they have evolved to withstand the high temperatures, lack of water, and salination in the scant water supply.[20]

Yet this inhospitable desert has inspired Euro-Americans to seek to transform Death Valley to serve human purposes and desires. Death Valley has been mined (more or less successfully for borax), planted with date trees, searched for a legendary gold mine, sold to gullible would-be pioneers as a lush and fertile place to settle (which it is not!), and is now part of the national park system with restaurants, inns, and marked hiking trails. In short, even as unpromising a place as Death Valley has inspired Euro-Americans to try to make Death Valley humanly useful and even lucrative. Perhaps most characteristically Euro-American is the extent to which Death Valley has figured in the con schemes of the hucksters who sold dreams of gold mines or fertile farm land (neither of which exist in Death Valley) to naïve easterners. It surely says something significant about the Euro-American character that this stark and hostile terrain has inspired so many get-rich-quick schemes.[21]

Interestingly, while Death Valley has been a place of dreams that brought great hardship and occasionally death to Euro-Americans, the Timbisha Shoshone people have lived in this brutally harsh place for over a thousand years.[22] They knew where the few natural springs are, and they were willing to eat a lot of chuckwalla, the rather plump lizards still plentiful in the canyons. It should also be noted that the Timbisha were not stupid—or arrogant—enough to stay on the valley floor during the summer, but retreated into the cooler mountains. Still, in a place where there is so little of what is essential to life, the fact that the Timbisha Shosone survived here without the food and (especially) the water trucked into the lodge and restaurants today is truly impressive.

The Timbisha adapted carefully to the conditions in Death Valley, learning to live on very little and respecting their surroundings. Euro-Americans, with a tendency to see wilderness as a source of utopian possibilities, have had a less happy history of struggle, failure, limited success at best, and a lot of grief in Death Valley. The wilderness-inspired freedom to create and re-create ourselves and our surroundings can be a significant, and positive, force of reform but, as the remains of mines and ghost towns in Death Valley remind us, nature is not entirely at our command and will be here long after we are gone.

Wilderness as Eviction: A Critical Public Theology (Thomas Hughson)

Ecofeminist theologian Sallie McFague has criticized identifying Christian love for nature with subscribing to protection of areas designated as wilderness. McFague points out that urban parkland, not wilderness, is the portal through which many more millions of urban fellow citizens, especially lower-income folks, walk into proximity with and grow in love with nature.[23] Her observation serves to steer public theology toward critical reflection on ideas, practices, and debates regarding wilderness.

Critical interrogation of the concept and legal status of wilderness has been under way for about twenty years. Until then three positions contended in the public sphere. One supported laissez-faire commercial interest in timber, ore, oil, hydroelectric power, and real estate development. A second commitment sought to preserve intact large areas without development, permanent structures, roads, even marked trails, in order to maintain either a biotic, scientific reserve or to offer a primordial relation to nature that offsets the pressures of modern life. A third position, more common in Europe, advocated "wise use" that mixes respectful conservation of mountains, rivers, and forests with readiness for some extraction of natural resources and some recreational development.

However, the preservationist and wise use positions have to deal with a telling critique of the concept of wilderness that has arisen in the last twenty years. Independently of each other, Mark David Spence and Holly Miller have shown how the Euro-American concept of wilderness has had the effect of oppressing Native Americans.[24] What is public theology to say in response to Spence's irrefutable argument that "uninhabited wilderness had to be created before it could be preserved"?[25] Consider three instances of "preservation." In 1865, landscape architect Frederick Law Olmsted, designer of Manhattan's Central Park, advised the California legislature to preserve Yosemite Valley. This involved emptying Yosemite Park of the Yosemite tribe.[26] In 1872, President Ulysses S. Grant inked the Yellowstone Park Act, preserving more than 2 million acres in Wyoming as Yellowstone National Park. The purpose was to prevent private acquisition and commercial exploitation of waterfalls, geysers, and hot springs. However, protecting wilderness partially caused Shoshone, Crow, and Bannock to be pushed out of Yellowstone and onto reservations. Similarly, preserving wilderness in Glacier Park impelled evicting the Blackfeet from the territory.

Black Elk, the Oglala Sioux shaman become Catholic catechist, saw this clearly. "Black Elk," notes Spence, "understood only too well that wilderness preservation went hand in hand with native dispossession."[27] Compounding the dispossession, by 1893 an estimated 30 million bison on the Great Pains had been reduced to 400. A relentless slaughter took place that, intended or not, amounted to conquest of the land, food, culture, travel, and peoples of buffalo-hunting tribes.[28]

In light of the difference between foraging and farming, the following can be asserted: The concept of wilderness not only describes geographical areas but also perpetuates a pre-understanding of agriculture as superior to hunting and gathering. Native Americans relied heavily on hunting and gathering, though some tribes cultivated some plants, had dogs, and eventually used horses. Consequently, they and their way of life have borne the brunt of the ingrained Euro-American assumption of the superiority of agriculture that cannot be dissociated from the differential meaning of wilderness.

What, consequently, might public theology wish to say about the apparent paradox of wilderness as colonization rather than preservation? An unmet task will be to prevent the critique from ending up in political and corporate arguments as a premise for further neoliberal, capitalist commodification of nature. Perhaps the following offers a path both practical and theoretical. Postmodern anthropology recognizes contentious heterogeneity within any society and culture.[29] No matter a common language and an aggregated history, diverse interests lead people and groups in any society to interpret the common situation variously. So too studies of the public sphere have pointed to plural public spheres in the United States.[30] Several smaller public spheres revolve around minority experiences, interpretations, and debated opinions. One or more of the smaller public spheres may be a space for numerical minorities that provides opportunities for expressing a minority's resistance to domination by the majority.

The resistant spheres are subaltern public spheres.[31] They may, or may not, form a mobilized subaltern public opinion that, as in the case of Americans of African descent, womanist, Latino/a, feminists, and LGBT associations, makes inroads into the main public sphere. Native Americans have not had a comparable subaltern public sphere. It is hard to see how public theology can uphold its purpose on the topic of wilderness without promoting the nascent, fragile, subaltern public of Native Americans. That probably involves meeting, listening to, reading, standing with, and arguing on the side of Native Americans about particular issues in their pre-US relationship to the land.[32] For example, in the lower forty-eight states there are issues over joint management of national parks by Native Americans and the National Park Service, protection of and regained possession of ancestral burial grounds such as the Black Hills. In Wisconsin and Minnesota, disputes have arisen over privileged access to ancient hunting and fishing locales.

Additional public theological topics pertinent to Native American interests include:

1. The Creator's primary relationship to the whole earth as a "first ownership" grounds Catholic social teaching on the universal destination of earth's goods. In that regard public theology could also explore public implications of the natural, cosmic dimensions of liturgy.
2. Niels Henrik Gregersen's "deep Christology" opens the Incarnation to full cosmic, planetary, and biological extension.[33]
3. The vaunted First Amendment protection of the free exercise of religion has not benefited Native Americans because the amendment's eighteenth-century concept of religion excluded a diffuse, diurnal, and seasonal, sacral relation to land, water, sun, moon, stars, and cosmos. How then could the First Amendment religion clauses protect free exercise of religion in preserving ancestral burial areas or buffalo hunting?

Public Attitudes, Public Theology

Wilderness is a human construct, a way of experiencing nature that is deeply embedded in Euro-American history, identity, and political imagination. This concept of nature as wilderness, whether to be conquered, transformed, or preserved, informs public attitudes not only about land use but also about national purposes and even about which peoples are recognized and included as partners in the public conversation. Our mutual explorations confirm that an adequate public theology, one that contributes to a more liberating public life in the United States, must critically interrogate the role and function of wilderness as part of a colonial mentality that has a history of claiming to serve God while abusing land and people.

Notes

[1] See especially David Tracy, *Blessed Rage for Order: The New Pluralism in Theology* (New York: Seabury, 1975).

[2] This argument is developed in Mary Doak, *Reclaiming Narrative for Public Theology* (Albany: State University of New York Press, 2004).

[3] See especially the historical and literary analysis provided by David R.

Williams, *Wilderness Lost: The Religious Origins of the American Mind* (Cranbury, NJ: Associated University Presses, 1987).

[4]Roderick Frazier Nash, *Wilderness and the American Mind*, 4th ed. (1967; New Haven: Yale University Press, 2014), 268. See also a fifth e-book edition with a foreword by Char Miller.

[5]Nash chronicles this history but relies too much on Lynn White Jr.'s well-known 1967 blame of biblical religion for modernity's scientific-technological exploitation of nature and consequent ecological crisis.

[6]Nash, *Wilderness and the American Mind*, 261, quoting Gertrude Stein, *The Geographical History of America* (New York: Random House, 1936), 17–18.

[7]Nash, *Wilderness and the American Mind*, 189, quoting Aldo Leopold, "The Green Lagoons," *American Forests* 51 (1945): 414.

[8]Nash, *Wilderness and the American Mind*, ix–7.

[9]For surveys of research see Jared Diamond's Pulitzer Prize–winning *Guns, Germs, and Steel: The Fates of Societies* (New York: W. W. Norton, 1999) and Graeme Barker's more technical *The Agricultural Revolution in Prehistory: Why Did Foragers Become Farmers?* (Oxford: Oxford University Press, 2006), as well as Barker's "Archaeology: The Cost of Cultivation," *Nature* 473, no. 7346 (May 12, 2011): 163–64.

[10]Richard B. Lee and Richard Daly, "Introduction: Foragers and Others," in *The Cambridge Encyclopedia of Hunters and Gatherers*, ed. Richard B. Lee and Richard Daly (Cambridge: Cambridge University Press, 1999).

[11]Jacques Cauvin, *The Birth of the Gods and the Origins of Agriculture*, trans. Trevor Watkins (Cambridge: Cambridge University Press, 2000). Barker outlines Ian Hodder's and Barbara Bender's positions in *The Agricultural Revolution*, 33–41.

[12]Cauvin, *Birth of the Gods*, 51–66.

[13]Ibid., 67–95.

[14]Nash, *Wilderness and the American Mind*, xiii, quoting Standing Bear, *Land of the Spotted Eagle* (Boston: Houghton Mifflin, 1933), 38.

[15]See the Wilderness Society website at www.wilderness.org. A Wilderness designation can be placed on land in national parks, national forests, Bureau of Land Management acreage, and Fish and Wildlife Service areas. Information on protection comes from the Wilderness Society website.

[16]See Williams, *Wilderness Lost*, esp. 25, 46.

[17]Ibid, 11.

[18]Ibid., 111. See also Nash, *Wilderness and the American Mind*, 69.

[19]Williams, *Wilderness Lost*, 15, 252.

[20]National Park Service, "Death Valley," at www.nps.gov.

[21]See especially John Soennichsen, *Live! from Death Valley: Dispatches from America's Low Point* (Seattle: Sasquatch, 2005).

[22]National Park Service, "Timbisha Shoshone Tribe of Death Valley," at www.nps.gov.

[23]See Sallie McFague, *Super, Natural Christians: How We Should Love Nature* (Minneapolis: Fortress Press, 1997), 120–29.

[24]Mark David Spence, *Dispossessing the Wilderness: Indian Removal and the Making of the National Parks* (New York: Oxford Press, 1999), and Holly

Miller, "Reconceptualizing the Wilderness: Native American Landscapes and Euro-American Control in America's National Parks," *Hohonu: A Journal of Academic Writing*, University of Hawai'i at Hilo, 9 (2011): 101–8, at http://hilo.hawaii.edu.

[25]Spence, *Dispossessing the Wilderness*, 4.

[26]Ibid., 3.

[27]Ibid., 6.

[28]Andrew C. Isenberg pins the destruction of the buffalo on both changing environmental conditions and "the American industrial economy," in *The Destruction of the Bison: An Environmental History, 1750–1920* (Cambridge: Cambridge University Press, 2000), 143. See Eric Freedman, "When Indigenous Rights and Wilderness Collide: Prosecution of Native Americans for Using Motors in Minnesota's Boundary Waters Canoe Wilderness Area," *American Indian Quarterly* 26, no. 3 (Summer 2002): 378–92, and Joy Porter, *Native American Environmentalism: Land, Spirit, and the Idea of Wilderness* (Lincoln: University of Nebraska Press, 2014).

[29]See Kathryn Tanner, *Theories of Culture: A New Agenda for Theology* (Minneapolis: Fortress Press, 1997), and Delwin Brown, Sheila Greeve Davaney, and Kathryn Tanner, eds., *Convergence on Culture: Theologians in Dialogue with Cultural Analysis and Criticism* (New York: Oxford University Press, 2001), 122–39.

[30]See essays in Craig Calhoun, ed., *Habermas and the Public Sphere* (Cambridge, MA: MIT Press, 1992) that respond to Jürgen Habermas's groundbreaking *The Structural Transformation of the Public Sphere: An Inquiry into a Category of Bourgeois Society*, trans. Thomas Burger and Frederick Lawrence (Cambridge, MA: MIT Press, 1989).

[31]Nancy Fraser, "Rethinking the Public Sphere: A Contribution to the Critique of Actually Existing Democracy," in *Habermas and the Public Sphere*, ed. Craig Calhoun, 109–42, and Michael Warner, *Publics and Counterpublics* (New York: Zone Books, 2002).

[32]See Miller, "Reconceptualizing the Wilderness"; Freedman, "When Indigenous Rights and Wilderness Collide"; and Porter, *Native American Environmentalism*.

[33]Niels Henrik Gregersen, "The Cross of Christ in an Evolutionary World," *Dialog: A Journal of Theology* 40, no. 3 (Fall 2001): 192–207, and "Deep Incarnation: Why Evolutionary Continuity Matters in Christology," *Toronto Journal of Theology* 26, no. 2 (2010): 173–88.

PART V

EXPLORING A PARTICULAR WILDERNESS

Wilderness or Wasteland?

Assessing Contemporary Resource Extraction in Light of the Appalachian Pastoral

This Land Is Home to Me (1975)

Jessica A. Wrobleski

The accounts of the first Europeans to experience the Appalachian Mountains tell of a wild and rugged land, abundant in plant and animal life, largely untouched—and certainly untamed—by humankind. In the travel journal of the expedition of Batts and Fallam in 1671, the explorers recorded their encounters with the wilderness of Appalachia:

> We came to the foot of a great mountain and found a very steep ascent so that we could scarce keep ourselves from sliding down again. . . . When we were got up to the top of the mountain and set down very weary we saw very high mountains lying to the north and south as far as we could see. . . . It was a pleasing tho' dreadful sight to see the mountains and Hills as if piled upon one another. . . . Going forward we found rich ground but having curious rising hills and brave meadows with grass about a man's height.[1]

Other accounts from the eighteenth century describe the buffalo and elk, bear and deer, and the diverse range of plants that they found among these mountains and the creeks and rivers that wound their way through them. In his 1906 history of the town of Thomas, West Virginia, T. Nutter dramatically notes that even at late as the 1880s, "Thomas was surrounded by a howling wilderness of pine and laurel, and wild beasts could be seen and killed from the very house doors."[2]

When you drive into West Virginia on an interstate highway today, you are greeted by a sign saying "Welcome to wild & wonderful West Virginia"[3]—and indeed, there is still much that is wild and wonderful about the state, including some of the mountainous and verdant terrain that the first settlers described. But there is also much about West Virginia, and the region of which it is at the core, that is neither of these things. In addition to the ordinary signs of human civilization, it is not uncommon to find large areas of land that have been stripped of soil and vegetation (or even leveled flat), and streams that are bright orange from acid mine drainage and chemicals. Moreover, measures of health and human development in the region are typically well below what one finds across much of the country, as they have been for decades. In 2011, more than half of all children in West Virginia were considered low-income or poor.[4] Last year, a study of the "hardest places to live in America" based on data regarding education (percentage of residents with at least a bachelor's degree), median household income, unemployment rate, disability rate, life expectancy, and obesity indicated that six of the ten lowest ranking counties—that is, the places that are "hardest to live"—were located in Central Appalachia.[5]

For those unfamiliar with the history of the region or the dynamics of extractive industries worldwide, such a situation might present a conundrum: Why is an area that is apparently so rich in natural resources so poor in terms of human well-being? Is there truth in the stereotypes of Appalachians as backward hillbillies who are unsuited to contemporary life? On the contrary, a brief look at the way that Appalachia has functioned as a "resource colony" for outside interests will shed light on the dynamics that have shaped this region and how they mirror those which operate in parts of the "developing" world. Following an examination of this history, I'd like to look at one noteworthy statement from the Catholic Bishops of Appalachia, who took a theological stand against the destruction of land and communities in 1975. As the church receives Pope Francis's ecology encyclical some forty years later, it is worth revisiting this important milestone in the evolution of the church's ecological awareness, particularly in light of a new wave of resource development in the Appalachian region.

Resource Colony—Resource Curse?

Montani semper liberi—"mountaineers are always free"—is the motto of the state of West Virginia. In his history of the state, John Williams writes, "Whether or not mountaineers were always free, they were almost always poor. . . . They have tried in every age to find their way over, under, or through the barriers to prosperity that the mountains raised."[6] Had the Appalachian region been simply a place of wild and mountainous terrain, its fate might have been like that of other rural areas, with a small economy based on agriculture or tourism, but the mountains of Appalachia contain acres of valuable timber and large deposits of bituminous coal and shale gas. Although recent research documents an agrarian capitalism within the region as early as the eighteenth century,[7] large-scale development did not come to Appalachia until after the Civil War, when the need to fuel the nation's expanding industrial sector made the region's resources newly valuable.

While certain aspects of pre-industrial mountain life have been romanticized, it is undisputable that the corporate acquisition of land and mineral rights dramatically reshaped both the land and the life of the people of Appalachia. Rights to minerals were often given over through "broadform deeds" that allowed mineral owners to have rights of access to them by any and all means necessary. A century ago, this may have meant an access road and a mine opening in a hillside; today, these same deeds allow modern drilling equipment to do serious damage through surface mining. The move to strip mining and mountaintop removal mining, which has been fueled by technological development and a drive for greater profitability, has also meant a net loss of jobs in the industry because these forms of extraction are less labor-intensive than deep mining. They are at the same time far more destructive to the natural environment and consequently to the health of communities around them.[8] Some might argue that the development of the region's energy resources has provided extensive benefits both within and outside Appalachia, but these same resources have also been at the root of some of the region's most devastating problems, both economic and environmental. Williams writes, "In its repetitive cycle of boom and bust, its savage exploitation of men and nature, in its seemingly endless series of disasters, the coal industry has brought grief and hardship to all but a small few of the people whose lives it touched."[9]

It may seem a stretch to compare Appalachia to parts of the world that have experienced the brutality and injustice of colonialism,[10] but the idea of the region as an American "internal resource colony" or "energy sacrifice zone"[11] has been an important model among Appalachian scholar-activists.[12] Although the differences are significant, an important commonality between the Appalachian experience and that of former colonies is that ownership and control of the land is in the hands of investors and companies based elsewhere. As can be seen throughout the developing world, access to land and local control over its use are key variables in regional power dynamics and the well-being of rural people worldwide. "It is ownership that determines who is wealthy . . . and who is poor, who exploits and who is exploited by others," wrote the authors of the Appalachian Land Ownership Task Force report in the early 1980s.[13] The Task Force survey found that the top 5 percent of owners—most of whom were companies based in New York or London—held 62 percent of the land, in contrast to the bottom 5 percent of land holders who owned only 0.25 percent. With the consolidation of corporate entities into large national or multinational energy conglomerates, a single corporate decision can dramatically affect both the land and the communities that are based on and around it. Such decisions are seldom made with the good of the local community in mind.

The negative impacts of economies based on extraction and absentee ownership can be seen beyond Appalachia, as well. Though the theory of a "resource curse" is debated to some degree among political economists,[14] there is widespread evidence from many developing nations that natural resource abundance has a negative correlation to GDP and economic growth. "From the diamond mines of South and West Africa to the oilfields of Iraq and the timber-rich forests of the Amazon, millions of people in these resource-rich countries have seen their lives devastated by the mishandling of vast revenues from natural resources. This pattern has reaffirmed the well-established resource curse: resource-rich countries are less wealthy and less competently governed than those lacking in natural resources."[15] The paradox of a resource curse may be explained by the fact that local governments often encourage investment in a particularly profitable resource to the detriment of a more diverse and stable economy. Economic dependence on a single extractive industry can make it difficult to plan long-term because of the volatility of markets and the availability of resources themselves (as was the case in many "boomtowns" within the United States).[16] Moreover, such dependence tends to foster docility and desperation among workers, who may be willing to work for low wages, face health risks, and accept the primary burden of externalities such as damage to infrastructure and the environment, because work in the industry is perceived as necessary to the economic livelihood of the region. In other cases, the value of these resources and a nation or region's dependence on them can be a potent source of conflict and corruption.

Each of these factors has been a part of the history of Appalachia—but they are not the end of the story, for the region also has a rich history of activism and citizen resistance. From the early struggles of organized labor and the formation of the United Mine Workers of America, to current efforts at stopping mountaintop removal mining and holding companies accountable for environmental pollution, a vibrant and vocal minority has spoken out for justice in the region, including those who are motivated to speak out of their commitment to Christian faith in action.

Theological Reflections on Power and Powerlessness: The Catholic Committee of Appalachia

In the 1960s, John F. Kennedy's visit to West Virginia brought increased visibility to the issues faced by the region, which soon came to be understood as a major front in the nation's War on Poverty. The Commission on Religion in Appalachia (CORA) was established in 1965 as an ecumenical organization to focus Christian efforts to meet the needs of the people of the region. In 1970, a Catholic caucus was formed, which in 1972 became the Catholic Committee of Appalachia (CCA), "a network of lay, religious, and ordained Catholics working in a variety of 'social outreach' ministries in mountain communities."[17] Due to contact with both domestic and international liberationist movements of the 1960s and '70s (such as the civil rights movement, Black Power, antiwar and feminist movements, and Latin American theologies of liberation) as well as a new wave of regional activist scholarship, CCA's activity soon shifted from a paternalistic idea of "helping poor people" to an approach that can be described in terms of "accompaniment" and liberationist praxis emerging "from below."[18]

In addition to these movements, the leadership of women religious—in particular, that of the Glenmary sisters—was especially significant to the development of the Catholic Committee of Appalachia. As a result of their encounters with the people there, the Glenmarys developed an approach to ministry that involved listening to the people and learning from their struggles as the first and foundational step in relating to the communities that they were called to serve.[19] Inspired by the work of these sisters, in the spring of 1973 CCA members held listening sessions with over thirty groups, Catholic and non-Catholic, throughout Appalachia to hear the people's experience of injustice and their insights into possible solutions. A document based on these sessions was drafted by a young theology student in a free-verse style and was commented on by the CCA, the bishops of the region, and at least one thousand readers who raised important questions. Although *This Land Is Home to Me* was officially promulgated by the twenty-five bishops of Appalachia who signed the document in February 1975, its theological method and writing process represented a break from top-down Catholic social teaching, "such that the letter has been praised by liberation theologians as a liberationist approach to generating church teaching."[20] In his forthcoming dissertation, Michael Iafrate describes how the letter and its successor *At Home in the Web of Life* (1995) "represent popular expressions of a North American liberationist theology rooted in a particular geographical region, its diverse cultures with some sense of shared connection to place, and its peoples' dreams for liberation from social injustice and ecological devastation."[21]

In terms of its content, the letter's subtitle—"A Pastoral Letter on Powerlessness in Appalachia"—offers a clue to its major concern. Responding to "the cries of powerlessness" from Appalachia which are echoed in the suffering of the poor "across the earth" (10–11), the letter's sharpest critiques are directed at an economic system built upon the principle of profit maximization— "a principle which too often/ converts itself into an/ idolatrous power" (17).[22] "Profit over people/ is an idol" (17), the letter claims, and "those who claim that they are/ prisoners of the laws of economics/ only testify that they are prisoners/of the idol"

(19). Both within Appalachia and around the world, poor and "plain" people struggle to get by, while "corporate profits/ for the energy conglomerates,/ who control our energy resources,/ keep on skyrocketing" (20). This critique is set within a framework of biblical and Catholic social teaching, with particular emphasis on the preferential option for the poor and the dignity of the human person. Like Pope Francis's message in *Laudato Si'*, the Catholic Bishops of Appalachia were keenly attentive to the ways that the poor are most gravely affected by environmental degradation.

In its final section, the letter discusses a way forward through "dialogue and testing," stating that while the bishops do not have answers to all of the problems they address, they do offer several principles to guide the process—namely, closeness to the people, careful use of scientific resources, and "a steeping in the presence of the Spirit" (32). They write, "We must listen/ to the vast majority of plain people/ who would not be called poor,/ but who are not rich,/ and who increasingly share in the/ powerlessness of the poor" (32). The goal of all such listening is "citizen control, or community control" in which "the people themselves/ must shape their own destiny" (32).

Appalachia's Evolving Energy Landscape

Of course, the Appalachian energy landscape and the "ethic of extraction"[23] that has given it shape together constitute an important theme throughout the letter. Although the bishops write that Appalachia is "all tied together by the mountain chain/ and by the coal at its Center/ producing energy within it," they also note that there is more than just coal here: There are also timber, oil, farms, steel mills, chemical manufacturers, and gas (12). Indeed, though the coal industry still exerts significant power within the region, its economic centrality has declined sharply in recent years, with some 38,000 coal industry jobs in Kentucky and West Virginia eliminated since 1983[24] and coal production down 46 percent (from 226 to 127 million tons) between 2008 and 2013.[25] The explanation for coal's decline is multifaceted, but a primary reason is the growth in domestic supplies of natural gas, as horizontal drilling and "fracking" technologies have made this resource more readily available and profitable.[26] The national quest for energy independence and that much of northern and central Appalachia sits atop the

Marcellus Shale—a source of methane and other gases that can be used in heating, the generation of electricity, and other industrial uses—have renewed interest in the area, much as the drive for independence from foreign oil led to renewed interest in Appalachian coal in the 1970s. At that time, the CCA described how

> . . . The corporate giants
> turn their eyes
> to the mountains once again.
> Slowly, but powerfully,
> their presence rumbles in
> the heavy trod
> of the powerful among the powerful,
> those who control
> finance and credit
> information systems
> and energy resources. (16)

Anyone who has lived in the areas affected by the development of the Marcellus Shale in the past eight to ten years can appreciate the appropriateness of this statement: On a daily basis in many areas, one can observe the heavy, rumbling presence of tanker trucks and drilling equipment that are necessary for the extraction process and that symbolize the presence of powerful energy companies in the region. Both the number of well pads and the amount of gas produced have increased exponentially in recent years, igniting a fierce debate over the economic and environmental impacts of this development. Does natural gas represent a more secure and sustainable future for American energy needs and the economy of Appalachia? Or is this simply the latest iteration of its resource curse, a new wave of exploitation from outside[27] that preys on the desperation of this vulnerable region?

In a working paper on the economic impacts of shale gas drilling in the Marcellus region, David Kay (a senior associate with the Community and Regional Development Institute at Cornell University) argues that "neither riches nor ruin are inevitable" with respect to this resource, but much will depend on how such development is managed by the communities that are affected. He acknowledges that although the benefits of natural gas extraction are real, mixed results are likely even in the short run:

The rising tide is not likely to lift all boats: there will be losing constituencies among communities and individuals who are displaced or left behind. Moreover, the experience of many economies based on extractive industries is a warning that their short-term gains frequently fail to translate into lasting, community-wide economic development. Most alarmingly, in recent decades credible research evidence has grown showing that resource-dependent communities can and often do end up worse off than they would have been without exploiting their extractive sector reserves. When the metaphorical economic waters recede, the flotsam left behind can in some circumstances be seen more as the aftermath of a flood than of a rising tide.[28]

Much of Kay's analysis is concerned with the inadequacy of models predicting productivity and economic impacts as well as the long-term problems associated with dependence on a single industry, but others point to social and environmental problems associated with fracking. While the growth of new businesses and markets can appear to be positive, residents of areas experiencing this kind of growth describe how they have been priced out of the rental market due to the demand created by the "pipeliners," who are often transient, out-of-state workers with no ties to the area.

One article discussing the experience of communities affected by drilling states: "Fracking takes rural communities and turns them into industrial zones—and citizens have little recourse. . . . Operations can go on around the clock, with constant noise, light and air pollution. A cornerstone of the industrialization that comes with fracking is all the truck traffic—hundreds of trucks a day travel on country roads never built for large trucks or the amount of wear and tear."[29] The resources that drilling and fracking require are also a concern for many: The average well requires three to five million gallons of water to drill and frack, which is often taken from local streams and rivers. The management and disposal of the "flowback"—that is, the mix of water, chemicals, and naturally occurring radioactive and organic materials that returns to the surface following a fracking job—is a further concern. Whether the produced water is pumped underground into injection wells or transported to a treatment facility, it represents a significant danger to water supplies if not handled with extreme care.

Although some operators take this responsibility very seriously, the industry as a whole has not exactly inspired public confidence. According to citizen action groups such as PennEnvironment and FracTracker, gas companies in the region were cited for more than four thousand violations of regulations between 2008 and 2011, many of which posed a direct environmental threat.[30] It may be possible to develop the natural gas resources of Appalachia in a way that is less destructive to the land and its people than coal has been, but this will require vigilance and fortitude on the part of communities to hold powerful companies responsible for their actions and to encourage development that is diversified and sustainable.

Whether the development of natural gas will be a benefit or a catastrophe for the region remains an open question, and hope for the former is often difficult to sustain in light of the powerful interests at work pushing development in ways that seem irresponsible. As the Catholic bishops of the region wrote in 1975, "Despite the theme of powerlessness/ we know that Appalachia/ is already rich here/ in the cooperative power/ of its own people" (33). Tapping into that cooperative power will be essential to ensuring that the "wild and wonderful" hills of Appalachia are not reduced to a human and ecological wasteland—for if nothing else can be learned from looking at extractive economies in Appalachia and beyond, here one can see clearly that harm done to the land is also harm done to human people and communities. Building ecumenical and interfaith coalitions of concerned citizens will be essential to responsible development.

Some forty years after it was written, the concerns and language of *This Land Is Home to Me* are still powerful. In its attention to environmental justice and inequities of wealth and energy consumption, the letter demonstrates an ecological and global consciousness that was well ahead of its time. Its critiques of consumer culture and corporate media also ring as true as ever today. The letter's theological method of listening to the voices of the people was not only innovative in its time, but also was recently affirmed by Pope Francis, who told the Vatican's International Theological Commission that they should "humbly listen" to the concerns of the "ordinary faithful" in their theological work.[31] But the letter's most poetic and enduring moments call its readers to join the struggle to defend the dream "of a life free and simple" that is rooted in a sense of place and an understanding of land as not simply a commodity, but a home (21). Caring for the earth as Pope Francis has recently called for in *Laudato Si'* will require that all people of good will recognize that not only is the earth our "common home," but that *this* land—the local, particular places where we live and work and even the places that remain wild and untamed—is home *to me*.[32]

Notes

[1]Arthur Fallam, *A Journey from Virginia to beyond the Appalachian Mountains, in September 1671,* reprinted in *West Virginia: Documents in the History of a Rural-Industrial State,* by Ronald Lewis and John Hennen (Dubuque, IA: Kendall/Hunt 1991), 25.

[2]"Settling Thomas, West Virginia," www.historicthomaswv.com.

[3]This phrase was adopted as a state slogan in 1975. In 2006, under Governor Joe Manchin, the highway signs were changed to read "West Virginia: Open for Business." Within the year, thousands of people petitioned to have "Wild & Wonderful" put back on the signs.

[4]West Virginia Center for Budget and Policy, *Child Poverty in West Virginia: A Growing and Persistent Problem* (Charleston, WV, February 2013), 11.

[5]Alan Flippen, "Where Are the Hardest Places to Live in the U.S.?" *New York Times,* June 26, 2014, http://www.nytimes.com. The author notes that "this combination of problems is an overwhelmingly rural phenomenon. Not a single major urban county ranks in the bottom 20 percent or so on this scale, and when you do get to one—Wayne County, Mich., which includes Detroit—there are some significant differences. While Wayne County's unemployment rate (11.7 percent) is almost as high as Clay County's, and its life expectancy (75.1 years) and obesity rate (41.3 percent) are also similar, almost three times as many residents (20.8 percent) have at least a bachelor's degree, and median household income ($41,504) is almost twice as high."

[6]John A. Williams, *West Virginia: A History* (Morgantown: West Virginia University Press, 2001), 200.

[7]See Wilma Dunaway, *The First American Frontier: Transition to Capitalism in Southern Appalachia, 1700–1860* (Chapel Hill: University of North Carolina Press, 1996).

[8]"Not only has mountaintop removal permanently destroyed more than 500 Appalachian mountains, but people living near the destruction are 50% more likely to die of cancer and 42% more likely to be born with birth defects compared with other people in Appalachia" ("The Human Costs of Coal: Mountaintop Removal's Effect on Health and the Economy," West Virginia Highlands Conservancy, www.ilovemountains.org).

[9]Williams, *West Virginia*, 206.

[10]See David Walls, "Internal Colony or Internal Periphery? A Critique of Current Models and an Alternative Formulation," in *Colonialism in Modern America: The Appalachian Case,* ed. Helen M. Lewis (Boone, NC: Appalachian Consortium Press, 1978), 319–49.

[11]"Fairly or unfairly, Appalachia is often perceived as an energy sacrifice zone—a place where human lives are valued less than the natural resources

that can be extracted from the region," write Geoffrey Buckley and Laura Allen in "Stories about Mountaintop Removal in the Appalachian Coalfields," in *Mountains of Injustice,* ed. Michele Morrone and Geoffrey Buckley, (Athens: Ohio University Press, 2011), 171. See also Jedediah Purdy, "An American Sacrifice Zone," in the same volume.

[12]This model of "internal colony" is usually set in contrast to what is sometimes called a "culture of poverty" model: whereas the former recognizes the ways that a region has been subject to exploitation from outside forces, the latter blames the cultural "backwardness" of mountain people for their poverty. Scholars influenced by the colonial model have made fascinating comparisons between the racism directed toward colonized peoples in the global south and the rhetoric of inferior culture and "otherness" that was used to describe Appalachian people—rednecks and hillbillies—throughout the nineteenth and twentieth centuries (and which to some degree still shapes the wider popular imagination regarding the region). Although the notion of Appalachia as an "internal colony" has been discussed in many places, a classic collection of essays on the theme is Helen M. Lewis, ed., *Colonialism in Modern America: The Appalachian Case* (Boone, NC: Appalachian Consortium Press, 1978).

[13]Appalachian Land Ownership Task Force, *Who Owns Appalachia? Land Ownership and Its Impact* (Lexington: University Press of Kentucky, 1983), 2. Following major flooding in the region in the 1970s, the federally funded Appalachian Regional Commission (ARC) was formed, and in cooperation with local citizens' groups it undertook a survey of land ownership in the region, published in this report.

[14]The seminal statement of this thesis by Jeffrey D. Sachs and Andrew M. Warner ("Natural Resource Abundance and Economic Growth," NBER Working Paper #5398, October 1995, revised November 1997, www.cid.harvard. edu) has been called into question along several lines. One paper argues that it is not resource abundance but resource *dependence*—that is, an economy with significant dependence on one primary (or extractive) sector—that leads to a "curse." This is significant, as it means that underdevelopment is not inevitable, but a factor of a wider set of variables that are subject to human manipulation.

[15]Nadira Lalji, "The Resource Curse Revised," *Harvard International Review,* December 31, 2007, www. hir.harvard.edu.

[16]See, e.g., Brian Black's treatment of the boomtown of Pithole, PA, in "A Legacy of Extraction: Ethics in the Energy Landscape of Appalachia," in *Mountains of Injustice*, ed. Morrone and Buckley, 32–48.

[17]Michael J. Iafrate, "Decolonizing Appalachian Theology: Liberation and Beyond in the Post-Vatican II Grassroots Appalachian Church" (PhD dissertation proposal, University of Toronto, 2013), 2.

[18]Michael Iafrate, "Liberating Appalachian Theology: Paternalism and Praxis in Faith-Based Social Justice Movements in Appalachia" (paper presented at Appalachian Studies Association Annual Conference, Huntington, WV, March 2014), 7.

[19]"This listening posture furthered the sisters' 'conversion' and they continued to question and redefine their rules, constitutions, and mission, drawing scrutiny from the church hierarchy who eventually intervened. In response, 70 sisters left Glenmary and 44 of them decided to continue their work as

a new group called FOCIS, cutting themselves off from the institutional church, but finding new life in projects of activism, community building, and the arts" (ibid., 7–8).

[20]Ibid., 20. Here Iafrate cites the following: Gregory Baum, "Statement by Gregory Baum," in *Theology in the Americas*, ed. Sergio Torres and John Eagleson (Maryknoll, NY: Orbis Books, 1976), 390–93; Gregory Baum, "The Christian Left at Detroit," in *Theology in the Americas*, ed. Torres and Eagleson, 399–429; M. Shawn Copeland, "Reconsidering the Idea of the Common Good," in *Catholic Social Thought and the New World Order*, ed. Oliver F. Williams and John W. Houck (Notre Dame, IN: University of Notre Dame Press, 1993), 309–27.

[21]Iafrate, "Decolonizing Appalachian Theology," 3.

[22]All page numbers refer to the joint publication of *This Land Is Home to Me* and *At Home in the Web of Life* issued by CCA and available at www.ccappal.org.

[23]See Black, "Legacy of Extraction."

[24]Brad Plumer, "Here's Why Central Appalachia's Coal Industry Is Dying," *Washington Post,* November 4, 2013, www.washingtonpost.com.

[25]Ted Boettner, "7 Things You Need to Know about Why Coal is Declining in West Virginia," *WV Center on Budget and Policy Evidence Counts Blog,* October 23. 2014, www.wvpolicy.org.

[26]Hydraulic fracturing involves using a mixture of water, sand, and chemicals at high pressure to fracture shale and release the gases it contains. Although this technology itself is not new, the development of horizontal drilling technology that allows for access to a much greater volume of shale gas has been the key innovation enabling the utilization of formations like the Marcellus.

[27]The two companies most heavily involved in gas extraction in the Marcellus region are Range Resources and Chesapeake Energy, based in Texas and Oklahoma, respectively.

[28]David Kay, "The Economic Impacts of Marcellus Shale Drilling: What Have We Learned? What Are the Limitations?" (Cornell Working Paper Series, April 2011), 3. www.greenchoices.cornell.edu.

[29]Tara Lohan, "You Have to See It To Believe it: What It's Like to Have Fracking in Your Backyard," www.alternet.org.

[30]Edward Humes, "Fractured Lives: Detritus of Pennsylvania's Shale Gas Boom," *Sierra Magazine,* July/August 2012, www.sierraclub.org. See also information and graphics at www.fractracker.org.

[31]Associated Press, "Pope to Theologians: Listen to the Ordinary Faithful," December 5, 2014, www.cruxnow.com.

[32]The Catholic Committee of Appalachia remains active in the region today, through an annual fellowship and educational gathering as well as activism in issues of environmental and economic justice. In December 2014, the CCA issued a brief statement on systemic racism and police violence, and a statement on the protection of water resources is forthcoming. A "People's Pastoral" drawn from listening sessions around the region is also anticipated to commemorate the fortieth anniversary of *This Land Is Home to Me* in late 2015. See Sharon Abercrombie, "Pastoral Letter 'from the Trenches' Emerging in Appalachia," April 17, 2014, www.ncronline.org.

The Border between Wilderness and Garden

Cultivating a Benedictine Spirituality of the Land

Christine M. Fletcher

Benedictines live on the borderland of wilderness and garden. Historically, they have chosen sites for abbeys which would be on wastelands or in wilderness to achieve the seclusion, quiet, and withdrawal from the world that monasticism seeks. Once on the site, however, the community works together and creates gardens, pastures, and orchards in order to be self-supporting. This essay maintains that these environmentally friendly, sustainable communities grow out of Benedictine spirituality, which balances work and prayer, grows from a communal life, and practices stability, poverty, and stewardship of material goods.

These communities are facing a severe test in an age that has seen both far fewer monastic vocations and the loss of the vocation of the lay brother. In these circumstances, maintaining a self-sustaining monastery as envisioned by the Rule is almost impossible. However, faithfulness to Benedictine values regarding stewardship is still possible, and can guide monasteries as they face today's challenges. We can see this in the case of St. Procopius Abbey, located in suburban Chicago. The monks of St. Procopius Abbey faced a situation that demanded a radical change in land use. Their decisions and the values that guided their choices illustrate Benedictine stewardship and care for the environment.

Benedictine Stewardship, Wilderness, and Garden

The Benedictine relationship to the environment is a very different vision from that of St. Francis, the patron saint of ecology and modern environmental hero. Francis went beyond the harmony with nature that features in the stories of the saints such as Antony, Benedict and Cuthbert, and viewed himself as one with nature. His Canticle of the Sun, a poetic expression of an original Christian thinker, summarizes Francis's paradigm shift: "Rather than being at the top rung of the ladder of creation, Francis saw himself as part of creation. His spirituality overturned the spirituality of hierarchical ascent and replaced it with a spirituality of descending solidarity between humanity and creation."[1] Francis had a humble intimacy with the natural environment, the opposite of what most people understand as the biblical concept of dominion. His vision was of a truly radical dependence on God—a life of wandering evangelism that would require both absolute poverty and nonattachment to places or property.[2] The ideal life as envisioned by Francis resisted everything that Benedict valued: formal organization, permanent habitation, and extensive alteration of the environment.[3] Benedict himself followed the pattern of early monastic spirituality: withdrawal from the world (in Benedict's case to the cave at Subiaco), purgation, and transformation. This transformation was understood as bringing the person back to the state of Adam, when humanity and nature were at peace. This sort of dramatic, completely life-altering sanctity, as seen in the life of Benedict or in Francis, is rare. Knowing this, Benedict in his Rule sought to give a guide to ordinary people who are seeking God in a fallen world.

Bernard McGinn suggests that although Benedict himself may be an image of Adam, he is in his Rule closer to the figure of Noah, the first man to plant a vineyard. The covenant God makes with Noah repeats the primacy of man over animals:

> God blessed Noah and his sons, and said to them, "Be fruitful and multiply, and fill the earth. The fear and dread of you shall rest on every animal of the earth, and on every bird of the air, on everything that creeps on the ground, and on all the fish of the sea; into your hand they are delivered. Every moving thing that lives shall be food for you; and just as I gave you the green plants, I give you everything." (Gn 8:1–3 NRSVCE)

McGinn describes Noah as a type of a new though still fallen humanity, called to work out a more adequate living arrangement with the universe on the basis of divine providence. Such a living arrangement included both covenant and cult, and we find both these elements within the Rule of Benedict. The Rule is centered on worship: "from the cultic center of the monastic church, Benedictine resacralization radiates outwards. Of course that is the common task of all peoples; Benedict's insight is that it has to take place in a particular situation: so we get stability, limitation, localization, moderation and perseverance."[4]

Benedict sought to bring order out of disorder, which is not surprising for one who lived through a tumultuous age. The localization finds expression in the particular Benedictine vow of stability. Benedict was suspicious of the monks who claimed their vocation was to wander; he condemned these gyrovagues as "slaves to their own wills and gross appetites."[5] Benedictine stability is a challenge to the individual and the community; there is no running from the good or harm one has done to people or the environment. Benedict insisted on the importance of the monastery being self-contained, and limited the amount of contact the monk would have with the outside world. This is the battlefield of spiritual life, getting along with these people in this place for the rest of one's natural life. Benedictines are going to live and die in this place, and so care for the land was the heart of the community's work.

Into the sorry state of Europe in the sixth century, "Benedictinism brought a new system of order, a new pattern of life, a new commitment to the land and to life. Almost seven hundred years later, Cistercian groups again devoted themselves to reforestation, the replanting and the reclamation of some of the worst land in Europe."[6] Stability of the community is good for the land. "The Benedictine monk is the religious epitome of the patient peasant who in his dedication to tilling his own plot of land builds monuments that outlast kings and emperors."[7]

Manual work was a central part of the Benedictine life. Benedict begins the chapter on manual work with the clear statement that "idleness is the enemy of the soul."[8] Work and the discipline entailed by work were essential to growth in the spiritual life. "When they live by the labor of their hands, as our fathers and the apostles did, then they are really monks. Yet all things are to be done with moderation on account of the fainthearted."[9] Those who are weak or sick "should be given a type of work or craft that will keep them busy without overwhelming them."[10]

Work should make a garden out of the wilderness, thus making the monastery an image of Eden. Christ has redeemed humanity, and redeemed humanity in turn is called to work to bring nature back to the order and harmony of God's plan. We are called to tend the garden. Jean Leclerq describes the Benedictine attitude to nature:

> The cloister is a "true paradise," and the surrounding countryside shares in its dignity. Nature "in the raw," unembellished by work or art, inspires the learned man with a sort of horror: The abysses and peaks which we like to gaze at, are to him an occasion of fear. A wild spot, not hallowed by prayer and asceticism and which is not the scene of any spiritual life is, as it were, in a state of original sin. But once it has become fertile and purposeful, it takes on the utmost significance.[11]

Benedict saw the world as God's gift, but he saw work as a necessary part of the spiritual life. Benedictines live as co-creators, who get their sustenance from the land by adding their work to God's world. This is the same vision found in the documents of the Second Vatican Council, which called the laity to work to reorder the secular world to better reflect God's justice. The community's work was directed to the common good; rather than relying on the charity of others, the community, through work, should provide not only for their own needs but also for the "sick, children, guests and the poor."[12] Care for nature and care for other people are linked in the Benedictine vocation.

Benedict's understanding of stewardship permeates the Rule. His vision of material wealth and community makes present once again the early church of the Acts of the Apostles where the disciples held all things in common, and cared for those in need. While the community owned the land and tools and goods it needed, Benedict legislated against private ownership by the monk: "Above all, this evil practice must be uprooted and removed from the monastery. . . . All things should be the common possession of all, as it is written, so that no one presumes to call anything his own."[13]

But as we know, this can lead to the tragedy of the commons— what belongs to everyone is cared for by no one. To avoid this problem, the leaders of the community, the Abbot and the Cellarer, were to see that members had what they needed: clothing, bedding, and tools for their work. Those who need less are to thank God, and the one who needs more "should be humble because of his weakness, not self-important because of the kindness shown to him."[14]

The Rule gives explicit directions on keeping accurate inventory of goods, knowing to whom and for what purpose things were given, and tracking their return; no wasteful consumption in food, clothing, or tools was tolerated. A monastic who treated the goods of the monastery carelessly "should be reproved. If he does not amend, let him be subjected to the discipline of the rule."[15] The Cellarer is explicitly commanded to "regard all utensils and goods of the monastery as sacred vessels of the altar."[16]

Regarding goods as the sacred vessels of the altar shows us Benedict's understanding of dominion and stewardship. Dominion does not mean domination; it does not mean unlimited power to seek self-interest. Instead, it means being a good steward, a responsible co-creator who has duties and responsibilities toward all creation. Benedictine stability means that past and future generations as well as the physical environment of the monastery are always kept in mind. The Benedictine values of humility, poverty, and community act as a brake on the selfish desires that would consume without limit. For those not called to the heroic sanctity of St. Francis, Benedictine stewardship provides a model for everyone, whether lay or monastic, to truly care for the environment. Joan Chittister sums it up best:

> We are choosing between a philosophy of consumption that gobbles up the world for its own satisfaction and a philosophy of co-creation that is committed to preserving natural resources for the sake of those to come. . . . Clearly the whole world needs Benedictinism again, needs a mindset that cares for the tools of life "as if they were vessels of the altar."[17]

St. Procopius Abbey provides a case study of how these values were lived in the history and stewardship of the land when circumstances, such as falling vocations, meant that adjustments to the agricultural life of the monks were inevitable.

St. Procopius Abbey

St. Procopius Abbey was founded by the Benedictine missionary Boniface Wimmer. He was aware of the large Czech population in Chicago and the lack of priests who could minister to them in their own language. On March 2, 1885, monks were sent from St. Vincent's Abbey in Latrobe, Pennsylvania, to St. Procopius parish in the Pilsen neighborhood of Chicago, the largest Czech parish in the nation at the time. There they built a small priory, established a school and the Bohemian Benedictine Press. As the city continued to grow, the monks found their situation difficult. They had no room to expand, and "urban temptations had proven too strong for some of the monks."[18]

In April 1896, Abbot Valentine Kohlbeck traveled to the farmland west of Chicago and purchased the 104-acre Neff farm in Lisle. In 1897, the monks purchased the Rott farm, southeast of the abbey property. The community in Lisle grew till it consisted of the abbey; St. Procopius Academy, a boarding school; St. Procopius College, an orphanage for boys; and Sacred Heart Monastery, the women's community. The large Czech migration in the early years of the twentieth century meant that by 1938 St. Procopius had the largest number of professed brothers (32) in the American Cassinese Congregation, "a preeminence lasting a decade."[19] The lay brothers were the builders of the community—quite literally, for they were carpenters, farmers, plumbers, and handymen who built the buildings and furniture, tailored the habits, maintained the heating systems, and fed the community. Most of these lay brothers were of Czech or Slovak extraction and brought the wisdom of the peasant farmers and craftsmen with them to the monastery.

By the late 1950s, St. Procopius Abbey was actually five communities under the same roof: the priests; the clerics; the clerical novices; the "older brothers," those builders of the community whose primary language was Czech; and the "younger brothers," those newer members whose primary language was English. The brothers supported the work of the monks in the school and college with the produce of the farm.

The farm around that time cultivated 365 acres growing corn, wheat, barley, alfalfa, oats, and hay, in addition to the truck gardens and orchards. There was a herd of 150 head of Brown Swiss cows, 3,000 chickens, 500 turkeys, and a large number of hogs. A cannery begun in 1948 preserved the produce from the gardens and from expeditions to pick peaches in nearby orchards. The monks had forty beehives, which produced one ton of honey a year. The farm provided 100 percent of the milk and eggs, 65 percent of the beef, and 30 percent of the poultry served to the 1,000 monks and students. Unlike the abbey, college, and school, the farm property was assessed and was subject to tax, but the sale of produce, eggs, and meat was sufficient to meet this obligation.

The remaining 285 acres were improved pasture and woodland. These were the responsibility of Hilary Jurica, OSB, the first American Benedictine monk to obtain a PhD from a secular university, in his case in biology from the University of Chicago. In this phase of the abbey's history, they were truly following Benedict's Rule: "The monastery should, if possible, be so constructed that within it all necessities, such as water, mill and garden are contained, and the various crafts are practiced."[20] This community was demonstrating Benedictine stewardship and care for the environment by farming in a sustainable way, not pursuing cash crops and monoculture, but a traditional farming culture brought from Bohemia and enlightened by the science of the current day.

A Time of Change and Challenge

By the late 1950s, various forces converged on the abbey to disturb this seemingly idyllic state. Vocations to the lay brotherhood dried up, regulations regarding food production changed, religious life itself changed in the renewal of Vatican II, and the population in the western suburbs of Chicago grew dramatically.

The decrease in the number of new brothers meant that the average age of the brothers as a group was increasing. A smaller, older group of brothers was less capable of the ongoing physical labor of running a farm and monastery. At the same time, new regulations on the pasteurization of milk and the butchering of meat meant that much of the animal husbandry was no longer viable. The pig herd was gone by 1958, and the chickens a few years later. The dairy herd was next: On May 10, 1966, the last cow was sold, a day celebrated each year by Brother Sebastian Kuhn, one of the former dairymen.

The renewal of religious life following Vatican II also had a lasting impact. By 1966, the American Cassinese Congregation had received indults from the Congregation of Religious allowing communities to grant solemn vows and chapter rights to their nonordained members. This was received as a mixed blessing at St. Procopius. The older brothers had a tradition of spirituality based on the rosary, litany of the saints, and other prayers recited together in Czech. They had never been required to attend Divine Office or the Chapter meetings. The younger brothers followed that pattern of spirituality, but in English. With the reform, most of the younger brothers opted to profess solemn vows; one, however, refused, saying that "he had joined the abbey neither to be a songbird nor to engage in capitular talk-fests, but to do the physical work that would free his ordained confreres to exercise their priestly ministry."[21]

Postwar prosperity created a demand for housing in suburbs, such as Lisle, which had good train service to Chicago. Equally, the college and school were growing. Ben Hall, which had until then served as the monastery, college dormitory, and classroom building, was no longer adequate. A new abbey was needed for the monks—and outside the abbey, new homes were also needed for laypeople in Lisle.

Given all these factors, the community deliberated about the future of the farm. They wanted to use their resources in the best way for the abbey, the college and school, and the town of Lisle. As then Abbot Kucera explained:

> The question then was, What are we to do? do we simply find a buyer and get rid of the 600 acres and walk away from it? Or do we take a look around us, as our campuses were developing and as people were moving in, to see what's going to happen. . . . It was about that time that we started holding conversations with representatives from Four Lakes, with Paul Hoffman, and with Elmhurst-Chicago Stone and began to say—look, we have a unique opportunity and perhaps a responsibility as four major landowners in a highly developing locality to have some way of predicting what would

happen, rather than getting into a haphazard development zoned haphazardly as developers come in with diverse ideas for land use. This was an opportunity. And the community felt, I think rightly so, that it was a responsibility as well.

If we could have some input into what would happen in the so-called Green Trails area, we would be completing our sense of responsibility and complementing the work of the schools and the Abbey in this particular area, especially in terms of the environment and open space. It would be the kind of development that would be useful to the people who would live in the community but also to the kind of contemplative and reflective types of activities of the monastery and its educational apostolate.[22]

After many discussions, the community voted to sell the farm. Abbot Hugh Anderson, then a young monk, remembers spending the night weeping. To him, the land was the community; to give it up was like cutting off a limb.

Together, the four landowners commissioned planners for a common development known as Green Trails, a sustainable community. The plans called for single and multifamily housing, with open spaces for parks and recreation. Walking trails, lakes, parks, and other outdoor recreation areas made up 40 percent of the total land. The abbey donated 134.5 of its acres for these public amenities, including one of the lakes dug by the original monks on the site in the 1800s.

The entire development was oriented toward back yards rather than front. The monks believed that since people lived in their back yards, creating a system of walking trails accessible from those rear yards would protect children from road traffic. The result of this farsighted plan is a garden community with housing for all income levels. The Green Trails website notes, "An important historical fact is that Green Trails was not originally planned to be the high-priced, prestigious development that it has become."[23] The high-priced, prestigious development wasn't the monks' plan, but was the result of their designing a development that was and is very attractive to buyers.

The difference Benedictine stewardship makes is clearly visible in Green Trails in the large amount of common areas for people to gather, and in the mix of housing: large and small single-family units, low-rise condominiums, and high-rise apartment buildings. For an American suburb, this is a relatively economically diverse community, with local shops, schools, and walking paths, parks, and recreation areas.

How different the Benedictine vision is from the normal land use can be seen by comparing Green Trails to the new development west of Benedictine University, Arbor Trails. Arbor Trails is an example of a typical suburban development where the maximum number of single-family houses, within a high and relatively narrow price band, $300,000 to $700,000, is built on the smallest possible plot of land.[24] There is one very small green space and two large retention ponds. The community has a few trees on the borders, but no common playground or meeting space where a community would naturally gather. The idea of common land is minimized. Architecturally, the suburb reinforces the ethic of the consumerist society: large houses to store the consumer goods, large garages for the vehicles. Had the monks not discerned as a community how to dispose of their farmland, most of Lisle could look like this development. Abbot Hugh calls it "the abomination."

When they sold the farm for Green Trails, the monks retained 80 acres surrounding the abbey. This property faces the two main roads, and is primarily grass, which, in another example of Benedictine stewardship, is not treated with cosmetic pesticides. Some of the area east of the abbey is being restored as native prairie. Woodland runs to the east and south. The vineyard and the orchard to the south of the woodland were preserved, and today both are worked by volunteers, many of them oblates of the abbey. The peace of the abbey was preserved, good environmental practices followed, and the link to the land maintained, albeit in a new form.

Green Trails is an example of Benedictine stewardship of the environment in a situation when the agricultural life envisioned by Benedict could no longer be sustained. The long-range planning that went into Green Trails reflected the Benedictine value of stability: The monks were going to be there, and so were invested in planning for a sustainable future for themselves and their new neighbors. It also demonstrates the Benedictine value of community as a cooperative venture that benefited the original landowners as well as the new and existing residents of Lisle. It shows the Benedictine attitude to nature, which is under human care to meet human needs: The garden is balanced by the wilderness.

Notes

[1]Timothy Vining, "A Theology of Creation Based on the Life of Francis of Assisi," *Cord* 40 (1990): 105.

[2]Roger D. Sorrell, *St. Francis of Assisi and Nature: Tradition and Innovation in Western Christian Attitudes toward the Environment* (New York: Oxford University Press, 1988), 37.

[3]Ibid.

[4]Bernard McGinn, "Concepts of Nature, Land Stewardship and Stability in the Benedictine Tradition," in *The Benedictines of Lisle: Centennial Celebration of a Monastic Land Ideal* (Lisle: Illinois Benedictine College, 1986), 9.

[5]Timothy Fry, ed., *RB 1980: The Rule of St. Benedict in Latin and English with Notes* (Collegeville, MN: Liturgical Press, 1981), 171.

[6]Joan Chittister, foreword to *Listening to the Earth: An Environmental Audit for Benedictine Communities,* by William L. Bartlett, Margarita Dangel, Pat Lupo, and Annette Marshall (Erie, PA: Lake Erie-Allegheny Earth Force, 2006), vii.

[7]McGinn, "Concepts of Nature," 10.

[8]Fry, *RB 1980,* 249.

[9]Ibid., 249–51.

[10]Ibid., 253.

[11]Jean Leclercq, *The Love of Learning and the Desire for God: A Study of Monastic Culture* (New York: Fordham University Press, 1982), 130.

[12]Fry, *RB 1980,* 229.

[13]Ibid., 231.

[14]Ibid.

[15]Ibid.

[16]Ibid., 229.

[17]Chittister, foreword to *Listening to the Earth,* vii–viii.

[18]James Flint, "The Builders of the Community: The Lay Brother Vocation at St. Procopius Abbey," *American Benedictine Review* 55, no. 4 (December 2, 2004): 399.

[19]Ibid., 414.

[20]Fry, ed., *RB 1980,* 289.

[21]Flint, "Builders of the Community," 434.

[22]Daniel Kucera, "Green Trails: Land Stewardship and Suburban Development," in *The Benedictines of Lisle: Centennial Celebration of a Monastic Land Ideal* (Lisle: Illinois Benedictine College, 1986), 72.

[23]http://www.greentrails.org.

[24]In Green Trails, prices range from $100,000 for condominiums and from the low $200,000s up to the $700,000s for single-family homes. The average lot size is a third of an acre compared to a quarter acre in Arbor Trails.

Sisters in the Wilderness

Toward a Theology of Depression
with Delores Williams

Jessica Coblentz

"Midway through our life's journey, I went astray/ from the straight road and woke to find myself/ alone in a dark wood. How shall I say/ what wood it was! I never saw so drear, so rank, so arduous a wilderness!/ Its very memory gives shape to fear."[1] The opening lines of Dante's *Inferno* are a popular reference in memoirs about depression.[2] They present one of many wilderness images found throughout contemporary autobiographical literature about this mental health condition. Therese Borchard, recalling her struggles with anxiety and depression, wrote that she "felt [her] way, blindfolded, through the woods of depression and anxiety."[3] When Andrew Solomon wrote about what he would have done at the depth of his depression had friends and family not taken responsibility for his care, he mused, "I would have found a place to lie down in the woods and would have stayed there until I froze and died."[4] Jeffery Smith called depression "another landscape."[5] It is a dark, mountainous, "impassable wilderness of flowerless, tangled limbs and harsh thistles."[6]

In an essay exploring "melancholic" landscapes, philosopher Jennifer Radden argued that visual motifs in art bridge natural scenes and our understandings of experiences like depression.[7] We call a landscape "melancholic" when it exhibits the pictorial language of "darkness" and "dreariness" that we often employ to describe melancholy.[8] Something similar is at work in how the depressed use wilderness language. The forest wilderness is dark, and metaphors of darkness pervade sufferers' descriptions of

193

depression. Depression is a "black struggle,"[9] a "harrowing darkness,"[10] a "black despondency,"[11] an "abyss,"[12] a "dark night."[13]

For many who experience depression—a condition that is
notoriously difficult to convey—the wilderness image, especially
the forest wilderness, expresses something about what it is like to
be depressed.[14] Depression, like the woods, is lonely,[15] harsh, and
inhospitable; it can feel endless, skewing one's sense of time,[16] and
its unpredictability leaves people feeling utterly helpless in their
circumstances.[17] Other qualities of depression, such as fatigue,
anhedonia, recurrent thoughts of death, self-hatred, and guilt elude
our typical associations with the forest.[18] Yet the ubiquity of the
wilderness in depression narratives and the correlation of so many
depression symptoms with our experiences of the forest evince its
effectiveness for conveying what depression is like for so many.

The image of depression as wilderness also offers us an avenue
into theological reflection. Delores Williams took up the wilderness
as a theological starting point in *Sisters in the Wilderness: The
Challenge of Womanist God-Talk*, in which she read the biblical
story of Hagar's journey in the wilderness through the lens of
African American women's experience.[19] What resulted was an
account of God's accompaniment of those enduring a "wilderness
experience." According to Williams, this "wilderness experience"
is ambivalent because it contained the healing presence of God
and immense danger and suffering.

In addition to the resonances between depressive experience
and the wilderness already mentioned, Williams's unique charac-
terization of wilderness illuminates another theological correlate
between depression and the wilderness. I demonstrate that, precisely in its ambivalence, the wilderness experience of depression
is similar to black women's wilderness experience.[20] Furthermore,
Williams showed that this ambivalence has soteriological implications. Following her lead, I argue that theologies of depression need
Williams's survivalist/quality-of-life soteriology to supplement the
liberationist soteriology that dominates contemporary theological
responses to suffering.

Williams's Ambivalent Wilderness

Williams was originally drawn to Hagar's story because of its
prominence in the tradition of African American biblical inter-

pretation. She recognized numerous features that explained her community's resonance with Hagar. Like many black women in American history, Hagar was a slave. Hagar was also forced into surrogacy like many American slave women and the generations of black domestic workers who raised white children.

In addition, Hagar's journey in and out of the wilderness resonated with the unique symbolism of wilderness in African American experience.[21] In the antebellum period, wilderness was a refuge for escaped slaves and a physical place known for encounters with God.[22] The wilderness took on a different meaning in the lives of newly emancipated African Americans in the postbellum era, however. Wilderness symbolized the economic, political, and social strife of the unfamiliar world into which African Americans ventured.[23] Thus, for African Americans in the postbellum period, wilderness had both positive and negative connotations: It was a sacred place where one encountered God, as well as a symbol for the harsh reality that greeted them in the postbellum United States.[24]

In Hagar's story, Williams recognized a similarly ambivalent wilderness experience: Hagar's wilderness contained the healing presence of God and immense suffering. Capturing this tension well, Williams defined wilderness as "a symbolic term used to represent a near-destruction situation in which God gives personal direction to the believer and thereby helps her make a way out of what she thought was no way."[25]

Readers meet Hagar in Genesis 16:1–16, where Sarai, the barren wife of Abram, gave Hagar to her husband for childbearing. When Hagar became pregnant with her son, Ishmael, Sarai was jealous and treated her slave harshly. The abuse compelled Hagar to flee from her slaveowners into the wilderness. There, pregnant and without the support and physical sustenance that she needed, Hagar encountered God.[26] Surprisingly, Yahweh instructed Hagar to return to the house of Abram. "Go back to your mistress and submit to her," Yahweh ordered (16:9). This is "no liberator God," noted Williams.[27] But it was a God who was concerned with Hagar's well-being. God promised Hagar the survival of her progeny, and Williams suggested that it was God's commitment to the flourishing of Hagar and her family that motivated the directive to return to the slaveowners she fled (16:10). Without the stability of Abram's household, the survival of Hagar and her son would have been unlikely.

Genesis 21:9–21 picks up Hagar's story again. Sarai—now Sarah—had birthed her own son, Isaac. On watching Ishmael and Isaac play together, Sarah ordered Abram—now Abraham—to cast out Hagar and her son. God instructed Abraham to concede to Sarah's request, promising that Ishmael would inherit a great nation of his own. Hagar and her son were exiled and found themselves in the wilderness again. When their water dwindled, Hagar cried out to God to spare her child. God comforted Hagar, instructing her on how to care for her son and then "open[ing] her eyes" to a well (21:19). "God was with the boy" as he grew up in the wilderness. Ishmael became an "expert with the bow," which enabled him and his mother to survive their inhospitable environment (21:20).

In the second part of Hagar's story, God again did not act as readers might expect or desire. Although Hagar and Ishmael did in fact survive, they did not return to any sort of community or civilization; rather, they survived in the wilderness. Yet Williams exhorted readers to take up the "black American community's way of appropriating the Bible so that emphasis is put upon God's response to black people's situation rather than upon what would appear to be hopeless aspects of African American people's existence in North America."[28] This is a hermeneutic of Christian hope that Williams called a "survival/quality-of-life" approach, and it engendered soteriological insights that would challenge the liberationist tradition that dominated the black theology of her day.

Delores Williams on Salvation in the Wilderness

The black liberationist tradition emphasized God's salvific work as our liberator from sin and from the effects of evil in history, especially social oppression. Whereas liberation soteriology located God's work in freedom from suffering, Williams's survivalist soteriology expanded African American soteriology to include the ways that God's grace assists us amid persistent oppression.

We witness the value of this soteriological shift in Williams's reading of the Hagar story. The story, read solely through a liberationist lens, is absent of salvation, for God did not liberate Hagar and her son. In contrast, Williams's survival/quality-of-life approach asserted that liberation is not the only way that God relates to the oppressed. She emphasized how God aided Hagar and Ishmael's survival by sending them back to food, shelter, and the community of Abram's house. God opened Hagar's eyes to the resources she needed to survive in the wilderness, such as the water she and her son desperately needed. God accompanied Ishmael as he grew into a hunter who could protect and provide for his family in the wilderness. God did not liberate Hagar and her son from the oppression of the wilderness, but God enabled survival and a better quality of life for them there. For Hagar and Ishmael—and Williams's African American sisters—survival was part of salvation.

In contrast to liberation's emphasis on God's agency, the survival/quality-of-life hermeneutic also drew out the role of human agency in salvation. Hagar spoke boldly to God throughout her story, initiating God's assistance. What's more, God repeatedly assisted Hagar and Ishmael in actualizing their own survival. While God offered instructions, opened Hagar's eyes to survival resources, and provided Ishmael with hunting skills, it was Hagar and Ishmael themselves who faithfully employed the resources afforded to them.[29]

Williams's soteriological shift stemmed from the ambivalence of wilderness experience. A liberationist soteriology presumes that God's salvific work resides in God removing people from the wilderness. This overlooks how God works in and through the wilderness experience of suffering. To be sure, attention to God's work in and through suffering is not motivated by beliefs that God works only in and through suffering, or that God does not dwell outside of wilderness experience. It is because African American women live so much of their lives in the wilderness that Williams focused on how God works amid suffering, something the liberationist tradition too easily overlooked.

Those who live with depression—a condition that is chronic, recurrent, and incurable for many—also spend much of their lives in the wilderness. Many long for deliverance from depression, in accord with the tradition of liberation theology. Yet in the process of making sense of their extended and repeated suffering, many also identify goods that depression engenders, including greater compassion for others,[30] deeper spirituality,[31] a new experience of community and care from those around them,[32] and a better quality of life in the long run.[33] Firsthand accounts of depression share the ambivalence of profound suffering and the work of God's grace. Often, sufferers do not confine grace to deliverance from suffering. They testify to the good that arose amid their suffering. For this reason, I consider how survivalist/quality-of-life soteriology may better suit a theology of depression than the liberationist approach that one might typically look to for developing a project on suffering and salvation today.

Soteriological Insights for a Theology of Depression

Williams's exploration of the wilderness experience showcased the complexities of suffering, and it raised the question of whether liberation is adequate for conveying God's salvific work in response to such complicated wilderness experiences. Since the publication of *Sisters in the Wilderness*, others have echoed Williams in questioning whether a liberation soteriology is sufficient for addressing the complexities of suffering. In the remainder of the essay, I engage theological responses to liberation soteriology that deepen and expand Williams's soteriological insights about ambivalent suffering. In the process, I will demonstrate their relevance to developing a soteriology in the context of depression.

My first concern follows Williams's insight that a liberationist soteriology oversimplifies salvation as freedom from suffering. This has led some theologians to charge that liberationist thinking reinscribes the stigmatization of suffering bodies. Nancy Eisland, author of *The Disabled God*, raised this concern in a theology of disability.[34] The logic of liberationist thinking posits that God frees us from the imperfections of evil that pervade our world. Where disabled bodies are cast as "imperfect," salvation is construed as liberation from the disabled body. This view of salvation reinforces the social stigmatization of disabled bodies, linking them to the sin and evil from which we need liberation. Theologian Grace Jantzen articulated a similar concern about Christian soteriological discourse. She went so far as to suggest that we rid ourselves of the language of "salvation" because it is too often used to demean and dismiss the body as something from which we need liberation.[35]

A liberationist soteriology of depression runs the risks that Eisland and Jantzen identified. As with disability, the stigma of depression is a source and magnifier of suffering for those living with this condition. A liberationist framework that positions depression as something from which we need liberation risks reinscribing social norms that already deem depression an evil.

Now, it is conceivable to construct a liberation soteriology that obviates bodily stigma. However, the insights of Eisland and Janzten shed light on a more vexing question: Does salvation merely reside in delivering our bodies from suffering? Those living with long-term conditions like disability and depression offer complicated replies. Nobody experiences depression as a good; by definition, it feels terrible. For many who experience it recurrently, however, they reach a point of ambivalence. Depression is at once a source of immense suffering, and, as a permanent dimension of their lives, it is a context for growth and transformation. To conceive of salvation in a way that postpones it until death (when we will be free of all suffering) is to ignore the more complicated relationship to suffering that many depression sufferers experience. We need a theology that acknowledges the difficulty of depression without casting salvation merely as an escape from suffering and all that it brings.

I also question the sufficiency of liberation because it implies a binary distinction between suffering and liberation, between creation's fallen state and salvation. Such a binary glosses over the ongoing salvific work of God's grace amid persistent suffering. This was a central concern of Williams, and Shelly Rambo drew attention to it in *Spirit and Trauma*, where she observed that redemption is often construed as a two-step process from the cross to resurrection.[36] Rambo challenged the applicability of this soteriological model for survivors of trauma who live between the cross and resurrection.[37] Like trauma, depression is often a persistent condition. Subsequently, a liberationist view of God's relation to suffering could leave the depressed on their knees, waiting for liberation and God's presence in their lives. A theology of depression needs a more capacious soteriological vision that invites sufferers to witness to and participate in the salvation always unfolding in their lives, even amid the wilderness.

Williams's survival/quality-of-life soteriology obviates the pitfalls of a liberationist soteriology while offering an alternative vision of God's work for the widespread, complex, and persistent suffering of depression. First, Williams's interpretation of Hagar's story presented a God who accompanies sufferers amid suffering that does not necessarily go away. God did not liberate Hagar from the wilderness, just as many never live beyond the bounds of depression. But God pointed Hagar toward the means by which she could live a better life. For depression sufferers, such resources may include medication, therapy, support groups, and any number of other coping strategies that improve their quality of life. Just as God provided Hagar with a skillful son who would aid the family's survival, so too God strengthens caregivers to support the depressed in times of need.

Because Williams's survivalist soteriology recognizes the suffering body as a site of salvation rather than an obstacle to it, her project obviates the weakness of a liberation approach identified by Eisland and Jantzen. It is not in the eradication of these needs and vulnerabilities that divine salvation unfolds. Salvation does not reside in liberation from the body. In Hagar's story, God uses embodied agency as a means for salvation. Because depression is defined by feelings of self-hatred, inappropriate guilt, and a loss of free will, this affirmation of human agency sends an especially profound message to those who suffer. Williams's reading of the Hagar story shows that small acts—from crying out to God, to acquiring food and water, to seeking out help from those who have resources of support—were the difference between death and survival. So too among the depressed. God uses even the smallest actions for salvation.

Williams suggested that God not only empowered acts of survival, but also Hagar's actions of resistance. Williams's interpretation suggests that God would likewise empower the sufferers of depression to resist the social mores that magnify their struggles. Social resistance is a component of a survivalist soteriology in addition to personal survival and quality of life.

Revealed by God's Grace

Like the wilderness of Hagar and African American women, depression is a "near-destruction situation in which God gives personal direction to the believer."[38] God helps the depressed "make a way out of what she thought was no way" through vital provisions and by gracing even the smallest acts of self-affirmation, including acts of resistance to one's personal and social suffering.[39] It is Williams's survivalist/quality-of-life hermeneutic that gives us the eyes to see the wilderness of depression as an ambivalent space that is nonetheless a land of salvation for those who live in it.

Let me emphasize that although Williams argued for a survival/ quality-of-life hermeneutic and soteriology, she maintained that God relates to the oppressed in both a liberationist and survival- ist fashion at the same time.[40] The Hebrew Scriptures' numerous, often entangled conceptions of God's relation to creation bolster Williams's suggestion.[41] Her motivation was not the absolute rejection of liberationist soteriology, but rather "the issue is an understanding of biblical accounts about God that allow various communities of poor, oppressed black women and men to hear and see the doing of the good news that is meaningful for their lives."[42] Likewise, I believe Williams's survival/quality-of-life read- ing of Hagar's story reveals an account of meaningful good news about God for those who suffer with depression.

I opened this essay with Dante's description of a dark, bitter wilderness. I conclude by repeating those words with the addi- tion of his next, more hopeful stanza. The addition of this stanza captures something about what I have drawn out of Williams's reading of the Hagar story—namely, that a survivalist hermeneutic can help us see what God reveals for our salvation in the wilder- ness. Dante wrote: "Midway through our life's journey, I went astray/ from the straight road and woke to find myself/ alone in a dark wood. How shall I say/ what wood it was! I never saw so drear, so rank, so arduous a wilderness!/ Its very memory gives shape to fear./ Death could scarce be more bitter than that place!/ But since it came to good, I will recount/ all that I found there revealed by God's grace."[43]

Notes

[1] Dante Alighieri, *Inferno*, trans. John Ciardi, Modern Library Edition (New York: Random House, 1996), 3–4.

[2] See Therese J. Borchard, *Beyond Blue: Surviving Depression & Anxi- ety and Making the Most of Bad Genes* (New York: Center Street, 2009), 129–30; Jeffery Smith, *Where the Roots Reach for Water: A Personal and Natural History of Melancholia* (New York: North Point Press, 1999), 74; and William Styron, *Darkness Visible: A Memoir of Madness* (New York: Vintage Books, 1992), 83.

[3] Borchard, *Beyond Blue*, xxvi.

[4] Andrew Solomon, *The Noonday Demon: An Atlas of Depression* (New York: Scribner, 2001), 66.

[5] Smith, *Where the Roots Reach for Water*, 30.

⁶Ibid., 62–65.

⁷Jennifer Radden, *Moody Minds Distempered: Essays on Melancholy and Depression* (Oxford: Oxford University Press, 2009).

⁸Ibid., 182.

⁹Styron, *Darkness Visible*, 83.

¹⁰Borchard, *Beyond Blue*, 92

¹¹Styron, *Darkness Visible*, 31.

¹²Borchard, *Beyond Blue*, 176; Solomon, *Noonday Demon*, 28, 133; Styron, *Darkness Visible*, 72, 84.

¹³Borchard, *Beyond Blue*, 3, 45, 128; Solomon, *Noonday Demon*, 145, 225. For additional examples see Kathryn Greene-McCreight, *Darkness Is My Only Companion: A Christian Response to Mental Illness* (Grand Rapids, MI: Brazos Press, 2006); Kay Redfield Jamison, *An Unquiet Mind: A Memoir of Moods and Madness* (New York: Vintage Books, 1995); Martha Manning, *Undercurrents: A Life Beneath the Surface* (New York: HarperOne, 1994). Meri Nana-Ama Danquah criticizes the widespread use of "blackness" as a metaphor for the negative dimensions of depression. See *Willow Weep for Me: A Black Woman's Journey through Depression* (New York: One World, 1998).

¹⁴David Karp, *Speaking of Sadness: Depression, Disconnection, and the Meaning of Illness* (Oxford: Oxford University Press, 1996), 12, 28; Smith, *Where the Roots Reach for Water*, 21; Styron, *Darkness Visible*, 36–37.

¹⁵James Aho and Kevin Aho, *Body Matters: A Phenomenology of Sickness, Disease, and Illness* (Lanham, MD: Lexington Books, 2008), 116–20.

¹⁶Ibid., 49–53; Matthew Ratcliffe, "Varieties of Temporal Experience in Depression," *Journal of Medicine and Philosophy* 37, no. 2 (2012): 114–38.

¹⁷Matthew Ratcliffe, "Depression and the Phenomenology of Free Will," in *Oxford Handbook of Philosophy and Psychiatry* (Oxford: Oxford University Press, 2014), 574–91.

¹⁸My presentation of depression combines insights from Western medicine, psychoanalysis, and phenomenology. For a thorough account of depression, see Ian H. Gotlib and Constance L. Hammen, eds., *Handbook of Depression*, 3rd ed. (New York: Guilford Press, 2014) for Western medicine; Sigmund Freud, "Mourning and Melancholy," in *The Freud Reader*, trans. Peter Gay (New York: W. W. Norton, 1989), 584–88, and Julia Kristeva, *Black Sun*, translated by Leon Roudiez, reprint ed. (New York: Columbia University Press, 1992) for psychoanalysis; Matthew Ratcliffe, *Experiences of Depression: A Study in Phenomenology* (Oxford: Oxford University Press, 2015) for phenomenology. Also depression manifests differently across cultures. For the sake of brevity I focus on contemporary Western iterations; see Arthur Kleinman and Byron Good eds., *Culture and Depression: Studies in the Anthropology and Cross-Cultural Psychiatry of Affect and Disorder* (Berkeley: University of California Press, 1985).

¹⁹Delores S. Williams, *Sisters in the Wilderness: The Challenge of Womanist God-Talk* (Maryknoll, NY: Orbis Books, 1993).

²⁰Williams invites theologians outside black theology, such as myself, to engage her notion of "wilderness experience." See *Sisters in the Wilderness*, 127–57. However, I hope it is clear that the African American female experi-

ences that informed Williams's original notion of wilderness experience cannot be reduced to the experiences of depression, or vice versa.

[21]I am indebted to Emily A. Holmes for her incisive analysis of "wilderness experience" in "Delores Williams' Theology of the Wilderness Experience: Incarnation in the Wild," *Union Seminary Quarterly Review* 48, no. 3–4 (2004): 13–26.

[22]Williams, *Sisters in the Wilderness*, 103–4.

[23]Ibid., 103–6.

[24]Ibid., 104–6.

[25]Ibid., 103.

[26]Genesis 16:7 states that "the angel of Yahweh" appears to Hagar. Drawing on biblical commentaries, Williams explained that the angel of Yahweh is not distinct from God, but is God in visible form. See Williams, *Sisters in the Wilderness*, 19.

[27]Williams, *Sisters in the Wilderness*, 20.

[28]Ibid., 5.

[29]Williams does not reduce salvation to human agency. See Catherine Keller's consideration of Williams's distinction between the agency of creation and God in "Delores Williams: Survival, Surrogacy, Sisterhood, Spirit," *Union Seminary Quarterly Review* 48, no. 3–4 (2004): 86–87.

[30]Manning, *Undercurrents*, 171; Solomon, *Noonday Demon*, 436.

[31]Solomon, *Noonday Demon*, 130–33, 441; Tim Farrington, *A Hell of A Mercy: A Meditation on Depression and the Dark Night of the Soul* (New York: HarperOne, 2009); Borchard, *Beyond Blue*, 122–23.

[32]Manning, *Undercurrents*, 146, 151, 186; Solomon, *Noonday Demon*, 436.

[33]Danquah, *Willow Weep for Me*, 265–66; Manning, *Undercurrents*, 161; Solomon, *Noonday Demon*, 437–41; Borchard, *Beyond Blue*, 128–29, 159.

[34]Nancy L. Eisland, *Disabled God: Toward a Liberatory Theology of Disability* (Nashville, TN: Abingdon, 1994).

[35]Grace M. Jantzen, *Violence to Eternity*, ed. Jeremy Carrette and Morny Joy (New York: Routledge, 2009), 205–18. See also Elaine Graham, "Redeeming the Present," in *Grace Jantzen: Redeeming the Present*, ed. Elaine L. Graham (Burlington, VT: Ashgate, 2009), 9–11.

[36]Shelly Rambo, *Spirit and Trauma: A Theology of Remaining* (Louisville, KY: Westminster John Knox, 2010).

[37]Drawing on Hans Urs von Balthasar and Adrienne von Speyr, Rambo called trauma a "Holy Saturday" space. Notable for this conference, Balthasar described Holy Saturday as a "wildness." See Rambo, *Spirit and Trauma*, 51n18.

[38]Williams, *Sisters in the Wilderness*, 103.

[39]Ibid.

[40]Ibid., 172, 176.

[41]See Denis Edwards, *What Are They Saying about Salvation?* (New York: Paulist Press, 1986), 3–13; Joel B. Green, *Salvation* (St. Louis, MO: Chalice, 2003); and Gerard O'Collins, *Jesus Our Redeemer: A Christian Approach to Salvation* (Oxford: Oxford University Press, 2007), 1–18.

[42]Williams, *Sisters in the Wilderness*, 176.

[43]Dante, *Inferno*, 3–4.

Contributors

Regina A. Boisclair, professor of religious studies and Cardinal Newman Chair of Theology at Alaska Pacific University, Anchorage, AK, earned her PhD from Temple University, STM and MDiv from Yale University, Élève Titulaire at the École Biblique and MA from Providence College. Publications include: *The Word of the Lord at Mass: Understanding the Lectionary*, LTP, 2015; "The Lectionary: A Canon within the Canon," in *Anselm Academic Study Bible*; "Amnesia in the Catholic Sunday Lectionary: Women Silenced from the Memory of Salvation History" and "Conflicting Messages? Sunday Lections and Official Church Teachings " in annual volumes of the College Theology Society.

Agnes M. Brazal obtained her STL/MA and STD/PhD in Theology at the Katholieke Universiteit Leuven. She is co-founder and past president of the Catholic Theological Society of the Philippines, former Coordinator of the Ecclesia of Women in Asia, and currently associate professor at De la Salle University, Manila, Philippines. She is co-author of *Intercultural Church: Bridge of Solidarity in the Migration Context* and co-editor of *Feminist Cyberethics in Asia: Religious Discourses on Human Connectivity* and has published numerous articles in anthologies and journals such as *Theological Studies, Concilium, Questions Liturgiques, Asian Christian Review, Asian Horizons*, and *Hapag*. Her awards include a senior research fellowship at the Center for World Catholicism and Intercultural Theology, DePaul University in 2012, and the 2003 MWI (Institute of Missiology, Missio, Aachen) prize for the international academic essay contest on Contextual Theology and Philosophy. She has been a planning committee member of the Catholic Theological Ethics in the World Church since 2007, board member of the Institute for Church and Social Issues, editorial board member of the journals *Asian Christian Review* and *Budhi*, and international advisory board member of *Louvain Studies*.

Julia Brumbaugh is an associate professor of religious studies at Regis University in Denver, Colorado. She holds a PhD from Fordham University in contemporary systematic theology. She is co-editor of *Turnings: Theological Reflections on a Cosmological Conversion: Essays in Honor of Elizabeth A. Johnson* (forthcoming), and is active in the Catholic Theological Society of America where she is a co-convener of the Women's Consultation in Constructive Theology. Her teaching and writing focus on Christian spiritualities and ecclesiology.

Colleen Mary Carpenter is an associate professor of theology and the Sister Mona Riley Endowed Chair of the Humanities at St. Catherine University in St. Paul, MN. She has an MA in English literature from the University of Wisconsin-Madison, an MA in theology from the University of Chicago Divinity School, and her PhD, in religion and literature, is also from the University of Chicago. She is author of *Redeeming the Story: Women, Suffering, and Christ* (2004) and various articles on ecotheology and ecospirituality, suffering, the religious imagination, and women's experiences of God. She is currently finishing work on an undergraduate textbook titled *Is the Earth Holy? An Introduction to Ecotheology*.

Jessica Coblentz is a PhD candidate in systematic theology at Boston College. Her dissertation examines depression as a starting point for theological reflection, critiques dominant trends in contemporary discourses about suffering and salvation, and retrieves insights from the Christian tradition for a constructive soteriology. Her other research explores feminist and black theologies, theologies of the body, narrative and theology, and eschatology. Coblentz's popular writing has appeared online at *Patheos, God's Politics, Religion & Politics*, and *Daily Theology*, and in print in *Catechetical Leader Magazine* and *From the Pews in the Back: Young Women in Catholicism* (2009).

Mary Doak is an associate professor of theology at the University of San Diego. She has an MA and a PhD in theology from the University of Chicago Divinity School, and an Honors BA from Loyola University of Chicago. Her publications include *Translating Religion* (2013), co-edited with Anita Houck, and *Reclaiming Narrative for Public Theology* (2004), as well as various articles on public theology, eschatology, and ecclesiology. She is currently working on a book in public ecclesiology, addressing the specific challenges the twenty-first century raises for the mission of the church.

Christine M. Fletcher is an associate professor of theology at Benedictine University and an oblate of St. Procopius Abbey, Lisle, IL. She holds a master's in politics and philosophy from Oxford University and a PhD in theology with subspecialties in business ethics and literature from Anglia Ruskin University in Cambridge, England. She has worked in various fields, including merchant banking and IT consulting, and has edited a magazine on business ethics. She is the author of *The Artist and the Trinity*, which discusses Dorothy L. Sayers's theology of work, and *24/7 Christian: The Secular Vocation of the Laity*.

David Gentry-Akin, a priest of the Diocese of Stockton, is professor of Roman Catholic theology at Saint Mary's College of California, where he is in his twenty-second year of ministry. Dave holds the MDiv from the University of Notre Dame, and the pontifical STL and STD from the Katholieke Universiteit Leuven (Belgium), and is currently serving as the executive director for National Conventions of the College Theology Society. A fundamental systematic theologian, Dave's teaching and research interests include questions around the nature and existence of God and the claims posed by various forms of atheism; mining the ancient and classical tradition to recover diverse ways of imaging and talking about God; ecological and feminist theology; the genius of the Catholic imagination; the relationship between science and theology; the future of Catholic higher education; and the study of early Christian Rome as a source of insight into the nature of Catholic thought and belief.

Katherine A. Greiner is a PhD candidate in theology and education at Boston College School of Theology and Ministry and currently teaches in the theology department at Carroll College in Helena, Montana. Her current research focuses on questions concerning identity, charism, spirituality, and mission in Catholic colleges and universities founded and sponsored by women religious communities. Her research interests include Christian spirituality in contemporary society and education, American Catholicism, and feminist and contextual theologies. She currently serves on the editorial board for the blog *Daily Theology*.

Elizabeth Groppe is an associate professor at Xavier University in Cincinnati, Ohio, where she teaches systematic theology. She received her PhD from the University of Notre Dame, where she was a participant in a program that took students to an international gathering of Jews and Christians at the Centre for Dialogue and Prayer in Oświecim, Poland, near Auschwitz. Her publications include the book *Yves Congar's Theology of the Holy Spirit* and articles on trinitarian theology, Jewish-Christian relations, and theological responses to the ecological crisis.

Thomas Hughson, SJ, became emeritus in theology at Marquette University in 2010. Superior and dean at the Pontifical Biblical Institute-Jerusalem 1986–89, he has been an associate editor of *Theological Studies*. Recent publications include "Creation as an Ecumenical Problem: Renewal of Belief through Green Experience," *Theological Studies* (2014); "Liberal Theology: An Ecumenical Future," *Modern Believing* (2014); *Connecting Jesus to Social Justice: Classical Christology and Public Theology* (2013). The edited volume, *The Holy Spirit and the Church: Ecumenical Reflections with a Pastoral Perspective* is in press. Pastoral service in Ignatian spirituality has accompanied his academic theology.

Catherine Keller is professor of constructive theology at the Theological School of Drew University, where she has taught since 1986. She is author of *From a Broken Web: Separation, Sexism and Self* (1988); *Apocalypse Now and Then: A Feminist Guide to the End of the World* (1996); *The Face of the Deep: A Theology of Becoming* (2003); *God and Power: Counter-Apocalyptic Journeys* (2005); *On the Mystery: Discerning Divinity in Process* (2008); and most recently, *Cloud of the Impossible: Negative Theology and Planetary Entanglement* (2014). She is also co-editor of several volumes and author of many essays, book chapters, and journal articles on process thought, poststructuralist philosophy, feminist theology, and ecotheology.

Bridget E. O'Brien is a doctoral candidate in systematic theology at the University of Notre Dame, where she also serves as an in-residence minister in a women's residence hall. Her dissertation, "A Doctrine of God's Fidelity," joins the theology of Catherine Mowry LaCugna with theological fruits of Jewish-

Christian dialogue in order to propose a postsupersessionist theology rooted in God's trinitarian fidelity to creation. Her other research interests include feminist and political theologies, interreligious dialogue, and theologies of hope in the midst of oppression and suffering.

J. Leavitt Pearl is a PhD student at Duquesne University completing doctoral work on French phenomenology's account of the sexual body. In addition to his work in phenomenology, he also writes and presents on radical theology—with a particular focus on the dialectical theologies of Hegel, Altizer, and Žižek.

Nancy M. Rourke is a moral theologian at Canisius College in Buffalo, NY, where she teaches courses in Catholic ethics and world religions and directs the Catholic Studies program. Her PhD is from St. Patrick's college of Maynooth (Ireland) and master's degrees are from the Boston University School of Theology. She is a member of the Catholic Theological Society of America, the Society of Christian Ethics, the Rochester People of Faith for Climate Justice, and other groups. She has several publications in the areas of bioethics, environmental ethics, and metaethics.

John Thiede, SJ, is an assistant professor in systematic theology at Marquette University, specializing in Christology and Latin American theology. Originally from Minnesota, he is a Jesuit priest of the Wisconsin Province. His current book project utilizes martyrdom as a lens for reading the Christology of Jon Sobrino and proposes a more expansive definition of martyrdom in our postmodern world. He also enjoys writing about Jesuit missiology in Latin America and has an article forthcoming on the Jesuit missions in Bolivia.

Jessica A. Wrobleski is originally from West Virginia and is currently assistant professor of religious studies and theology at Wheeling Jesuit University. Wrobleski received her PhD from Yale University in 2009 with a focus on theological ethics. Her first book, *The Limits of Hospitality* (2012), addresses the spiritual practices and virtues necessary to the formation and discernment of hospitable boundaries. She currently serves as a member of the National Seminar on Jesuit Higher Education and has been active in the College Theology Society since 2009.